AN INTRODUCTION TO
THE PHILOSOPHY OF BERNARD LONERGAN

D0914004

Sage mir, *wie* du suchst, und ich werde dir sagen, *was* du suchst (Wittgenstein, *Philosophische Bemerkungen*, 67)

An Introduction to
THE PHILOSOPHY OF
BERNARD LONERGAN

Hugo A. Meynell

Second Edition

University of Toronto Press
Toronto and Buffalo

© Hugo A. Meynell 1976, 1991

First edition published by the Macmillan Press Ltd 1976

Second edition published in North America by University of Toronto Press 1991

Printed and bound in Great Britain

ISBN 0–8020–5869–8 (cl)
ISBN 0–8020–6792–1 (pa)

Canadian Cataloguing in Publication Data
Meynell, Hugo A.
 An introduction to the philosophy of Bernard Lonergan

2nd ed.
Includes bibliographical references.
ISBN 0–8020–5869–8 (bound)   ISBN 0–8020–6792–1 (pbk.)

1. Lonergan, Bernard J. F. (Bernard Joseph Francis), 1904– . I. Title.

BX4705.L7133M49 1990   191   C90–095631–3

For Jenny

Contents

6 God and Philosophy

ACKNOWLEDGEMENTS

My thanks are due to Alec Dolby and Harry Lewis, who read and criticised parts of the manuscript. I owe a great deal to the encouragement of Eric Mascall.

H.M.

NOTE TO SECOND EDITION

I have added an Afterword to take into account salient developments in philosophy over the last fifteen years, and expanded the bibliography to include recent books and articles about Lonergan's philosophy. In doing the latter, I have been helped greatly by Fr. Frederick Crowe. I would like to say that, if the book as a whole had been written now, I would have attended to the problem of inclusive language.

Introduction

Of all contemporary philosophers of the very first rank, Bernard Lonergan has been up to now the most neglected. In what follows I shall attempt to summarise his philosophical position, in such a way that attention may be drawn to it from a wider audience than has been so far forthcoming.

In my own opinion, *Insight*, the largest work Lonergan has written, is at a conservative estimate one of the half-dozen or so most important philosophical books to have appeared in the course of the present century. 'Thoroughly understand what it is to understand, and not only will you understand the broad lines of all there is to be understood, but also you will possess a fixed base, an invariant pattern, opening upon all further developments of understanding.'[1] *Insight* pursues this thesis through mathematics, empirical science, common sense, depth psychology, and social theory, into metaphysics, hermeneutics,[2] ethics, and natural theology. The hint from which the argument of the book originates, that study of the human understanding is the way to determine the fundamental nature of the world revealed to that understanding, is of course the starting-point of the classical British empiricists Locke, Berkeley, and Hume; but the metaphysical consequences of the method as pursued by Lonergan are not, to say the least of it, the same as those arrived at by the empiricists.

Though Lonergan's style is well-suited, as I believe, to his method and material — all the technical terms in *Insight* are deliberately introduced and carefully justified — he is not at first sight the easiest of authors to understand. Nor does his obscurity have the glamour of the technical jargon associated with the two most influential schools of contemporary philosophy, the analytical and the existentialist. The difficulty is partly due to the mathematical examples of which the earlier part of *Insight* is full; and which, to many people, will be far the least readily intelligible aspect of the book, and probably have made many give it up who would have been perfectly capable of grasping the fundamental purport of the work as a whole. For the basic principles of Lonergan's philosophy are not at all difficult to grasp. They are at least as easy, for example, as those of Descartes or Locke or A.J. Ayer, and much easier than those of Hegel, Kant or Heidegger. The term 'insight' gives a clue to the fundamental theory of knowledge and science which is at the basis of Lonergan's philosophy. The physicist, the chemist, the historian and the sociologist are all confronted at first sight with diverse scraps of information; an insight is the mental act by which these diverse scraps are grasped as cohering in an orderly and intelligible whole. Now since Hume and Kant it has been very usual among philosophers to attribute the intelligible order which we seem to find in the universe simply to the activity of the human mind, and to deny that it can be rightly inferred to exist in reality itself prior to the imposition of a conceptual framework by the human mind in the process of understanding it. But according to Lonergan, who in this matter follows Aristotle, Aquinas and (I would have thought) the common sense of mankind, both the phenomena which we experience and the intelligible pattern within which they are found to cohere are aspects of the real objective world which confronts the human inquirer, and which would exist even if there were no intelligent beings to inquire into it. Hence the investigation of insight, of *how* it is and hence in general terms *what* it is that the human mind comes to know, will have implications not only about the nature of the human knower but also about everything that there is for him to know.

Insight is an occurrence familiar to everyone, however recondite and obscure some of its manifestations and implications. There are insights when it suddenly occurs to the astronomer that the queer anomalies in the orbit of an observed planet are due to the presence of another planet which has not yet been observed; to the theoretical physicist that the streaks on the photographic plate before him are to be accounted for by the postulation of a new sort of fundamental particle; to the man of common sense that the strange looks in his neighbour's eye and unexpected runs of bad luck in his own business are due to the man's attempt to cheat him. The process by which we come to know the truth about the world consists of a repetition over and over again of the three steps, experience, understanding, and judgement. Experience only gives us uncoordinated scraps of data; understanding grasps by 'insight' the intelligible unity in these scraps of data, in the act of concocting a theory which accounts for them; in judgement, which is that whereby reality is known, we affirm that the theory is true, or that the postulated state of affairs is the case, verifying or falsifying the judgement typically by renewed appeal to the data.

In a passage now well-known, Eddington asked which was the real table, the solid heavy coloured article of common sense and elementary experience, or the almost empty space inhabited by swarms of colourless particles in continuous motion as alleged by the physicist.[3] According to Lonergan, each way of talking, the common-sense and the scientific, has its own kind of validity and propriety, since common sense bears on the relations of things to our senses, science on their intelligible relations to one another. This relation of things to one another may indeed be grasped by understanding, but the data provided by our senses can only provide clues to it, and, once a plausible theory has been arrived at, material for the verification and falsification of judgements couched in terms of it. Now empiricism and materialism both presuppose, in their different ways, that it is only experience, and not the whole process of experience, understanding, and judgement, which actually puts us in touch with the real world; real knowledge of the real world, for these philosophies, is fundamentally a matter of taking a look at what is open for inspection rather than of inquiring intelligently and reflecting reasonably. Science in its earlier stages gave some excuse for such views; but now that physics blatantly treats of entities which are not observable or even imaginable, they have become quite incredible once their full implications are realised.

Insight is relevant not only to scientific and metaphysical

investigation; it also plays a fundamental role in the life of each man and the social and institutional framework within which he lives out his life. How I live and act depends on my own insight and lack of insight, including my insight and lack of insight into the insight and lack of insight of others. Unfortunately, human life is largely determined not only by mere lack of insight but by deliberate flight from insight, when individuals and groups refuse to attempt an honest understanding of themselves and their relations with others. To the flight from understanding is due not only personal self-deception and neurotic dissociation, but a very large proportion of the evils with which men afflict themselves and one another. A thorough understanding of insight will include an understanding of the flight from insight.

Our mental life does not seem fairly to be described as merely a flow of sensations and memory-traces as empiricists tend to assume. On the contrary, on the basis of what we experience and imagine, we are always raising questions and trying out theories and hypotheses about what is the case, and finding out that these are more or less right or wrong. I wonder about the meaning of a damp patch spreading over the ceiling of my living-room, and jump to the conclusion that my water-tank is overflowing; I may test this conclusion by climbing up to the attic to look. From various puzzling expressions on the face of one of my colleagues, I come to think that he is constantly stifling the impulse to laugh at my manner of behaviour or style of dress, and later events may justify me in this. A theoretical physicist examines a recurrent pattern of streaks on a series of photographic plates, and it suddenly occurs to him that they may be evidence for the existence of a previously unknown kind of fundamental particle; further thought and examination may lead him to assert his hypothesis with confidence, or to give it up. From a collection of reports from the front, a general may infer that a severe artillery barrage directed upon his centre is really a feint, and that the enemy intends to deliver the main attack on his right. Here again, and perhaps with momentous consequences, events are likely to prove whether he was right or wrong. From a series of pencil drawings, a young geometer suddenly jumps to the conclusion that the

angles at the base of an isosceles triangle are necessarily
equal. All these examples have in common an initial
puzzlement at a mere series of scraps of data; a sudden grasp
of them as exhibiting an intelligible order; and subsequent
reflection establishing whether the pattern grasped was really
immanent in the data or not.

David Hume, generally considered the greatest of the
British empiricists, concluded as a result of sustained inquiry
and argument that mental life consisted of nothing but a
series of sense-impressions and of ideas which were copies of
these impressions. No *reason* whatever, he declared, could be
given for what we assumed upon instinct: that there was a
real external world to cause the impressions and ideas, or a
real internal mind or soul to have them. However carefully I
look about me, I can perceive nothing but sense-impressions;
by no exercise of my senses or my reasoning powers can I
discover real material bodies which somehow transcend these
sense-impressions.[4] Similarly, however carefully and persistently I look within myself, I always come across some
particular feeling or memory or sensation, never on some
'self' existing somehow prior to or independently of such
feelings or memories or sensations. Twentieth-century empiricism has been much indebted to Hume. For Bertrand Russell,
whose theory of knowledge was largely a development of and
continuation of that of Hume, minds and bodies were alike
'logical constructions' out of sensations; in other words, to
talk of minds and bodies is in the final analysis simply to talk
of sensations.[5] The central thesis of logical positivism, that
any statement (provided it is not true by definition) which is
in principle impossible to validate in terms of 'sense-data' or
'sense-contents' is simply nonsensical, depends on the same
assumption.[6] Now Hume's own inquiry as to the existence of
his own inquiring mind, over and above the experiences and
memory traces which it contained or of which it consisted, is
worth a little consideration. What is really going on in the
famous passage which concludes with the assertion that we
have no impression, and therefore no idea, of the self?[7] It is
not just that Hume has introspected and found nothing but a
stream of impressions and ideas. On the contrary, the little
thought-experiment which he describes is designed to test a

hypothesis to the effect that Hume's mind or soul consists of something over and above impressions and ideas. His argument may be set out as follows. 'If I have or am a substantial self over and above my sense-impressions and ideas, I will be able to find this substantial self by the same kind of introspection as that with which I advert to my current sense-impressions and ideas. But when I engage in this kind of introspection in search of this kind of entity, I find nothing. Therefore I have no reason to think that I have or am such a substantial self.' Hume has considered a popular theory which is deemed to account for the facts of mental life, has tested the theory in relation to the facts as he apprehends them, and has accordingly found it wanting. Involved in this process are not only a stream of impressions and ideas, but also the intelligence and reflection which Hume has exercised with respect to them. It does not appear how this intelligence and reflection are to be reduced to the experiences upon which they are exercised.

Lonergan's philosophy as a whole is a following-through of the hint afforded by this example that our mental life, and so our relation to whatever extramental reality there may be, is to be understood not simply in terms of experience, but also in terms of the inquiring intelligence which achieves insights and propounds judgements on the basis of that experience. That the real world is not simply the object of our experience, but the object of judgements framed in terms of insights made on the basis of this experience, can be made clear, as will be shown, by an analysis of human cognition itself; but the discoveries of modern physics bring this truth home with far greater clarity and force than was available in earlier times. To put it tersely, electrons, according to the world-view of contemporary science, form a part of the real world. But this is inconsistent with the view that the real world consists simply of what is observable, of what can be apprehended by 'taking a look';[8] since electrons cannot and could not possibly be objects of experience. Physicists have come to be convinced of the existence of electrons as a result of a repeated process of observation, the propounding of hypotheses, and the testing of these hypotheses by more observation and experiment — in other words, by forming judgements in terms of insights, and testing these judgements in experience. It appears to follow from the validity of contemporary physical theory that the real world is not that which is apprehended by mere observation; but it appears to be perfectly consistent with it that the real world is that which is known through the three-fold process of experience, understanding and judgement.

Reality does not consist simply of the flow of sensations, nor are things as we are acquainted with them mere chunks more or less arbitrarily chopped out of that flow. There is also the questioning subject that each of us is, which is characterised by the wonder that Aristotle declared was at the basis of all science and philosophy. This subject is that which asks, What is this? Why does this happen? Does that exist? Is that so? The questions which we ask can be divided into two basic kinds, those for intelligence and those for reflection. Those for intelligence are those which we ask when we are looking for some explanation of a set of data, some theory to account for it. Those for reflection are those in which we ask whether the theory we have arrived at is so or is not so, whether the kind of thing that we have postulated exists or does not exist, whether the state of affairs which we have conjectured is so or is not so. Questions for reflection are unlike those for intelligence in that they may all be answered Yes or No. It is absurd to answer Yes or No to questions like, 'What is the boiling point of water?', or 'What kind of courtship ceremony is characteristic of Great Crested Grebes?', or 'What were Julius Caesar's intentions in visiting Britain?' But having come by provisional answers to these questions, it is appropriate to ask further whether these provisional answers are correct; and such further questions can appropriately be answered Yes or No. These examples illustrate another fact about cognition which is of some importance; that every question for reflection presupposes the answer to a question for intelligence.

A study of human understanding, such as Lonergan undertakes, may be expected to throw light on a number of important, persistent and puzzling problems. Do the methods and achievements of science somehow prove or presuppose that the world of common sense is an illusion? Do they prove or presuppose that men have no freedom of will? Are the actual or potential deliverances of science exhaustive of real knowledge, or is there knowledge which can only be achieved in other ways? What relation do psychology and the other sciences which treat of man have to the purely natural sciences? Is there a radical difference between the methods of the natural sciences and those of the sciences of man, and, if so, what is the nature and what are the grounds of these differences? Can there be a rational basis for a science of interpretation such that we may gain insight into the insights of others however remote from us in space, time, or physical or cultural situation? What bearing does the nature of human inquiry and understanding have on the nature of the reality about which it inquires and which it progressively comes to understand? What help, if any, is afforded by the methods and achievements of science to those who are perplexed by the ancient problems of philosophy? Can there be a rationally grounded ethics, and if so, what are its principles? Can good reasons be given either for affirming or for denying the existence of a God, and, if there were good reasons for affirming the existence of such a being, how could we come to any reliable knowledge of him?

These are a few of the more momentous of the questions posed and answered in the course of Lonergan's investigation of the human understanding.[9]

1 Elements of Insight

1.1 *Insight and Discovery*

Insight is a phenomenon with which everyone is acquainted at least to some extent. It occurs whenever anyone comes to understand anything. It is a release from the tension of inquiry, and is apt to come suddenly and unexpectedly (when, as it were, the pieces of the puzzle which one had been working at apparently in vain suddenly fall into place). Once acquired, an insight is not readily lost, but becomes part of the habitual texture of one's mind. A good paradigm case of the occurrence of an insight is provided by the famous story of Archimedes. He had been given a particular problem to solve, of finding out whether a crown supposed to be of pure gold had in fact had baser metals added to it. In the baths of Syracuse he suddenly hit on the solution, to weigh the crown in water; and was so elated at this that he rushed out into the streets naked, shouting 'I've got it!' Anyone who has come by the solution of a problem after long and arduous thought about it knows something of the elation of Archimedes, though he may express it with less eccentricity.[2]

Discovery is a new beginning; you cannot get the knack of discovery by learning rules, or there would be no difference in kind between the genius and the mere hack. On the contrary, insights are themselves the origin of rules. What holds for the making of discoveries holds also for the imparting of them to others. The teacher cannot undertake to make his pupils understand; he can but 'present the sensible elements in the issue in a suggestive order and with a proper distribution of emphasis', leaving the pupils to achieve understanding themselves, which they do, notoriously, with very different measures of ease and rapidity. Here is one obvious difference between insight and sensation. Unless one is blind, one has only to open one's eyes to see; unless one is deaf, one can hardly avoid hearing. The occurrence and content of sensation stand in a fairly immediate correlation with outer circumstance. But the occurrence of insight seems to depend more on inner endowment; one can say, pretty accurately, that it is what occurs frequently in the intelligent and seldom in the stupid. 'Many frequented the baths of Syracuse without coming to grasp the principles of hydrostatics. But who bathed there without feeling the water, or without finding it hot or cold or tepid?'[3]

A further important feature of insight is that it pivots between concrete and abstract. (You may count pebbles or biscuits in order to gain an insight into the arithmetical truth that seven plus five equals twelve; but once you have gained it, you know something that is true quite independently of the existence of any particular assemblage of pebbles or biscuits at any particular place or time. Again, you may convince yourself that the mixing of hydrochloric acid and caustic soda in certain proportions yields a solution of common salt in water by doing an experiment and investigating the results of it; but the chemical formula which expresses this fact is not just a matter of particular things happening in particular places at particular times. It is not the case that one set of physical laws obtains in Australia, another in Canada, or one kind of chemistry on Mondays, quite another on Tuesdays. Particular occurrences and our observation of them are a matter of particular places and times; but the content of the insights to which they give rise need not be so.) 'By its very nature, insight is the mediator, the hinge, the pivot. It is insight *into* the concrete world of sense and imagination. Yet what is known by insight, what insight adds to sensible and imagined presentations, finds adequate expression only in the abstract and recondite formulations of the sciences.'[4]

It is worth looking more deeply into a single example, so that one may apprehend more clearly just what is involved in this grasp of abstract principles through concrete data. How does one come by the definition of a circle? Consider a cartwheel. What is the reason for its roundness? It might be suggested that the wheel is round because the spokes are equal. But evidently this will not quite do, since it would not be round all the same if the rim of the cartwheel were flat between the spokes, or if the spokes were sunk unequally into hub and rim. Yet the suggestion does seem to provide some kind of a clue. 'Let the hub decrease to a point; let the rim and the spokes thin out into lines; then, if there were an infinity of spokes and all were exactly equal, the rim would have to be perfectly round.' Now it is important to grasp that these points and lines which we have *supposed* cannot be *imagined*. The points and lines of the geometer are obvious cases of what is conceivable yet unimaginable. An imagined line has to have thickness as well as length, an imagined dot has to have size; but the geometer invites us to suppose that the line has only length, that the dot has only position.[5] Now concepts are not a matter of imagining, but are constituted by the activity of 'supposing, thinking, considering, formulating, defining', and that activity occurs in conjunction with insights. Points and lines, necessity and impossibility, cannot be imagined. Yet 'in approaching the definition of the circle, there occurred some apprehension of necessity and of impossibility. As we remarked, if all the radii are equal, the curve must be perfectly round; and if any radii are unequal, the curve cannot avoid bumps or dents.' It may be remarked that the image, for all that the insight goes beyond it, is necessary at least in the first instance for the occurrence of the insight; in this case 'the insight is the act of catching on to a connection between imagined equal radii and, on the other hand, a curve that is bound to look perfectly round'. Now the question 'Why?' comes from a kind of mental tension which is resolved in the joy of discovery. This drive to know the answer, this original question, is prior to all insights, and to all the concepts which insights generate and the words in which insights are expressed. The original question is about the concretely given or imagined, just as insight is insight into it.[6]

There is an old philosophical puzzle about primitive terms; since every definition presupposes terms, and these terms cannot be defined without pre-supposing others, one seems to be involved in an infinite regress. Fortunately, definitions do not occur in a vacuum, but emerge in solidarity with experiences, images, questions and insights. It is not the case that every insight pre-supposes further insights. On the other hand, each insight has to be expressed in more than one term. 'For every basic insight there is a circle of terms and relations, such that the terms fix the relations, the relations fix the terms, and insight fixes both. If one grasps the necessary and sufficient conditions for the perfect roundness of this imagined plane curve, then one grasps not only the circle but also the point, the line, the circumference, the radii, the plane, and equality. All the concepts tumble out together, because all are needed to express adequately a single insight. All are coherent, for coherence basically means that all hang together from a single insight.'[7]

Insights may occur either in isolation or in related fields. In the latter case they cluster and coalesce into the mastery of a subject. At some point later insights may show the shortcomings and limitations of earlier ones — this is what may be called the emergence of a *higher viewpoint*. A good example is the transition in arithmetic from the viewpoint which includes only the positive integers to that which includes negative numbers, fractions and surds. Let us begin by giving a definition of the positive integers, 1,2,3,4 and so on. We presuppose as familiar the notions 'one', 'plus' and 'equals'; and we get the following infinite series of definitions for the infinite series of positive integers.

$$1 + 1 = 2$$
$$2 + 1 = 3$$
$$3 + 1 = 4$$

etc. etc. etc.

Now it is evident that the important thing here is the 'etc. etc. etc.'; this presupposes that the insight has occurred, that the reader understands how to go on for himself to define any positive integer whatever.[8] As has already been said, a single insight is expressed in many concepts. 'In the present instance, a single insight grounds an infinity of concepts.' Other addition and multiplication tables may easily be derived (to multiply a number being to add it to itself so many times), and tables of powers by way of multiplication; tables may also be constructed for the inverse operations of subtraction and division.[9]

The need for a higher viewpoint will make itself felt when these inverse operations are allowed full generality, and are not restricted merely to bringing one back to one's starting-point. (3—2 =1, and 2÷2 = 1 — one is still safe within the range of the positive integers. But what will happen if one subtracts 3 from 2, or divides 1 by 4? No answer can be given in terms of the positive integers; one has to introduce negative numbers in the first instance, fractions in the second.) 'Subtraction reveals the possibility of negative numbers, division reveals the possibility of fractions, roots reveal the possibility of surds.' (The higher viewpoint reached in this way thus encompasses all the numbers and types of operations encompassed by the lower viewpoint, but in association with the negative numbers, fractions and surds which are beyond that viewpoint. Rather similarly, the higher viewpoint of Einstein explains all the results of observation and experiment which were explained by Newton's lower viewpoint, but also explains other phenomena, like the increase in the mass of objects as their velocity approaches the speed of light, which could not be explained by it.) Now the instructed mathematician can move easily through the series of higher viewpoints of which mathematics consists, from that of the positive integers to that of group theory. But one cannot learn mathematics in that way. On the contrary, the learner has to perform, over and over again, the same kind of move from lower viewpoint to higher as has just been illustrated; only so far as he does so can he become a competent mathematician.[10]

The importance of an apt symbolism is that it facilitates the achievement of insight and the consequent solution of problems. 'It is easy enough to take the square root of 1764. It is another matter to take the square root of MDCCLXIV.' The symbolism provides the inquirer with a heuristic technique, a method of cutting the corners in the road towards finding out what he wants to know. A mathematician can name his unknowns, and set out their properties in equations. Furthermore, the symbolism appropriate to each stage of mathematical development provides an image in which may be grasped the insights constitutive of the next stage.[11]

1.2 *Inverse Insight and the Empirical Residue*

An important distinction is to be drawn between direct insight, of which all the cases considered up to now are instances, and *inverse insight*. While direct insight gets the point, or sees the solution, an inverse insight is to the effect that the point is that there is no point, the solution is that there is no solution. An inverse insight is not the same as a correction of insights previously reached; it finds fault not with answers but with questions. Its essence is the denial of an expected intelligibility. 'In a demonstrative science it is to prove that a question of a certain type cannot be answered. In an empirical science it is to put forward a successful hypothesis or theory that assumes that certain questions mistakenly are supposed to require an answer.' Now the significance of such insights can only be seen in the context of a wide range of human thought, and with reference to 'later systems that positively exploit... their negative contribution.'[12] One example is provided by the existence of irrational numbers. One would naturally expect that the square root of two, which is the proportion between the length of the diagonal and the side of a square, would be the proportion between some two integers of which neither is a factor of the other. But there is a proof that this cannot be so. If $\sqrt{2} = m/n$, where m and n are two integers, then $m^2/n^2 = 2$. But if m and n have no common factor, then m^2 and n^2 cannot have any common factor either; so m^2/n^2 cannot be 2, and therefore m/n cannot be $\sqrt{2}$. Our initial supposition thus leads to a contradiction, and hence cannot be true. 'The argument is easily generalized and so it appears that a surd is a surd because it is not the rational fraction that intelligence anticipates it to be.' Another example is provided by the surprising part of Newton's first law of motion — that a body unless interfered with continues in its state of motion. Spontaneously, one thinks of continued uniform motion needing explanation, as something requiring some external cause. Yet another example can be derived from the basic postulate of the Special Theory of Relativity 'that the mathematical expression of physical principles and laws is invariant under inertial transformations.' This means, in effect, that though there are differences in the spatio-temporal viewpoint from which the relevant data are considered, still there is no difference in the intelligibility grasped in them or in the mathematical expression of that intelligibility. Now of course it is common to have differences in data or in viewpoint without a corresponding difference in intelligibility. There is, for instance, a considerable difference between large circles and small circles, but no one expects different definitions and different theorems to hold for them. But the trouble with the invariance postulated by Special Relativity is that it implies a drastic revision of our ordinary notions of space and time (making nonsense as it does of such common-sense conceptions as absolute rest and the absolute simultaneity of events at a distance from one another). The last two examples as opposed to the first, being matters of empirical science rather than of mathematics, are validated only through the testing of their consequences by observation and experiment.[13]

The significance of inverse insight may be brought out by the introduction of the notion of an *empirical residue*. This empirical residue consists in positive empirical data, is to be denied any immanent intelligibility of its own, and yet is connected with some compensating higher intelligibility. Particular places and times pertain to the empirical residue; each differs from every other, as a matter of fact. As differences in place and time have no immanent intelligibility, they do not modify that of anything else. Mere difference in place or time as such does not involve difference in observations or experimental results. If it did so, each place and time would have to have a physics, chemistry and biology of its own; and since a science cannot be worked out instantaneously in a single place, science would be impossible. On the contrary, of course, it is actually the case that scientists can collaborate, and pool results gained from observations at many places and times. Still more important for science than collaboration is generalisation. Each chemical element and compound differs from every other, and these differences have to be explained. But there is also a sense in which every single atom of hydrogen differs from every other, and these differences, fortunately, do not have to be explained. Here is another aspect of the empirical residue — that it is so simply as a matter of fact, without explanation. Again, the physicist offers explanations of red and blue and each of their shades; but he does not aspire to obtain as many different explanations as there are instances of each. 'In brief, individuals differ, but the ultimate difference in our universe' (between individual instances of exactly the same kind) 'is a matter of fact to which there corresponds nothing to be grasped by direct insight'.[13]

Abstraction is properly speaking a matter of grasping the essential and avoiding the inessential. (The colour of the cartwheel, and the material out of which it was made, were not matters relevant to the determination of why it was round). For any insight or cluster of insights the essential or important consists of those aspects of the data necessary for the insight to occur, and the set of concepts necessary to express the insight. In the study of insight itself, the particular examples of insight chosen to provide insight into insight are of course irrelevant; the reader can substitute examples of his own. In any subject, 'one comes to master the essentials by varying the incidentals' — and so it is with the study of insight.[15]

2 Scientific Insight

2.1 *Classical and Statistical Method*

Galileo's discovery of the law of falling bodies is at once a model of scientific procedure, and notably similar to the process already described 'from the image of a cartwheel to the definition of a circle'. Just as we started from the clue of the equality of the spokes, so Galileo 'supposed that some correlation was to be found between the measurable aspects of falling bodies'. Then he did three things: he showed by experiment the wrongness of the old view that the speed of their fall varied with their weight; turned his attention to two measurable aspects of a fall, the distance traversed and the time taken; and discovered that the measurements provided by experiment satisfied a general rule, that the distance traversed is proportional to the square of the time taken. This correlation, of course, has been verified, directly and indirectly, ever since. Now in the case of the cartwheel and the circle we moved into the realm of the supposed from that of the merely imagined. Something rather similar applies in the case of the law of falling bodies. We *suppose* the existence of a vacuum — which of course can never actually be obtained. All that we find in actual fact is that the closer one gets to a vacuum, the more exactly the law of falling bodies is obeyed in actual instances. However, there are notable dissimilarities as well. First, in the case of the establishing of the reason for the roundness of the cartwheel, there was no need for field-work, as there is in the case of arriving at and verifying the law of falling bodies. Second, the phenomena observed in the case of the law of falling bodies are discontinuous. If you plot individual results of experiments on a graph, and join the resulting points with a line, the line will not itself represent known data, but your presumption of what understanding will grasp in them. Third, the insight into the image of the wheel grasps necessity and impossibility; if the radii are equal, the curve *must* be a circle; if they are unequal, it *cannot* be. But insight into the discontinuous series of points on a graph representing results of experiments on falling bodies simply grasps a possibility. The simple curve with which one joins the points could represent the actual law; but there is an infinite number of other curves each of which could pass through all the known points, and hence represent the law.

In both mathematics and empirical science the inquirer tries to get to know what he does not yet know on the basis of what he already knows. In algebra one says, Let x be the required number, and finds out what x is by constructing and solving an equation. What Galileo was after was *the nature of* a free fall; and it is characteristic of empirical inquiry that the unknown to be reached is the nature of something. In every empirical inquiry there are knowns and unknowns — the knowns being typically the data of sense, which are apprehended whether or not one understands. The unknown are what one will grasp by insight and formulate in conceptions and suppositions. 'Once Galileo discovered his law, he knew that the nature of a free fall was a constant acceleration. But before he discovered the law, from the mere fact that he inquired, he knew that a free fall possessed a nature, though he did not know what that nature was.'[1] Now individuality belongs, as we have seen, to the empirical residue, 'the nature of' to the universal. (One does not inquire into the nature of each particular hydrogen atom, but applies experiments on particular samples of hydrogen to the understanding of 'the nature of' hydrogen in general.) Similars are similarly understood; to understand one set of data is to understand all exactly similar sets. It is of the utmost importance to notice, however, that there are two sorts of similarity, similarity of things in relation to us (roughly, sensible similarity), and similarity of things in relation to one another (intelligible similarity). Galileo differed from his Aristotelian contemporaries, basically, by his insistence that one must move on from the first step to the second, from attending to sensible

similarity to looking for intelligible similarity, from attending
to things as related to us to seeking out the nature of things
as related to one another. Thus was modern science inaugurated.[2]

(The distinction between things as related to us, as sensed,
and things as related to one another, as understood, is of
cardinal importance for the understanding of Lonergan's
theory of knowledge and reality, and of the relation of his
thought to Scholastic Aristotelianism. Aristotle rightly saw
that to come to know was to grasp the universal in particular
instances — to gain an insight — and then to judge that
such-and-such existed or was the case.[3] Correspondingly, the
medieval Scholastic philosophers distinguished between two
kinds of question about anything: *quid sit?* — what is it? Of
what nature is it? — and *an sit?* — whether it exists, whether
it is the case. In more modern terms, one has to distinguish
between the steps of forming a hypothesis, and judging
whether there are adequate grounds for thinking the hypothesis true.[4] But what Aristotle for all his genius did not
apprehend, and what the Aristotelians of Galileo's time failed
to advert to, was the fact that sensible similarities only
provide a preliminary classification of reality; that the
scientific mind cannot be content until it can explain
individual things and occurrences in terms of a set of
similarities that are explanatory.) Similarities are of two
kinds. 'There are the similarities of things in their relations to
us. Thus, they may be similar in colour or shape, similar in
the sounds they emit, similar in taste or odour, similar in the
tactile qualities of hot and cold, wet and dry, heavy and light,
rough and smooth, hard and soft. There are also the
similarities of things in their relations to one another. Thus,
they may be found together or apart. They may increase or
decrease concomitantly. They may have similar antecedents
or consequents. They may be similar in their proportions to
one another, and such proportions may form series of
relationships such as exist between the elements in the
periodic table of chemistry or between the successive forms
of life in the theory of evolution.'[5]

While scientific inquiry seeks out the nature of things as
related to one another, common sense remains in the realm

of things in relation to us, its further questions being bounded by the interests and concerns of daily living. But insight is relevant to common sense as well, since human intelligence is exercised not only in mathematics and physics; in every walk of life, there are opportunities for getting the point or for failing to do so. Each man has a drive to understand, each community has its common fund of tested answers and consequently its own kind of common sense. Someone might ask how those who share this common fund of insights define its terms and make its postulates. The answer, of course, which we obtain by an inverse insight, is that they do not. Common sense, as opposed to science, is a specialisation of the intelligence in the particular and concrete. It tries to master each situation as it arises, and has no use for technical languages or formal modes of speech. It limits its ambition to the successful performance of daily tasks, to immediate solutions that will work. Just as science dismisses metaphysical questions, so men of common sense brush aside theoretical questions which make no immediate difference. Like science, common sense consists of a vast accumulation of insights; but unlike science, it has no theoretical aspirations. Someone might ask which was the rational choice, science or common sense. But the question is wrongly posed, since it is rational not to choose between them, but to follow the exigences of both, science to master the universal, common sense to deal with the particular.[6] (For the present, we are concerned with common sense only so far as it is to be contrasted with science; it will be considered in detail in a later chapter.)

Science, as has already been said, aspires to a degree of generality which contrasts radically with the preoccupation of common sense with the particular. Scientific discoveries are not true merely of a particular place and a particular time; they do not pertain to the empirical residue. The formulae for chemical compounds have the same meaning and intelligibility, and are patient of the same symbolic representation, no matter what the place or time. Of course, it is not the appearance of, say, colour, but the explanation in terms of wave-lengths of light, which is the same no matter what the state of the observer's eyes, or his motion relative to anything else.[7]

Scientists achieve understanding only at the end of an inquiry; and yet the inquiry is methodical. Now this evidently involves something of a paradox. Method implies the adjustment of means to ends; and the question arises of how means can be adjusted to the end of a knowledge which is not yet acquired. (How can we know how to find out what we do *not* already know, unless somehow we *do* already know it?)[8] The answer to this puzzle is the *heuristic structure*. Pre-scientific thought tries to understand 'the nature of' light, heat, weight, and so on; and 'the nature of . . .' is expected to be the same for all data which are similar. But 'the scientific anticipation is of some unspecified correlation to be specified, some indeterminate function to be determined; and now the task of specifying or determining is carried out by measuring, by tabulating measurements, by reaching insight into the tabulated measurements, and by expressing that insight through some general correlation or function that, if verified, will define a limit on which converge the relations between all subsequent appropriate measurements.' Once the initial difficulties are overcome, and the basic insights are reached, there comes a moment when all the data fall into a single perspective, sweeping yet accurate deductions become possible, and predictions on the basis of these regularly turn out to have been correct. This type of heuristic structure, which anticipates the kind of intelligibility that may be grasped by direct insight, may be called *classical*. Not only Galileo, but also Newton, Clerk Maxwell and Einstein provide paradigm cases of scientific theories arrived at by the classical heuristic structure. The account of it given here, it should be noted, is quite independent of any assumptions about corpuscles, waves, causality, mechanism, determinism and so on. All that is essential to it is that it anticipates the sort of intelligibility that is to be grasped by direct insight.[9]

But in recent science a new kind of heuristic structure, which may be called *statistical* as opposed to classical, has gained enormously in prestige; and the question arises of how far this structure is consistent or inconsistent with the assumptions governing earlier scientific inquiry. In order to clarify what is meant by the statistical type of heuristic structure, it is necessary to introduce the concept of *unsystematic process*. In unsystematic, as opposed to systematic, process, there is no single insight or set of insights from which the whole process and all its events may be mastered. ' . . The group of systematic processes is constructed on determinate principles. Therefore, by violating the principles one can construct other processes that are non-systematic.' In a number of ways, non-systematic process exhibits what may be called coincidental aggregates. 'An aggregate is coincidental if (1) the members of the aggregate have some unity based on spatial juxtaposition or temporal succession or both, and (2) there is no corresponding unity on the level of insight and intelligible relation.' Processes which exhibit such aggregates are grasped by different and unrelated insights. If such processes exist — and so far we have only considered their theoretical possibility — the difficulty of investigating them evidently increases with the number and diversity of the separate intelligibilities involved. In such cases, deductions have to be restricted to the short term, and predictions confined to indicating probabilities. To illustrate the difference between systematic and non-systematic processes, one may take as examples the motions of the planets and the vagaries of the weather. Astronomers can confidently tell us of the eclipses of past and future centuries, but meteorologists need a constant supply of fresh information to tell us about tomorrow's rainfall. While systematic process is a repetition of a story which is essentially the same, non-systematic process has to be followed through a sequence of situations in which radical changes occur, and when they do so, fresh insights are needed. An important corollary of this is that while systematic process is monotonous, non-systematic process is the womb of novelty. Another important difference between the two is that systematic process would run backwards in much the same way as forwards. Now whether the world process as a whole is systematic or non-systematic does not seem to be a matter which can be settled *a priori*. (Determinists assume, for good reasons or bad, that it is systematic; once you know the state of the universe at any particular time, and the laws according to which it develops,

you can work out what any event in the past or future will
be.) One can only work out the consequences of the
assumption that it is one or the other, and compare these
consequences with the observable facts. If world process as a
whole turns out to be non-systematic, it will follow that
some forms of science at least will be irreducibly statistical,
and hence that a science which is content with the assigning
of probabilities is not a mere cloak for ignorance.[10]

Classical investigations are concerned with what *would* be
so *if* other things were the case. (Galileo's or Kepler's laws do
not so much inform you of any particular matter of fact, as
of what may be expected to happen if something else does
so). Statistical investigation, on the other hand, is concerned
directly with aggregates of events, like sequences of tossings
of a coin, or of casts of a die, or births and deaths, or of
situations created by the moving molecules of a gas. The
theoretical considerations which may effect individual instances are set aside by the statistical investigator. Each fall of a
die observes the laws of mechanics, but these are not relevant
when one is determining the probability that a particular
number will be cast. Doctors, again, can usually assign the
causes of any particular death; but these are not relevant to
the determination of death-rates. Statistical investigation as a
whole is directed towards the establishment of frequencies,
how often an event of a given description occurs. It is of
central importance for statistical investigations that differences in actual frequency, provided only that they oscillate
about some average, are deemed to be of no account. (If the
number of deaths per thousand is above the national average
in your town in a particular month, there is little cause for
alarm; but if it remains so over a number of years, then some
explanation is called for. There is no objection, again, to a die
which falls three times with the six uppermost in just one set
of six throws; but if this happens as a rule, and the original
set turns out to represent the average, there is good reason to
object to it.) This deeming of differences to be of no account
evidently does not apply to classical types of inquiry. 'Had
astronomers been content to regard the wandering of the
planets as a merely random affair, the planetary system never
would have been discovered. Had Joule been content to

disregard small differences, the mechanical equivalent of heat would have remained unknown. But statistical inquiries make it their business to distinguish in their tables of frequencies between significant and random differences.' The radical difference in mentality between classical and statistical types of inquiry seems to demand something like an inverse insight. Classical investigation acts on the principle that no difference is to be neglected; statistical, that to seek intelligibility in random differences is merely silly. Even if one grants (what is held by determinists), that classical inquiry will ultimately lead to laws that explain every event whatever, it remains that classical science rarely bothers to explain the single events of non-systematic process; there can (as in the case of a series of falls of a die) be a defect in the intelligibility of a group of events even when each single event is determinate. Statistical inquiry finds intelligibility in what classical inquiry neglects; a defect in intelligibility of one kind is replaced by intelligibility of another kind.[11]

By the appropriate kind of insight, the inquirer abstracts from the randomness in frequencies and hits on regularities, which are expressed in constant proper fractions called probabilities. It is important to notice that both probabilities and the states that they define are merely the fruits of insight. (What is given to sense is simply an aggregate of observed events.) Probabilities are hypothetical entities whose existence has to be verified, and are in fact so to the extent that subsequent frequencies of events conform to expectations based upon them. The basic practical problem of statistical inquiry is finding representative samples, where by a representative sample is meant a set of relative actual frequencies which leads to an assessment of probability that turns out to be correct. The notion of probability has a general resemblance to the mathematical notion of a limit. Like a limit, a probability is a number; it is also similar in that it cannot be reached from the relevant data without an insight. In all methodical inquiry, one proceeds by naming what will be known when an act of insight shall have occurred; but whereas classical inquiry investigates 'the nature of x' as already described, statistical inquiry is rather concerned with 'the state of y'. In both cases, one gives a pre-scientific description of what is apprehended as given but not yet understood; and as classical inquiry consists of getting to know natures by understanding data of different kinds, so statistical inquiry comes to know states by understanding ordinary and exceptional, normal and abnormal runs of events. Both sorts of inquiry involve a leap of constructive intelligence, which apprehends what is universal and constant in what is particular and subject to extraneous or random differences. (Neither can be got at just by taking a careful or persistent look at the data.) The discoveries made by both methods are universal and abstract; but the type of abstraction involved is different in the two cases. 'Classical laws . . . abstract from coincidental aggregates inasmuch as they demand the qualification, "other things being equal". On the other hand, statistical states express an intelligibility immanent in coincidental aggregates and, to reach this intelligibility, they abstract from the random differences in relative actual frequencies.' Both sorts of theory have to be verified, since insight as such grasps only a possibility; but the mode of verification is different in the two cases. Roughly, classical laws state what *would* happen *if* conditions were fulfilled; statistical laws, *how often* one can expect conditions to be fulfilled. Thus the kind and manner of prediction involved differ from one another. Classical predictions can be exact within assignable limits; but statistical predictions cannot be so, just because relative actual frequencies differ at random from probabilities. If probable events do not occur sooner or later, this amounts to evidence for the interference of some systematic factor. (Fifteen successive falls of the die in which no six is scored may just be bad luck; after a hundred such falls, there is pretty good reason to suspect that the die is not a fair one.) A range of observations may be amenable either to classical or to statistical understanding; which is appropriate cannot be settled *a priori*, but only by trial and error.[12]

2.2 *Canons of Scientific Inquiry*

To explore further the nature of insight as exemplified in the physical sciences, it is necessary to pay some attention to the canons which guide their methods of discovery. Empirical science in general may be said to operate like a pair of scissors, of which the upper blade consists in the general principles which give rise to the methods employed and justify them, the lower blade in particular working hypotheses, deductions, revisions of hypotheses, and so on. The canons which are to be described constitute this upper blade. *The canon of selection*, firstly, states that if a hypothesis pertains to physical science, it will have consequences which are capable of being perceived, and which can be produced or at least observed. It will prescind from what does not involve such consequences, and reject what fails to be confirmed by them. But the apparent neatness and simplicity of this canon conceals traps for the unwary. The perceivable consequences may be so slight that an expert with a highly elaborate apparatus is needed to detect them. Hence the need for a division between theoretical scientists and fact-gatherers as science progresses. It is also very important to be clear that while questions failing to satisfy the canon do not arise in empirical science, it does not immediately follow that they do not arise at all.[13]

Second, there is the *canon of operations*. Inquiry into the data of sense leads to insights formulated in classical and statistical laws; conversely, 'the laws provide premises and rules for the guidance of human activity upon sensible objects. Such an activity, in its turn, brings about sensible change to bring to light fresh data, raise new questions, stimulate further insights, and so generate the revision or confirmation of existing laws and in due course the discovery of new laws.' Laws which prove successful guides to operations in a large range of situations are more and more confirmed. Now laws given by insights, as has already been argued, are abstract; but operations take place in concrete and often complex situations, to apply the abstract law to which more laws are required. 'The law of free fall holds in a vacuum. But operations do not occur in a vacuum. Hence, one is driven to determine the law of air resistance and the laws of friction.' The canon is likewise a source of higher viewpoints. In virtue of it, fresh data are constantly being brought to light which force on the scientific consciousness the inadequacies of existing hypotheses and theories, and which provide evidence in accordance with which they may be satisfactorily revised; 'and, in the limit, when minor corrections no longer are capable of meeting the issue, demand the radical transformation of concepts and postulates that is named a higher viewpoint'.[14]

Third, there is the *canon of relevance*. What have traditionally been known as final, material, and instrumental causes are not the primary concern of the empirical scientist; these are rather a matter of the uses to which science can be put than of science itself. In the case of the cartwheel which we considered initially, considerations of these sorts of causality would have led to the economics of transportation (what the wheel is for, its final causality), to forestry and mining (the wood and iron of which the wheel is made, its material causality), the man or men who put it together (its efficient causality), and so on. The canon of relevance lays down that the main and first thing for the scientist to do is to grasp the intelligibility immanent in the data. It notes, moreover, that 'this intelligibility, immanent in the immediate data of sense, resides in the relation of things, not to our senses, but to one another. Physics studies the relations of types of energy, not to our senses, but to one another. Chemistry defines its elements, not by their relations to our senses, but by their places in the pattern of relationships named the periodic table. Biology has become an explanatory science by viewing all living forms as related to one another in that complex and comprehensive fashion that is summarily denoted by the single word, evolution.' Now the intelligibility grasped by the scientist has to be verified; simply as an intelligibility it is merely a possibility, which may or may not be realised in fact. Empirical science, one might say, is science by virtue of its insights, empirical by virtue of the verification of these insights in experience. The intelligibility which it seeks in the world 'consists not in an absolute necessity, but in a realized possibility'.[15]

The fourth canon, *the canon of parsimony*, involves the exclusion from what is claimed to be known by the empirical scientist both of unverified and of unverifiable statements. In general, it may be said that this canon forbids the scientist to affirm (as opposed to merely suppose) what he does not know. It sounds obvious enough; yet 'it is difficult inasmuch as knowing exactly what one knows and what one does not know has been reputed, since the days of Socrates, a rare achievement'. Now verifications are of formulations which may state either the relation of things to our senses or the relation of things to one another (i.e. as explained rather than merely experienced). Thus the formulations contain two classes of terms, which may be named respectively *experiential conjugates* and *pure* or *explanatory conjugates*[16]. "Colours" will be experiential conjugates when defined by appealing to visual experience, "sounds" when defined by appealing to auditory experience; "heat" when defined by appealing to tactile experience; "force" when defined by appealing to an experience of effort, resistance, or pressure.' Experiential conjugates satisfy the canon of parsimony very clearly, since they are verified not only by scientists but by humanity at large. Explanatory or pure conjugates, on the other hand, are defined not directly by appeal to experience, but by empirically established laws and theories. An example of such a conjugate is mass as a correlative implicit in Newton's inverse square law. It is important that verification of pure conjugates is not directly in experience, but in insights into series of experiences. (One does not have direct experience of the mass of an object in the sense determined by Newton's law; however, the law does have implications for our experience, for example, our observation at successive moments of a falling apple, or on successive days of the position of the moon.) 'Events stand to conjugates as questions for reflection stand to questions for intelligence.' To think out an explanatory theory, in terms of pure conjugates, is one thing; to find out whether it is actually verified in the relevant events, another. Questions for reflection, unlike those for intelligence, can all be answered 'Yes' or 'No'. Once a law is enunciated, there arises the question for reflection, whether it is verified. When a term is defined (through the exercise of intelligence), the question is whether what is defined exists or occurs (which is a question for reflection). This is the clue to the relation between conjugates and events. Without events, conjugates cannot be discovered or verified. Without conjugates, events cannot be distinguished or related.[17]

Fifthly, there is the *canon of complete explanation*. The goal of empirical method is often ana rightly said to be the complete explanation of all phenomena. Unfortunately, at the very inception of modern science, Galileo made his distinction between primary and secondary qualities in place of the correct one between what we have called pure and experiential conjugates. A mistaken twist thus given to scientific method is now being overcome owing to the character of modern scientific discoveries; this makes a separate enunciation of this canon opportune. For Galileo, experienced extension and duration were primary qualities in that, according to him, there would be extension and duration and hence extended and enduring material things, even if there were no animals to have experience of them. (To use our terms, Galileo treated *experienced* extension and duration, as opposed to experienced colour, sound and so on, as though they were pure conjugates. This is the basis of modern materialism, which regards the very essence of scientific explanation to be the reduction of all descriptions of phenomena to that of matter in motion.) For us, however, extension and duration are not exceptional in this respect; they may be either experiential or pure conjugates, just like colours or sounds, according to whether they are envisaged as experienced or as explained. As experiential conjugates, extension and duration are correlative to familiar elements of our experience; as pure, it is quite another matter. 'On our analysis, the space-time of Relativity stands to the extensions and durations of experience in exactly the same relations as wave-lengths of light stand to experiences of colour, as longitudinal waves in air stand to experience of sound, as the type of energy defined by the first law of thermodynamics stands to experiences of heat, etc.'[18] What applies to extension and duration, of course, applies also to the local motion of objects which can be described only in terms of them; a preliminary description of local motion may thus properly be given in experiential conjugates, but the scientist may content himself only with complete explanation, that is to say, with verified description in terms of pure conjugates. (The trouble with the Galilean scheme is that its postulation of primary qualities involves the giving of a special privilege to one set of experiential conjugates, this is to say the matter and motion in the space and time of our experience. The working-out of this principle is best known to English philosophers through the work of Locke, the chief objection to it, that it involves *either* the postulation of what is utterly beyond our experience *or* the uncritical according of privilege to one kind of experience over another, through the philosophy of Berkeley.) If the canon of parsimony is applied as well as the canon of complete explanation, further objections arise to the Galilean account of scientific explanation. Experiential conjugates are verifiable, so one ought not to reject them as *mere* appearance. Inversely, Galileo did not base his claim as to the reality and objectivity of primary qualities on their verifiability. 'Accordingly, his affirmation was extra-scientific. It did not satisfy the canon of parsimony.'[19]

Sixthly and lastly, we come to the *canon of statistical residues*. This presupposes inquiry of the classical type, and from there argues to the existence of residues which call for statistical inquiry. There are a large number of schemes of recurrence in the world (where an event of the same description occurs over and over again at regular intervals), of which the planetary system is a clear and obvious example. But each such scheme 'presupposes materials in a suitable constellation that the scheme did not bring about, and each survives only as long as extraneous disrupting factors do not intervene.' Moreover, 'there does not seem to exist any universal scheme that controls the emergence and survival of the schemes that we know'. (I think it would have been quite reasonable, from the seventeenth century until the beginning of the twentieth, to suppose that classical mechanics provided such a scheme; but contemporary physics seems to have destroyed the grounds for confidence that it really does so.) Apparently there are and must be 'non-systematic conditions under which the systematic has its concrete realization'. The objection may perhaps be raised that while admittedly single laws are abstract since they do not cover all the data, the totality of such laws, once it was discovered, would be found to cover every aspect of the data. But the world process as it actually unfolds does not seem to support this conclusion, involved as it is in the essentially statistical devices of large numbers and long intervals of time, and exhibiting as it does a fluid rather than a rigid stability that promotes development and novelty as well as admitting breakdowns and false starts. Classical laws, it must be insisted, yield reliable predictions, but only *given* the necessary preconditions, and *given* the exclusion of extraneous factors. (Astronomical tables will enable one to predict reliably the motions of the planets far into the future, given that no large foreign body enters the solar system, given that none of the major planets disintegrates, and so on). And it appears that the series of pre-conditions is divergent. 'In the general case, any event, Z, is deducible from antecedent circumstances, Y, provided some P, Q, R ... continue to occur and provided some U, V, W ... do not intervene.' And each of *these* conditions is similarly conditioned. 'Since each event ordinarily has several conditions, the series ordinarily diverges.' Someone might urge that, all the same, world process in the last analysis will be found to be systematic. But this is only a hypothesis, and, withal, an exceedingly doubtful hypothesis; as has already been pointed out, world process so far as we are acquainted with it does not seem to support it. Further, 'while this doubtful hypothesis implies that statistical method is ultimately mistaken, there is no difficulty in framing opposite hypotheses of equal value which, if true, would imply that ultimately classical method is mistaken'. But, in fact, a little reflection will show that classical and statistical method are complementary. Statistical theories deal with events, which cannot be settled by classical laws without reference to further events. On the other hand, scientifically significant statistical laws will define events by reference to the pure conjugates which are the concern of classical laws. 'For events must be defined if they are to be assigned any frequency but unity. In other words, only the defined type of event is not occurring always and everywhere.' It has already been explained that mere reference to experience will not do for defining conjugates once science is sufficiently advanced. 'So pure conjugates will be used in defining the events of scientifically significant statistical laws. Hence, Quantum Mechanics defines its observables by appealing to classical physics, which developed the notions of Cartesian co-ordinate, linear and angular mementum, energy and so forth.' It may be added that indeterminacy is a general characteristic of statistical investigations, which presuppose that 'the concrete cannot be deduced in its full determinacy from any set of systematic premisses'. The basis of all these reflections, the reader should be reminded, is not contemporary physics, whose theories are likely to be in for plenty of revision with the passage of time, but analysis of the cognitional process itself and the nature of the insights to which it gives rise.[20]

2.3 *The World-View of Emergent Probability*

The two heuristic structures, together with the canons of method just outlined, constitute an *a priori*. (This is to say that the inquiring intelligence by its very nature anticipates an intelligibility in the world which is to be found in the manner and according to the principles described.) As in Galileo's case the method of inquiry employed issued in a world view of mechanistic determinism; as in Aristotle's case it led to a cosmic hierarchy; so on our case too a world view may be expected to result from our affirmation of the applicability to the world of both classical and statistical methods of inquiry. The problem, then, is to determine what is the immanent order or design of a universe in which both classical and statistical laws obtain. The account will be generic rather than specific, resting as it will do not on scientific doctrines of particular places and times but on the dynamic of inquiring human intelligence as such. An invariant structure, scientific method or the inquiring human intelligence, knits together successive stages of science — Renaissance, Enlightenment, present, and future. (If someone were to doubt whether future science will really presuppose the same 'invariant structure', he might be asked in reply how far any enterprise of the human mind could properly be called 'science' which did not seek understanding of the world at least approximately in the manner described.) 'The design of the universe, to which we shall conclude, will enjoy the invariance of the premise which we shall invoke.' Of course, this invariance is relative to the degree that our analysis of empirical method may be revised in detail.[21]

What kind of a universe is it, to revert to our question, in which classical and statistical laws both have application? Let us introduce the notion of a *scheme of recurrence*. From an abstract point of view, a scheme of recurrence is a combination of classical laws; concretely, schemes of recurrence begin, continue, and cease to function according to statistical probabilities. The diverging series of positive conditions for an event of a particular kind may coil round, as it were, in a circle. Thus, if A occurs, B will occur; if B, C; if C . . . , A will occur. This kind of scheme may be indefinitely complex, and include devices which have a tendency to exclude disruptive elements. Let F be such an element. Then, say, if F occurs, then G will occur; if G, H; and H will prevent the recurrence of F. Examples of such schemes of recurrence are the planetary system, the nitrogen cycle, and rhythms of animal and economic life. Such schemes will tend to include defensive cycles, such that a change will be offset by the opposite change, to restore the initial situation. (An infection in one part of an animal's body will stimulate that body as a whole to initiate processes which will restore health in the infected part.) Let us introduce the further notion of a *conditioned series* of such schemes of recurrence. Schemes P, Q and R constitute such a series when P can function though neither Q nor R exist, but Q cannot function unless P exists, nor R unless Q exists. The dietary schemes of animals are clear examples. All carnivorous animals cannot live off other carnivorous animals; some animals must be herbivorous. These in turn depend for their existence on plants, plants on chemical processes, and chemical processes on physical processes.[22]

The *possible*, *probable* and *actual* seriation of schemes of recurrence are to be distinguished. The actual seriation 'consists of the schemes that actually were, are, or will be functioning in our universe along with precise specifications of their places, their durations, and their relations to one another'. The actual differs from the probable according to the principle already explained,[23] by which the actual run of events differs non-systematically from the probable. The possible seriation is still more remote from the actual, including as it does all the schemes of recurrence which could be devised from the classical laws of our universe, including those whose probability is so slight as to be practically negligible. It is equally relevant to the actual universe and any other possible one with the same classical laws, 'no matter what its initial numbers, diversities and distribution of elements'. The probable seriation depends also on statistical laws; for each moment of world history, the most probable course of future events can be assigned in accordance with it. It would seem that there is a probability of schemes as well as of events, and that each scheme has one probability to be assigned for its emergence and another for its survival. In the case of any set of events, the probability of the occurrence of all of them is (other things being equal) the *product* of the probability of the occurrence of each one of them; the probability of the occurrence of one of them the *sum* of the probability of the occurrence of each. If you have a set of events A, B, and C, such that, if any one of them occurs, the others will occur as well (as in the case of a scheme of recurrence), the probability of the scheme will then be the sum of that of its constituent events. The probability of its survival is the probability of the non-occurrence of any of the events which would disrupt it.[24]

What is probable, sooner or later occurs; when it occurs, probability of occurrence is replaced by probability of survival; and as long as the scheme survives, it fulfils conditions for the possibility of later schemes. Such is the general notion of emergent probability. Spatial considerations are evidently involved, since later schemes become possible only *where* earlier schemes function. (You cannot have life as we know it where there are no organic compounds.) Thus however widespread the elementary schemes, there is a spatial restriction on each successive emergent scheme. Minimum probability pertains to the ultimate schemes of the series. But large numbers offset low probabilities, and so do long intervals of time. 'Just as a million million simultaneous possibilities yield a million probable realizations, whose possibility is one in a million, so also a million million successive possibilities yield a million probable realizations under the same expectation.' The distinction between probability of emergence and probability of survival is also important in this regard. If both are low, the scheme will be rare and fleeting; if both are high, frequent and enduring — and so *mutatis mutandis* when one probability is low and the other high.[25]

The emergent probability which we have been describing seems to be what we have been looking for, the immanent order or design of a world to which classical and statistical laws apply. There remains the task of working out its generic properties — its specific properties are not relevant to our present purposes. The difference between probability and chance is that while probabilities are what actual frequencies diverge from non-systematically, that non-systematic divergence itself is chance. World-process as probable realisations of possibilities neither runs along the iron rails postulated by determinists, nor is 'a non-intelligible morass of chance events'. It becomes, however, increasingly systematic, since 'the further the series of schemes is realized, the greater the systematization to which events are subjected'. Given sufficient numbers and sufficient time, even slight probabilities become assured. There may however be breakdowns of schemes and blind alleys of development; since some schemes with a high probability of emergence may block possible developments rather than allowing for them. The later a scheme in the conditioned series, the narrower its distribution. But the effect of large enough initial numbers is to ensure that at least one situation will be such that the whole series will win through. It must be pointed out that the analysis given here, at least in basic outline, presupposes only that there are schemes which operate according to classical laws and occur in accordance with statistical laws, but does not depend on assumptions concerning the determinate content of any particular scheme. Hence changes in scientific theory with regard to the actual formulation of classical or statistical laws will not affect it. The reader may also be reminded that whereas he was at first being invited to grasp the intelligibility immanent in the image of a cartwheel, he is now being asked to do the same thing in regard to the main features of the universe of our experience.[26]

The nature of the world-view of emergent probability may

be clarified by comparison and contrast with earlier world-views. Aristotle distinguished between what is 'necessary' and what is 'contingent', in the sense of what always happens and what sometimes or usually happens.[27] His notion of the necessary lumps together classical and one element of statistical laws (since classical laws tell you what will happen if . . . , statistical laws how often something happens). Emergent probability differs from Aristotle's world-view by its different account both of science and of law. The alleged 'necessary' motions of the heavens, as conceived by Aristotle, are, in terms of emergent probability, merely schemes of recurrence which arose and will survive in accordance with probabilities. Instead of an eternal cyclic recurrence, again, emergent probability involves the successive realization of ever more complex schemes of recurrence. (It is perhaps worth noting at this point that, for all this wide divergence between Aristotle's world-view and Lonergan's, Lonergan is closer to Aristotle's position on the central philosophical issues of epistemology and metaphysics than he is to that of most modern philosophers — as will appear in due course.)[28]

Galileo correctly grasped that explanation lies beyond mere description, though he failed to recognise the abstract character (already discussed) of his own law of falling bodies. And his methodology, involving as it did the assumption that the essence of scientific explanation is to achieve a description in terms of those 'primary' qualities whose equivocal nature has already been shown, was pervaded by misleading conceptions of reality and objectivity. The inadequacy of these conceptions comes clearly to light in the philosophy of Kant, 'where the real and objective bodies of Galilean thought prove to constitute no more than a phenomenal world . . . Our present concern is the fact that Galilean laws of nature are not conceived in abstraction from sensible or, at least, imaginable elements and, consequently, that the Galilean law stands in the field, not of our abstract classical laws, but rather of our schemes of recurrence in which classical laws and imaginable elements can combine'. From this concreteness of conception, two results ensue; first, a hostility of incomprehension against statistical laws; second, a mechanistic view of the universe as a whole. In the abstract, of course, it is quite true that classical laws are both universal and necessary. (It is of the very essence of phosphorus that it is related to the other elements in the ways specified by the periodic table of the elements.) 'The Galilean acknowledges this universality and necessity but cannot recognize its abstractness.' For him, the necessary laws attach to imaginable particles or an imaginable aether or both; thus, 'it is already concrete, and it is not in need of further determinations in order to reach concreteness'. As he sees it, the further determinations necessary for its concrete application, which are and must be non-systematically related to one another according to our view, simply do not exist. Thus he regards statistical laws as mere confessions of ignorance, since he is sure that there is some vast aggregate of discrete or continuous, but at all events imaginable, entities subject to universal and necessary laws, and that the business of the scientist is to determine these laws and thence to predict what cannot but occur. The negation of statistical laws thus leads to mechanism, a machine being a set of imaginable parts systematically related to one another. In the case of an ordinary machine, there are things apart from it which might interfere with its working; but in the case of the universe, what could there be to interfere from outside? So it is that mechanism inevitably issues in determinism. The Galilean viewpoint as here described was dominant in science until fairly recently; it survived the veiled implications of Darwinism, but was crippled by the overt claims of Quantum Mechanics.[29]

Darwin's *The Origin of Species* is the outstanding extant example of the use of probability as a principle of explanation. The immanent intelligibility in phenomena sought and found in that book is not at all of the kind typified by the work of Newton or Laplace. The follower of Laplace cannot reach determinate conclusions without fully accurate information on the basic situation, but 'the follower of Darwin is indifferent to the details of his basic situation; and he obtains his conclusions by appealing to the natural selection of chance variations that arise in any of a large variety of initial situations'. Evidently, natural selection of chance variations is a particular case of a more general formula to which we have already drawn attention. 'As chance variation is an instance of probability of emergence, so natural selection is an instance of probability of survival.' Nature effects this process not with the exact predictability of the changing phases of the moon, but only by a general tendency that increases in efficacy with increase of numbers and prolongation of time-intervals. Unlike the planets, and like the electrons which one may imagine to leap from orbit to orbit around their nucleus, a plant or an animal may enter any one of a range of alternative schemes of recurrence.[30]

Some indeterminists maintain a version of their own of the Galilean dualism of the real and the merely apparent, identifying the real with the sub-microscopic and random, the merely apparent with the macroscopic in which classical laws, as they see it, merely appear to be verified. Now it is certainly true that the only verification of what is *imagined* is in the corresponding sensation; but it is also true, as has already been shown, that one can verify conceptual formulations if they have sensible implications. Again, it may be argued that classical laws are determinate and precise, whereas data are irreducibly hazy; and so that the latter can never be held to count as verification of the former. But this argument would only be convincing so far as classical laws were interpreted concretely, which we have argued that they should not be. Classical laws merely assign limits on which, other things being equal, huge numbers of data converge. Does not admission of any divergence between data, and classical law, it might be asked, imply that classical laws are not really verifiable? Not at all, if their verification is understood in the way that we have described. The divergence only goes to show that classical laws cannot constitute the *whole* of our knowledge, not that they cannot be a part of it. Quantum physics, it is true, provides a general theory which includes Newtonian physics as a special case. But this is no proof that the special case has no analogue at all in the real world. It seems that an exact analogue would exist if schemes of recurrence were perfectly realised. The old determinism was mistaken not in looking for classical laws, but in failing to envisage the possibility of a development in heuristic structures such as would allow for the seeking and finding of statistical laws. It 'supposed the universal validity of a type of explanation that is possible only when schematic situations are realized perfectly', and overlooked the possibility that the probabilities of the non-schematic account for the existence of the schematic.[31]

2.4 *The Understanding of Development*

One of the most important consequences of acknowledging the existence of the non-systematic is that it leads to the affirmation of the existence of successive levels of scientific inquiry, and of different types of entity investigated by each of these levels. 'If the non-systematic exists on the level of physics, then on that level there are coincidental manifolds that can be systematized by a higher chemical level without violating any physical law.' And the same will apply to the biological level in relation to the chemical, the psychical level (of animal sensation and emotion) in relation to the biological, and the specifically human level of 'insight and reflection, deliberation and choice' in relation to the psychical. The existence of these separate kinds of entity, in the kind of relationship described, corresponds both to the immemorial convictions of common sense and to the divisions of the sciences as they actually exist. Now we have given a general description of the world process into which insights may be gained in terms of conjugates and events, and of schemes of recurrence according to which events defined by the conjugates occur. It may be asked what application there is, if any, for the notion of a *thing* on this view. The answer is that the notion of the thing involves a new type of insight, which, as we shall show, is indispensable to our understanding of the world. This type of insight 'grasps not relations between data' (as do the insights which grasp conjugates), 'but a unity, identity, whole in data'.[32] Things are extended in space, permanent in time, and subject to change; they possess properties and are subject to laws and probabilities. 'To say that Fido is black or that he is a nuisance, is to conceive both a unity in a totality of aspects and some aspect out of that totality and to attribute the latter to the former.' It can be shown that the notion of a thing is not one which is liable to be dispensed with as we get to understand the world better. The first reason for this is that without the notion of a thing there can be no sense given to the concept of change. Data simply come one after another, and abstractions are eternally whatever they are defined to be; hence neither can be subject to change. Change is nothing but what is to be known through correct, successive, and opposed affirmations about the same thing. As well as providing a basis for the concept of change, the notion of a thing is necessary for the continuity of scientific thought, since science moves from mere description to explanation, and something must remain identical throughout the process from the one to the other. The thing or things which are first merely described are later fully explained.[33]

Indeed, 'the thing is the basic synthetic construct of scientific thought and development'. The ancient list of elements, earth, air, fire and water has been rejected, and the new list provided in the periodic table of the elements has been set up by hypothesis and verification; but both old and new lists are lists of kinds of things. It is things which are said properly to exist, and in fact 'existence stands to the thing, as event or occurrence stands to the conjugate'. Now it is important to notice that things, as objects of insight, are not only *sometimes* something other than mere observables; they are never *mere* observables. 'If subatomic elements cannot be imagined, then atoms cannot be imagined, for one cannot imagine a whole as made up out of unimaginable parts. It follows that no thing itself, no thing as explained can be imagined.' The difference between a tree and an electron in this respect is that a tree can be perceived or imagined, *as well as* explained, whereas an electron cannot. A thing, as an intelligible unity-identity-whole, is not to be confused with a mere 'body' — in the sense of what is anticipated by mere animal extroversion as opposed to by intelligence and reasonableness. To think that all things are really 'bodies' is a recurrent temptation, since human beings are sentient and percipient animals as well as subjects of intelligent inquiry and reasonable reflection. To both scientist and layman 'as animals, a verified hypothesis is just a jumble of words. What they want is an elementary knowing of the "really real", if not through sense, at least by imagination'.[34] (A thing is, in fine, an intelligible unity-identity-whole to be grasped through insight from the data of sense, of whose existence and nature we may get to know by virtue of judgement framed in terms provided by insight on the basis of experience. It is not merely, and frequently is not at all, what may be the direct object of experience or imagination. The assumption that it must be so is one of the cardinal errors which bedevil science and philosophy.)

(The notion of development has still to be studied, since it is not coped with adequately by classical or statistical laws. Here it is not merely a matter of what will happen in certain circumstances, as with classical laws; or of how often such circumstances will obtain, as with statistical laws; but of how a single thing or group of things changes over time and in adaptation to a succession of circumstances. The method of inquiry into this kind of development will be called *genetic method*.) Developments in some things may occur on several levels at once. 'In the plant there is the single development of the organism; in the animal there is the twofold development of the organism and the psyche; in man there is the threefold development of the organism, the psyche, and intelligence.' Now organic, psychic and intellectual events occur with a certain regularity, but not with the rigid periodicity which characterises, for instance, the motions of the planets. There is in their case not a single scheme of recurrence, but a flexible cycle of schemes of recurrence. 'For the same organism, the same psychic habits and dispositions, the same intellectual development result in widely different operations under different conditions and in accord with different circumstances.' Physics differs conspicuously from biology, psychology, and intellectual theory, and this for two main reasons. First, the events studied by the latter group of sciences recur not in single schemes, but in flexible circles of ranges of schemes; and secondly, because these sciences are concerned with development — the performance of masses and electric charges, as opposed to that of animals and men, not being a function of age. 'There is not a different law of gravitation for each succeeding century.' There follows from this the outstanding difference between classical and genetic

method. 'Classical method is concerned to reduce regular
events to laws. Genetic method is concerned with sequences
in which correlations and regularities change.' To use a
mathematical analogy, 'genetic method is concerned with a
sequence of operations that successively generate further
functions from one initial function.' Development is from
generic indeterminacy to specific perfection; all organic
functioning becomes more alike as one mounts to the early
stages, and, conversely, psychic development is a matter of
character and temperament becoming set, and skills acquired
and perfected.[35]

Besides the characteristics of development in general, there
are special characteristics of simple development as in the
organism, twofold as in the animal, and threefold as in man;
thus the biologist, the psychologist and the intellectual
theorist have to operate not only in the light of the general
notion of development, but also with regard to more
specialised directives. (Each of them studies the development
of things from a primary stage, through stages of greater
development, to a fully developed and mature stage; each of
them is concerned at every stage with the question *why* the
last stage gave way to this one, *why* the present stage is to
give way to the next; but the kind of answer that is sought to
this question 'why' is evidently somewhat different as
between organisms, psyches and intellects.) Unfortunately,
the spectacular success of the physical sciences has tended to
stimulate investigators of the organism, the psyche, and the
intelligence to a servile rather than an intelligent adaptation
of the successful procedures. (In both sorts of inquiry, what
is sought is an insight, and the insight has to be one which is
verified in observable data; but the type of insight sought is
different in classical and in genetic forms of inquiry.) 'As
classical method is based on the assumption that similars are
to be understood similarly, so genetic method rests on the
assumption that an understanding of significantly dissimilar
individuals is to be reached by subsuming their respective
histories under common genetic principles.' (What is to be
understood is, for instance, how each biological species, and
each member of each biological species, comes to be as we
find that it is. Such understanding is to be obtained by

observation of successive stages, insight into the conjugates constituting each stage, and insight into why each stage gives way to the next.)[37]

'The biological species are a series of solutions to the problem of systematizing coincidental aggregates of chemical process.' An explanatory account of animal species will differentiate them according to their psychical characteristics (sensation, affectivity, aggressivity, and so on). That the psychic is more difficult for the investigator to get at than the physical and chemical (apparently at least, it is less reducible to the merely observable than they are) does not excuse the investigator from attempting to explain animals in terms of it. Science deals, after all, as we have already tried to show, not with 'bodies', but with the intelligible unities which are things. 'The study of animal behaviour, of stimulus and response, would reveal at any stage of development a flexible circle of ranges of schemes of recurrence. Implicit in such a circle of schemes, there would be correlations of the classical type.' Implicit in such correlations, there would be conjugates at the psychical level which would account for habitual perceptiveness and modes of aggressive and affective response, and would appear to systematise underlying neural configurations which otherwise would be unsystematic. But the point is not only to understand the organism at any particular stage of development, to get at the conjugates which together constitute what may be termed the *integrator* for that stage; the essential point of genetic method is to specify what we shall call the *operator*, or the intelligibility of the change from each particular stage to the next.[37]

One good example of a rather successful application of genetic method is the psychiatric theory of H.S. Sullivan. 'Roughly, Sullivan deals with ranges of intersubjective schemes of recurrence (dynamisms meeting needs,) their integrator (the self-system), and their operator (the avoidance of anxiety). From such elements he is in a position to construct any number of fortunate or unfortunate developments from a rather convincing extrapolation to infantile experience, through mischievous children, chums and gangs, early and late adolescence, either to the attainment of psychic maturity, or to the eruption of neurotic malfunctioning, or to the invasion of consciousness by the horrors of the 'not-me' in schizophrenia.'[38] (Apart from this rather brief instance, Lonergan does not adduce many examples to clarify his conception of genetic method; so perhaps it will be helpful for me to do so. Let us take as examples the origin of intra-specific aggression among fishes, reptiles, birds and mammals; and the origin of quasi-personal relations of love and friendship among some of these aggressive species. It is not at first sight at all easy to see why the universal operator in the evolution of animal species, random variation and natural selection, should in any circumstances favour intra-specific aggression. But a satisfactory explanation is that such aggression has the effect both of spreading a species over the available habitat, and of ensuring that the stronger of two males will tend to get possession of a female when competition arises; both these effects can readily be seen to favour survival. Here, the integrators concerned are the psychical characteristics of animals who were ancestors of those which are intra-specifically aggressive *before* the occurrence of that characteristic on the one hand, and the psychical characteristics of intra-specifically aggressive animals on the other. The operator is the explanation of the change, assuming that it is correct, as just described. Again, there is a problem about how quasi-personal bonds of friendship and love could have developed among animals, and of why all the animals who have developed these characteristics should also display intra-specific aggression.[39] It has been suggested that the redirection of aggression away from one or more conspecifics would tend to promote survival so far as young demand protracted care, and so far as animals tend to survive and flourish not only by aggressive behaviour between individuals, as already described, but by a degree of mutual assistance and co-operation. This suggestion is verified by the apparent existence of all degrees of ritualisation of aggression in the affectionate gestures between animal and human friends and lovers. Now whether this theory of the origin of love and friendship is true or false, it illustrates very well the principles of genetic method. Again, the relevant integrator is the behaviour of the ancestors of animals displaying love and friendship respectively before and after these characteristics were developed; and the operator is the intelligibility of the development from the one stage to the other.)

In clarifying the notion of genetic method, it will be useful to contrast our position briefly with other views of the nature of life. In agreement with the mechanist, we affirm the relevance of every insight which the physicist and chemist can offer to the biologist, since the organism is a higher system of underlying chemical and physical manifolds. But against mechanism, we deny that there is any prospect of biology ever being reduced to chemistry and physics, since 'the only evidence for that hope is the mechanist belief that reality consists in imaginable elements as imagined'. (It is clear that we cannot actually see the seeing of a rat, except on the implausible behaviourist view, which in any case is based on a view of reality which we have already given reasons for rejecting, that its seeing simply *is* that observable behaviour which constitutes our evidence for its seeing. But on our view, the seeing of the rat is the intelligibility to be grasped not only in the behaviour of the rat, but also both in the developed eye and optic nerve of the adult and 'proleptically in the developing eye of the foetus'. The behaviourist, or the mind-brain-identity theorist, will say that psychical events simply *are* their correlatives in brain-chemistry or in behaviour. Lonergan would agree with the man of common sense that there is something to the sight of the rat over and above what we can or conceivably could observe in the rat's brain or behaviour; and he would specify that what there is to it is the intelligibility which exists over and above the mere assemblage of observable data within which we find the intelligibility and by means of which we verify it.) There is, of course, from our point of view, a ready welcome for such discoveries as that of the conditioned reflex, which is one part of the flexible circle of schemes of recurrence which belongs to an organism at any given stage. Our rejection of mechanism is not to be taken as equivalent to an assertion of vitalism. Vitalism is insufficiently radical in its rejection of mechanism, which it seems indeed to accept in principle, merely adding that as well as imaginable elements, reality consists (in the case of living things) of unimaginable, vital entelechies. For our part, we affirm that real things are intelligible unities, and not mere objects of perception, at the level of protons, electrons, atoms, and chemical compounds, as well as of living organisms. This is not mystery-mongering; for us, things are purely and simply what are known in as far as one understands correctly. In our doctrine of the thing as an intelligible unity we agree with holism or organicism (which insist that an organism can be properly understood only as a whole, and not as a mere heterogeneous assemblage of elements); but we also affirm conjugates. This is necessary, since in emergent processes (such as living things) the classical laws which can be verified at their end are not the same as those which could be verified at their beginning. 'In determinate materials, there has occurred a change in what can be grasped by insight, formulated as law, and affirmed as verified.' (A mature blackbird, or fox, or man, differs in habits and capabilities from a nestling, cub or baby.) 'The process from one set (of conjugates) to the other is regular. But this regular process is not in accord with classical law, for there are no classical laws about changes of classical laws; nor is it in accord with statistical law, for it is not an indifferent choice between a set of alternative processes; so one is forced to recognize the fact of a third type of process to be investigated by a third, genetic method.'[40]

So far we have outlined three methods of inquiry, the classical, the statistical, and the genetic. Understanding leads to the formation of systems which are verified in phenomena; and such systems may be supposed either to be constant in time or to change over time. The anticipation that there is some constant system to be discovered grounds classical method; the anticipation that there is not a constant system to be discovered grounds statistical method; the anticipation that a changing sequence of systems will be intelligibly related grounds genetic method. Evidently there remains a fourth possibility, 'that the relations between successive stages of changing system will not be directly intelligible'. This grounds what we shall call *dialectical method* (which will prove relevant to the study of human ideas and the history of the institutions based on them). Since data either conform to system or do not do so, and since successive systems must be either related in a directly intelligible manner or not so related, it is clear that the four methods of inquiry when taken together are relevant to the study of any field of data whatever.

3 The Method of Metaphysics

3.1 *Judgement and Fact*

The central principle of Lonergan's epistemology is that knowledge is what is to be had by the threefold process of experiencing, understanding, and judging, and that reality is simply what is to be known by this process. There is presupposed in this account not only the mere flux of experience, as in the radical empiricism derived from Hume which has been thoroughly worked out by twentieth-century logical positivism, but also the inquiring intelligence which puts questions and expects answers. 'The Humean world of mere impressions comes to me as a puzzle to be pieced together.'[1] To follow through this viewpoint consistently is to obtain a theory not only of the knower and his knowing, but of the nature of the world which he is in process of coming to know; an adequate cognitional theory thus gives rise to an ontology or theory of reality.[2]

It is worth inquiring whether there is perhaps a generalised empirical method which can be applied to the data of consciousness, rather as the specialised empirical method of the natural sciences can be applied to the data of sense. After all, sensible data, contents of acts of seeing, hearing, tasting and so on, do not occur in a cognitional vacuum, but in a context determined by the subject's interests and preoccupations; this is just as true of the ordinary man, who adverts to what is relevant to his interests and concerns, as of the scientist. Now in every experience content and act may be distinguished, what is seen from the act of seeing, what is heard from the act of hearing, and so on. By correlating contents one moves in the direction of natural science; by correlating acts, and prescinding from contents, one moves in the direction of psychological[3] or cognitional theory.[4]

(Knowledge involves necessarily experience and understanding, but is complete only in the act of judgement, in which the knower grasps that this or that *is so*. What the knower rightly grasps to be so is what Lonergan terms the *virtually unconditioned*. Every matter of fact, everything that is the case, and can be found to be so by the process of experience, understanding, and judgement, is an example of the virtually unconditioned in Lonergan's sense. The concept of the virtually unconditioned is of cardinal importance in Lonergan's philosophy, enabling him to avoid Hegel's conclusion that thought ultimately has nothing to think of but itself, without embroiling him with Kantian 'things in themselves' such as somehow exist in utter transcendence of our cognitional processes.) The virtually unconditioned does have conditions; but these happen to be fulfilled. That the content of the relevant kind of judgement is absolute implies that it is not relative to the subject who utters the judgement. 'Caesar's crossing of the Rubicon was a contingent event occurring at a particular place and time. But a true affirmation of that event is an eternal, immutable, definitive validity. For if it is true that he did cross, then no one whatever at any place or time can truly deny that he did.' Here is a clue to the publicity of our knowledge. 'For the same reason that the unconditioned is withdrawn from relativity to its source, it also is accessible not only to the knower that utters it but also to any other knower.' Of course, the absolute objectivity of correct judgements is not to be confused with the invariance of the appropriate expression of particular kinds of judgement to which reference has already been made.[5] The identical truth expressed by the statement 'I am here now' has later to be expressed by the statement 'He was there then'. If knowledge is achieved, as we have argued, in the making of a judgement which has adequate grounds, an old sceptical puzzle, about how one seeking to know can ever achieve objective knowledge of what is other than himself, is easily resolved. The question is actually misleading, presupposing as it does that the knower knows himself. But the knower does not know himself until he intelligently and reasonably makes the correct judgement, 'I am'. But 'other judgements are equally possible and reasonable, so . . . through experience, inquiry and reflection there arises knowledge of other objects both as beings and as beings other than the knower' (since I may have good reason to judge both that there is a Queen of Britain, and that the Queen of Britain is other than myself). Objectivity in judgement is to be obtained, of course, by refusing to allow the cognitional process to be interfered with either by excessive rashness or excessive timidity, or by hope, fear or wishful thinking. To be objective in this sense is to give free rein to the questions for intelligence and reflection posed by the pure desire to know. Every logic and method is based on the exigences of the pure desire to know; 'a logic or method is not an ultimate which can be established only by a hullabaloo of starry-eyed praise for Medieval Philosophy, or for Modern Science, along with an insecure resentment of everything else'.[6]

3.2 *The Self-Affirming Subject*
How can I know that I am a knower? All knowledge is of the virtually unconditioned, and is based on a grasp at once of *what* the conditions are for what is known to be so, and of the fact *that* those conditions are fulfilled. In this case 'the link between the conditioned and its conditions may be cast in the proposition, I am a knower, if I am a concrete and intelligible unity-identity-whole, characterized by acts of seeing, perceiving, imagining, inquiring, understanding, formulating, reflecting, grasping the unconditioned, and judging. The fulfilment of these conditions is given in consciousness'. Now attention to one's acts of consciousness *heightens* them; but it does not *constitute* them as such. (I may see or hear or feel, but not attend to the fact that I see or hear or feel). Seeing and hearing as such have in common that they are both conscious acts. Some would object that in seeing one is aware of colour, but that any accompanying awareness of awareness is a fiction. But this objection does not seem quite to meet the facts. If seeing is an awareness of nothing but colour and hearing is an awareness of nothing but sounds, why are both termed 'awareness'? 'Is it because there is some similarity between colour and sound? Or is it that colour and

sound are disparate, yet with respect to both there are acts which are similar? ... One may quarrel with the phrase, awareness of awareness, particularly if one imagines awareness to be a looking and finds it preposterous to talk about looking at a look. But one cannot deny that, within the cognitional act as it occurs, there is a factor or element or component over and above its content, and that this factor is what differentiates cognitional acts from unconscious occurrences.' After all, there is unquestionably a difference between acts like seeing and hearing on the one hand, and merely biological acts (like digestion) of which we are not conscious on the other.[7]

If by consciousness is meant an awareness immanent in cognitional acts, it would seem that the awareness will differ in kind with the acts. (Each level of the cognitional process, so to speak, will have its own particular kind of consciousness.) 'There is an empirical consciousness characteristic of sensing, perceiving, imagining ... there is an intelligent consciousness characteristic of inquiry, insight, and formulation ... (and) on the third level of reflection, grasp of the unconditioned, and judgment, there is rational consciousness.' The point is not that I can uncover intelligence by introspection, as I can point out Calcutta on a map; it is only that I do in fact have (and have good reason to know that I have) conscious states and perform acts of intelligence and reasonableness. My repugnance at placing astrology and astronomy, or legend and history, on the same footing, is an expression of the fact that I am rationally conscious, that I demand sufficient reason. Though I never enjoyed such a remarkable insight as that of Archimedes, I do know what it is to get the point, to see how things hang together, to know the explanation or cause of some state of affairs. However, while the consciousness of an individual varies according to the nature of his conscious acts, it is also a unity. Rather as one thing can be the object of experience, understanding, and rational judgement, so there is one consciousness in the subject which is empirical, intelligent and rational. This must be so, or one couldn't make a rational judgement in the light of one's understanding and experience. Of course, it is one thing to be conscious, another thing to affirm rationally that one is a conscious being. (The object of the present section is precisely to induce the reader to take the step from the former position of merely being a conscious individual to the latter position of affirming that he is such.) 'As consciousness is not increased by affirming it, so it is not diminished by denying it, for the effect of denying it would be to add to the list of one's judgments and not to subtract from the ground on which judgments may be made.'[8] (It is fruitless, one might put it, to judge that one makes no judgements; and merely to judge that I make no judgements is by no means to prevent myself making them.)

I cannot coherently question that I am a questioner,[9] or coherently employ my intelligence to concoct theories to the effect that I am not intelligent. Again, I cannot be content with mere inquiry and theory, but want to get at the facts. All the revisions in the sciences are forced upon us by the facts, which may compel us to chuck away the theories evolved, however brilliantly, by previous understanding. 'Fact . . . combines the concreteness of experience, the determinateness of accurate intelligence, and the absoluteness of rational judgment. It is the natural objective of human cognitional process.' The sceptic, in denying that he really knows anything at all, is not in conflict with absolute necessity; he might not have existed at all, or he might not have been a knower. Contradiction only arises 'when he utilises cognitional process to deny it . . . The critical spirit can weigh all else in the balance, only on condition that it does not criticize itself. It is a self-assertive spontaneity that demands sufficient reason for all else but offers no justification for itself.'[10]

In the case of data of consciousness, as in that of the data of sense, one starts from description and moves towards explanation. But there is a very important difference between the resulting types of theory, cognitional and scientific. 'Explanation on the basis of sense can reduce the element of hypothesis to a minimum but it cannot eliminate it entirely. But explanation on the basis of consciousness can escape entirely the merely postulated, the merely inferred.' (I can be much more certain of the fact that I am an experiencing, inquiring and reflecting being, for example, than I can of any scientific theory, since my evaluation of any such theory can only be arrived at on the basis of such experience, inquiry and reflection.) Any scientific theory, for instance in mechanics, is accepted because it provides the simplest account available of the known facts. There may still be unknown yet relevant facts which will ultimately demand its revision. But this sort of limitation need not apply to the explanation of human consciousness. The certainty available in cognitional theory depends on the fact that any revision would itself presuppose cognitional theory. (This is because revision is a matter of developing and expanding insights, and their checking in relation to the virtually unconditioned; the generic nature of this process at least can be fully described by cognitional theory.) 'Revision cannot revise its own presuppositions. A reviser cannot appeal to data to deny data, to his new insights to deny insights, to his new formulation to deny formulation, to his reflective grasp to deny reflective grasp.' Popular relativism is inclined to argue that empirical science is the most reliable form of human knowledge, and yet that it is subject to indefinite revision. But 'one must definitely know invariant features of human knowledge before one can assert that empirical science is subject to indefinite revision; and if one definitely knows invariant features of human knowledge, then one knows what is not subject to revision'.[11]

Since something not unlike Kant's 'transcendental deduction' has been performed in the course of what has been said so far, it seems worthwhile to describe and justify the principal differences between our results and Kant's. Our distinction between the thing-for-us and the thing-itself, between the thing-as-described and the thing-as-explained, seems to have something to do with Kant's distinction between the phenomenon and the noumenon. Exactly what Kant meant by this distinction is disputed;[12] it seems likely to be derived, through successive alterations, from the Galilean distinction between the primary and secondary qualities of things. But our distinction, in any case, is identical neither with the Galilean nor with the Kantian; it is simply between things as described and things as explained. Also, it is to be observed that Kant's categories are at once inflexible and irreducibly mysterious; yet had he taken his 'Copernican revolution' further, and really disentangled himself from earlier misapprehensions concerning reality and objectivity, they need not have been so.[13] (Kant's unknowable things-in-themselves are the residue of real things as constituted by their primary qualities, subjected to a criticism which is not quite thorough enough; correspondingly, the categories which, according to Kant, we bring *a priori* to our understanding of the world, are the result of a not quite sufficiently rigorous analysis of the cognitional process.) 'Inquiry is generative of all understanding, and understanding is generative of all concepts and systems. Reflection is generative of all reflective grasp of the unconditioned, and that grasp is generative of all judgement. If the Kantian proscribes consideration of inquiry and reflection, he leaves himself open to the charge of obscurantism. If he admits such consideration, if he praises intelligent curiosity and the critical spirit, then he is on his way to acknowledge the generative principles both of the categories Kant knew and of the categories Kant did not know.'[14]

The account of the human subject's knowledge of himself that we have given puts us also at odds with the relativist, in his contention that fully correct judgements do not occur. Relativist thinking is quite correct in its insistence, against empiricism, that human thinking is not to be accounted for at the level of sense-presentations alone. But 'just as the relativist insists on the level of intelligence against the empiricist, so we insist on the level of reflection against the relativist.' In any case, the non-existence of any other matter of fact would itself be a matter of fact, even if it were the case. Now we do not simply theorise about what is given in our experience; we make judgements about it in terms of these theories which may, sure enough, turn out to be false. When you attempt to give a definite answer to such a plain question as 'Is this a typewriter?', the relativist will pounce on your inability to say exactly what 'is' and 'typewriter' mean. He will point out that human knowledge is limited, and that every system of conceptions and ideas which you care to mention has its weak points. The relativist may claim that as the universe is a pattern of internal relations (in which every thing and fact is inextricably related to every other thing and fact[15]), you cannot know any part or aspect of it in isolation from the rest. But what is required for particular judgements does seem to be less than the ideal of comprehensive understanding; it is merely that, whatever be the case about the rest of the universe, at least this particular fact is so. 'I may not be able to settle border-line instances in which one might dispute whether the name, *typewriter*, would be appropriate. But, at least, I can settle definitely that this is a typewriter. I may not be able to clarify the meaning of *is*, but it is sufficient for present purposes to know the difference between *is* and *is not*, and that, I know . . . You warn me that I have made mistakes in the past. But your warning is meaningless, if I am making a further mistake in recognizing a past mistake as a mistake.' And questions which are answered in terms of a pattern of internal relations (grasped by such direct insights as have already been described) are only those which ask for some explanatory system (such as is looked for by the heuristic structure of classical science); however, prior in our knowing to knowledge of things-as-explained is knowledge of things-as-described. And the single judgement (in such cases) is a limited commitment which does not pronounce on the universe; 'it is content to affirm some single conditioned that has a finite number of conditions which, in fact, are fulfilled'. And in any case, as appears from our earlier analysis, the universe is not just explanatory system; it is a universe of facts, which diverge non-systematically from pure intelligibility; and 'explanatory system has validity in the measure that it conforms to descriptive facts.' (Any theory, however self-consistent, must be verified before one has any grounds for saying that it is true.) As to the meanings of such terms as 'is' and 'this', it is certainly up to the cognitional theorist to explain them. 'He would do so by saying that *is* represents the *Yes* that occurs in judgment and that is anticipated by such questions as, Is it? What is it? Similarly, a theorist would explain *this* as the return from the field of conception to the empirical residue in the field of presentations.'[16] But we can employ such terms, which derive their significance from the basic drive of inquiring human intelligence, without such full definition.

The relativist might ask me to consider the enormous difference there would be in my notion of a typewriter if I understood fully the chemistry of its materials, the mechanics of its construction, its effect on literary style and commercial bureaucracy, and so on. But the very possibility of such increase in my *knowledge* of typewriters presupposes that I can at least *identify* this and similar machines as typewriters. 'In the last analysis, just as the empiricist tries to banish intelligence, so the relativist tries to banish fact and, with it, what everyone else names truth.'[17]

3.3 *The World as Everything to be Known*

We have discussed the knower and his knowledge of himself. What of the rest of reality, of things other than himself? 'Being . . . is the objective of the pure desire to know.'[18] It includes both all that is known, and all that remains to be known. It is what is to be known by the totality of true judgements, the complete set of answers to the complete set of questions. It is important to draw a distinction between the spontaneously operative notion of being (the sum of everything that is known and everything that is th: case but not yet known), and the theoretical account of its genesis and content. The first is universal and invariant (since everyone aspires to understand and to judge correctly, and being is that about which correct judgements can be made on the basis of understanding); the second varies with philosophical context, with the completeness of a thinker's observations and the thoroughness of his analysis. Mere thinking prescinds from existing and not existing; I can think of centaurs and phlogiston just as well as I can think of horses and oxygen. This has led some philosophers to conclude that being is one thing and existing another.[19] But, apart from the oddity of the implication that the non-existent somehow is, this overlooks the nature of the cognitional process as a whole. In one sense, certainly, thinking does prescind from existing and not existing. But there is another sense in which it does not, since thinking is purposive, and its purpose ultimately is 'determining whether what is thought does exist'. (I not only try to frame concepts; I also try to find whether there really exists anything that corresponds to them.) 'Intelligence, as obverse, looks for the intelligible, as reverse. Reasonableness, as obverse, looks for the grounded, as reverse.' The desire to know has as its object everything there is to be known — an 'unrestricted object named being, or the all, or everything about everything, or the concrete universe'.[20]

We do not have any insight into an 'essence of being', or anything like that; to do so, we would have to know everything about everything, which we do not. However, we *can* define what we mean by 'being', as it were at second remove, 'by saying that it refers to all that can be known by intelligent grasp and reasonable affirmation'. Thus, it is not an essence in the sense of what can be grasped by an act of understanding and expressed by a direct definition, since it does not prescind, as essences in this sense do, from questions of existence or actuality. To define 'being' in the way that we have suggested leaves open the general question of which particular kinds of question are appropriate, and which kinds of answer are correct — a general question answered in different ways by materialists, empiricists, idealists, and phenomenalists. 'Being' is capable of such diverse interpretations because it is determinate only at second remove; it is 'the notion of what is to be determined by correct judgments. If the strategic correct judgments are that matter exists and nothing but matter, the materialist is right', and the same obviously applies *mutatis mutandis* to the empiricist, the idealist, and the phenomenalist. The notion of being, of what there is, becomes determined only as correct judgements are made, and fully determined only when all correct judgements are made. 'However, the making of judgments is a determinate process, and one does not have to make all judgments to grasp the nature of that process. It is this fact that makes cognitional theory a base of operations for the determination of the general structure of the concrete universe.'[21] The notion of being is determined by the set of correct judgements; however, there is a larger set of possible judgements, within which are 'strategic sets that serve to define the general character of the concrete universe in accord with the varying viewpoints of different philosophies ... To determine what being is in any particular philosophy, one has to determine the strategic judgments of that philosophy; and to determine what is the correct meaning of being as being, one has to examine the strategic judgments of the correct philosophy'.[22]

Our own account of being may be clarified by contrast with that provided in other philosophies. The right way to find out 'the nature of being, of the concrete universe, is to inquire and reflect with respect to the whole of experience; and 'being' will be what one would know if one had exhaustively so inquired and reflected. Parmenides did not advert to the fact that being is subject to definition only in the indirect way we have described. So he was led to argue that 'because being is, it cannot be not-being, nor becoming, nor ceasing to be. Inversely, neither not-being nor becoming nor ceasing to be are being, and so they must be nothing'. So, since there cannot be any emptiness (not being), nor becoming, nor ceasing to be, being must be without origin or end, full and unchangeable. Another kind of misapprehension is enshrined in Plato's doctrine of Forms. This doctrine is derived from failure to distinguish between the level of intelligence and the level of reflection in the cognitional process; thus 'the unconditioned of judgment is surreptitiously attributed to mere objects of thought to transform them into eternal Forms' (the inevitable result of this is that luxuriant proliferation of entities which Quine has called 'Plato's beard').[23] The failure of Platonism to grasp the nature of judgement, and its distinction from understanding, resulted in a deviation from the concrete universe of fact to an ideal heaven. Aristotle made an advance of fundamental importance when he distinguished sharply between questions for intelligence (What is it? Why is it so?) and questions for reflection (Is it so? Does it exist?), with the result that he had a sane and clear-headed respect for fact, without reaching the full implications of the distinction he had made. For Aristotle, 'the function of explanation was simply to determine what things are and why they have the properties they possess. The intrinsically hypothetical character of explanation and its need of a further, verifying judgment of existence was overlooked'.[24]

The medieval followers of Aristotle thus inherited a central metaphysical problem from him. 'Aristotle broke with his Parmenidean and Platonist antecedents by identifying being with the concrete universe as, in fact, it is known to be. But Aristotle did not break with their supposition that the notion of being was a conceptual content.' (To the fundamental problem of the nature of the mind's conception of being or the concrete universe, discussed in the last paragraph but one, Aristotle had hit on a vital clue, the distinction between questions for intelligence and questions for reflection; but he still held that one could attain what we have termed a direct rather than an indirect conception of being.) The medieval philosopher Henry of Ghent seems to have held that the unity of being is merely a name (i.e., that there is nothing whatever in common to all that there is); while Duns Scotus, on the contrary, held that there was some minimal unity of content in all beings. 'What it is', on his view of the matter 'cannot be declared by appealing to other positive contents; for it is one of the ultimate atoms of thought; it is simply sim-ple[25]... The concept of being is the concept with least connotation and greatest denotation';[26] it is simply 'the negation of nothing'. Cajetan, in the sixteenth century, was as dissatisfied with Scotus' solution as Scotus had been with Henry of Ghent's. 'If a single name without a single meaning will not do, neither will a single meaning that as single seems restricted to the order of thought. Accordingly, Cajetan worked out his theory of the unity of a function of variable contents. Just as "double" denotes indifferently the relation of 2 to 1, 4 to 2, 6 to 3, and so forth, so "being" denotes indifferently the proportion of essence to existence or, as we might say, the proportion between what is formulated by thought and what is added to it by judgement.' It will be observed that, in relation to Aristotle, Scotus stands for those assumptions of Parmenides and Plato from which Aristotle never freed himself, Cajetan for those aspects of his thought that go beyond them[27] (Cajetan took advantage of, and followed through in his analysis of 'being', that difference between questions for understanding and questions for reflection which Aristotle had in effect emphasized without formulating explicitly.)

Cajetan's position has its limitations, for all its brilliance.

'It envisages an aggregate of concrete beings each of which is constituted by essence and existence' (i.e. of which it is to be found out not only *what* they are, but *that* they are). 'It offers as the unity of the notion of being the relation or proportion of what is conceived to its being affirmed. But it does not elucidate how that relation emerges in our knowledge as a single notion.' To complete his position, to show its full rationality and point, one has to go back to his master Aquinas. Aquinas recognised an unrestricted desire to know, which advances towards knowledge 'by asking the explanatory question, *Quid sit?* and the factual question, *An sit?*'[28] From his point of view 'it is easy to discern not only justification of Cajetan's theory of analogy but also the elements which that theory tends to overlook. Prior to conception and to judgement' (and thus to the 'essence' and 'existence' which are the object of these), 'there is the dynamic orientation of intelligent and rational consciousness with its unrestricted objective' (knowledge of everything there is to be known).[29] 'This orientation is man's capacity to raise questions and thereby to generate knowledge . . . As it is the common root of intelligent grasp and reasonable affirmation, so also it is the root of the relation or proportion between the conceived essence and the affirmed existence.'[30]

(*In fine*, being, or reality, or the concrete universe, is what is to be known by the process of experience, intelligent inquiry, and reasonable reflection. The true cognitional theory and metaphysics advert to this fact and consistently apply it; while false cognitional theories and metaphysical systems are all due, in some way or other, to neglect of it. Typically, they assume that knowledge is to be gained by a more or less crude or subtle kind of looking; this may be either a common-or-garden looking at what is immediately given in experience, or a spiritual look at the Platonic heaven of concepts which in fact result from intelligent inquiry on the basis of experience, but which are not necessarily confirmed as instantiated by reasonable reflection.) 'Against the objectivity that is based on intelligent inquiry and critical reflection, there stands the unquestioning orientation of the extroverted biological consciousness and its uncritical survival not only in . . . practical living but also in much of philosophic thought.'[31] Against the universe intelligently to be grasped and reasonably to be affirmed, there is the world which is the intentional object of the extroverted biological consciousness, of which the real and the apparent are deemed to be mere sub-divisions. 'Against the self-affirmation of a consciousness that at once is empirical, intellectual, and rational, there stands the native bewilderment of the existential subject, revolted by mere animality, unsure of his way through the maze of philosophies, trying to live without a known purpose, suffering despite an unmotivated will, threatened with an inevitable death and, before death, with disease and even insanity.' No-one is born with the mental habits and dispositions necessary for sustained thought, and no-one reaches them easily; merely biological factors, and prejudices deriving from a predominantly practical point of view, may and do interfere with them, and cause the subject to construe himself and his world in a manner quite different from what would be indicated by a consistent use of intelligent inquiry and reasonable reflection. Human consciousness is polymorphic, and each man is in tension between various aspects and possibilities of his consciousness. (He is subject to emotions and moods, harassed by the needs of his daily life, and entangled in the prejudices of his own particular cultural and social group.)[32] It is no wonder that there have been so many conflicting and disparate philosophies, since up to now the materials for grasping the polymorphic nature of the mind of man have not been available. But now we have the requisite materials — in mathematics, in a well-developed empirical science, in depth psychology, in historical theories, and in the epistemological discussions of Descartes, Hume and Kant. It is easy to despair, in the welter of conflicting philosophies, of ever getting at the truth in this field; it may not exist, one is inclined to conclude, or it may be otherwise unattainable. But this is to neglect the possibility that 'the many, contradictory, disparate philosophies can all be contributions to the clarification of some basic but polymorphic fact'. The philosophies have in common that they are products of inquiring intelligence and reflecting reasonableness; thus they have at least a unity of origin. And if the truth to which philosophy aspires is a general description of the nature of the reality to be known by inquiring intelligence and reflecting reasonableness, the philosophies will be unified in their ultimate goal as well.[33]

3.4.   *Philosophy and the Philosophies*

In any philosophy, one may distinguish on the one hand its cognitional theory (epistemology or theory of knowledge), and on the other hand its resulting pronouncements in the realms of metaphysics, ethics, and theology. (For example, in the version of Logical Positivism propounded in A.J. Ayer's *Language, Truth and Logic*, the cognitional theory is constituted by the Verification Principle. Accordingly, reality in effect consists of what can be the object of experience; moral discourse amounts to the evincing of feelings and the propagation of behavioural dispositions; and theological statements are nonsensical.) Let us label the two basic elements that we have just distinguished in any philosophy as its *basis* and its *expansion*. The philosophical component immanent in the formation of the cognitional theory will either be a *basic position* or a *basic counter-position*. 'It will be a basic position (1) if the real is the concrete universe of being and not a subdivision of the 'already out there now'; (2) if the subject becomes known when it affirms itself intelligently and reasonably and so is not known in any prior 'existential' state; and (3) if objectivity is conceived as a consequence of intelligent inquiry and reasonable reflection, and not as a property of vital anticipation, extroversion, and satisfaction.' It will be a basic counter-position, if it contradicts one or more of these principles. A philosophical pronouncement on any epistemological, ethical, metaphysical or theological issue will be named a *position* if it is consistent with the basic positions; a *counter-position* if it is coherent with one or more of the basic counter-positions, but not with the basic positions. Each of the counter-positions invites reversal, since it is inconsistent with the activity of grasping it intelligently and affirming it reasonably. (Hume's denial of the existence of a substantial self, discussed at the beginning of this book, would appear to be a counter-position, in that it utilises very acutely understanding and judgement to make nonsense of understanding and judgement.[34]) 'One can grasp and accept, propose and defend a counter-position; but that activity commits one to grasping and accepting; and the commitment involves a grasp and acceptance of the basic positions.' All positions invite development, so far as the actual stating of them in any instance is inadequate and incomplete. The shift of human consciousness backwards and forwards between the extroversion suitable for the immediate needs of living on the one hand, and the unrestricted desire to know on the other, and the infinite number of possible attitudes in between, is what gives rise to the positions and counter-positions. It is by acknowledging this shift that a metaphysics is critical, and only by being critical can it free itself from the many pseudo-problems which otherwise beset it.[35]

The dualism of Descartes is a very clear example of a philosophy containing both a basic position and a basic counter-position. The basic position is *'Cogito, ergo sum'* (I think, therefore I am); but this dictum has to be clarified and made more precise by a pursuing of the questions of what are the self, thinking, being, and the relations between them — questions which Descartes himself did not adequately pursue. The basic counter-position is the affirmation of the *res extensa* (extended thing) as well as the *res cogitans* (thinking thing); this in effect makes the real a subdivision of the already-out-there-now anticipated by animal extroversion. Hobbes got rid of the dualism by granting reality to the *res cogitans* only as another instance of the *res extensa*. 'Hume overcame Hobbes by reducing all instances of the "already out there now real" to manifolds of impressions linked by mere habits and beliefs.[36] The intelligence and reasonableness of Hume's criticizing were obviously quite different from the knowledge he so successfully criticized. Might one not identify knowledge with the criticizing activity rather than the criticized materials? If so, 'Cartesian dualism is eliminated by another route. One is back at the thinking subject and, at the term of this reversal, one's philosophy is enriched not only by a stronger affirmation of the basic position but also by an explicit negation of the basic counter-position.' Significant discoveries are not, of course, the prerogative of those with completely successful philosophies, and so may be expressed as counter-positions as well as positions. But since the counter-positions invite reversal, the free unfolding of thought should at length separate any discovery from the bias of its author.[37]

Metaphysics is the branch of human knowledge which underlies and unifies all other departments. Its principles are 'the detached and disinterested drive of the pure desire to know and its unfolding in the empirical, intellectual, and rational consciousness of self-affirming subject'. Other departments of knowledge are restricted to some particular subsidiary viewpoint and field. Metaphysics transforms the other branches of knowledge, since the consciousness of man, being polymorphic (and so subject to many impulses besides the desire to know), is always at the risk of formulating its discoveries as counter-positions. Common sense, which we will deal with at greater length later on, has indeed its uses, but gives rise to bias when evoked outside its proper field of the particular and practical; scientists share the bias of common sense so far as the special interests and concerns of each do not correct it; and so far as men have these many and conflicting biases (since common sense differs according to individual, class and cultural background), they are divided and at a loss for a coherent view of the world. Metaphysics urges the positions to fuller development, and by reversing the counter-positions liberates discoveries in philosophy and the sciences from the shackles in which they may at first be chained. Metaphysics unifies all other branches of knowledge, since 'it is the original, total question and it moves to the total answer by transforming and putting together all other answers. Metaphysics . . . is the whole in knowledge but not the whole of knowledge'[38] (co-ordinating as it does the rest of knowledge obtained through science, common sense, introspective psychology, or whatever other means there may be).[39]

Metaphysics appears to exist in three stages. There is a *latent* stage when efforts to unify knowledge are haphazard and spasmodic; a *problematic* stage when the need for unification is felt, but studies of knowledge are involved in the disarray of positions and counter-positions.[40] In its third and ultimate stage, it may be termed *explicit*. What is this explicit metaphysics? Let us prescind at present from the complicated question of man's knowledge of what lies beyond his experience. 'Accordingly, we introduce the notion of *proportionate being*. In its full sweep, being is whatever is to be known by intelligent grasp and reasonable affirmation. But being that is proportionate to human knowing not only is to be understood and affirmed but also is to be experienced. So proportionate being may be defined as whatever is to be known by human experience, intelligent grasp, and reasonable affirmation. Now let us say that explicit metaphysics is the conception, affirmation, and implementation of the integral heuristic structure of proportionate being... A heuristic notion ... is the notion of an unknown content and it is determined by anticipating the type of act through which the unknown would become known. A heuristic structure is an ordered set of heuristic notions. Finally, an integral heuristic structure is the ordered set of all heuristic notions.' This metaphysics would explicitly supply the questions which are answered by knowledge of other kinds, rather than doing it merely implicitly as does the inquiring mind which is the source of latent metaphysics. Moreover, 'heuristic notions and structures are not discovered by some Platonic recall of a prior state of contemplative bliss. They result from the resourcefulness of human intelligence in operation'. While other branches of knowledge tend to advance by discovering new methods of inquiry, metaphysics does so by adding these to its account of the integral structure of proportionate being. Such a metaphysics would neither dictate nor be subservient to the scientific and common sense knowledge which it would transform and unify; but it could and would take over the results achieved by such methods of inquiry, work them into coherence by reversing the counter-positions involved in them, and unify them by identifying them as parts of its own integral heuristic structure. Such a metaphysics, once it had got over its initial difficulties, would be basically stable; no doubt there would be incidental modifications and improvements in it, but there would be no revolutionary changes. Revolutions in science are due to the acquisition of new viewpoints; but there is no viewpoint beyond that of the inquiring and reflective intelligence itself. For instance, there are Aristotelian, Galilean, Newtonian, and Eisteinian accounts of free fall, all open to revision; but 'one cannot revise the heuristic notion that the nature of a free fall is what is to be known when the free fall is understood correctly'.[41]

Explicit metaphysics is a personal attainment for each individual, since no-one can understand and judge for another — though of course books and teaching can provide a useful stimulus.[42] It is true that human individuals differ a great deal from one another in their backgrounds and individual histories, and have various outlooks on the universe. Yet they, as they actually are, constitute the starting-point for explicit metaphysics. 'People cannot avoid experience, cannot put off their intelligence, cannot renounce their reasonableness. But they may never have adverted to these concrete and factual inevitabilities.' The move from latent to explicit metaphysics in the individual is primarily the development of his self-knowledge. At the beginning of the process the individual 'has not learnt to distinguish sharply and effectively between the knowing men share with animals, the knowing that men alone possess, and the manifold blends and mixtures of the two that are the disorientation and ground the bewilderment of people as they are'. The explicit metaphysics acquired through such self-knowledge does not destroy science or common sense, which are quite valid each within its own sphere. What it can do is remove from the knowledge one has acquired through science and common sense whatever is *not* due to experience, intelligent inquiry, and reasonable reflection. The subject as a result of his self-knowledge becomes aware of the polymorphism of his consciousness, how it reflects the bias of his individual situation, his class, and his culture, and how it intrudes into science confused notions about knowledge, reality, and objectivity. The re-orientation achieved by the subject through his self-knowledge will thus mount a steady pressure 'against the common nonsense that tries to pass for common sense and against the uncritical philosophy that pretends to be a scientific conclusion'.[43]

In its general form, the transition to explicit metaphysics is a deduction involving a major premiss, a set of minor premisses, and a set of secondary minor premisses. 'The major premiss is the isomorphism which obtains between the structure of knowing and the structure of the known.' The primary minor premisses are 'affirmations of concrete and recurring structures in the knowing of the self-affirming subject', the simplest being that every instance of knowledge of proportionate being consists of a unification of experiencing, understanding, and judging. 'It follows from the isomorphism of knowing and known that every instance of known proportionate being is a parallel unification of a content of experience, a content of understanding, and a content of judgment'. The secondary minor premisses are supplied by re-oriented science and common sense, and they provide what is to be integrated by the integrating structure. It is possible to use a different method to get the same results; one may, for example, begin from the secondary minor premisses, find in them their invariant structure, and generalise the result obtained. As a matter of fact this has been done by the Aristotelian and Thomist schools of philosophy, whose conclusions largely anticipate our own. But there is certainly something to be gained from the method which we have used here, since Aristotelian and Thomist thought has as a matter of historical fact been rather a lonely island in an ocean of philosophical controversy. Only the methodical reorientation of science and common sense (which may be achieved by analysis of the knowing subject and the nature of his knowing) can put a stop to the confusions caused by that inexhaustible matrix of muddle, the polymorphism of human consciousness. And the misconceptions in which metaphysics remains involved, unless these sources of confusion are stopped up, serve to deflect it from acting in the salutary way it should; 'what should provide an integration for the science and the common sense of any age risks taking on the appearance of a mummy that would preserve for all time Greek science and medieval common sense'. (This is what the Aristotelian and Thomist philosophies inevitably look like, unless there is added to them an extension and justification in cognitional theory of the kind that we have offered.) It is vital that the central question is not begged; explicit metaphysics (far from being a series of dogmas to be accepted on ecclesiastical or political or scientific authority, or any recondite matter) is based directly on what any inquirer can verify in his own empirical, intelligent and rational consciousness. A method can direct activity to a goal only by anticipating the general nature of the goal (as we showed in our discussion of the heuristic structures of scientific method); metaphysics anticipates the general nature of reality, but has to leave the filling-in of details to the sciences and common sense.[44]

We do not attempt here a general survey and discussion of metaphysical systems; however, metaphysical positions can be studied expeditiously by looking at the methods of argument that underlie them. As to these, we shall not merely tabulate but criticise them, since there is, as we have tried to show, only one method of metaphysics which is not arbitrary. A metaphysical system, when fully articulated, takes the form of a set of propositions, of which some are primitive, and the others arrived at by logical deduction from these. The main problem of a metaphysics is thus to make a correct selection of the primitive propositions. First, it may be held that the set of primitive propositions consists of universal and necessary truths; since *ex hypothesi* they are not deduced from anything else, it is commonly claimed that they are self-evident. But it is difficult to see how such universal and self-evident truths could include any proposition about matters of fact, without thereby ceasing to be universal and self-evident.[45] Awareness of this difficulty compelled Scotus and Ockham to complement their abstract systems with an intuition of the existing and present state of affairs as existing and present. (There is always a special problem of how a system of universally valid propositions can relate to ordinary matters of empirical fact, as appeared from our discussion of the relation of the theories of classical science to concrete situations.)[46] Furthermore, if the primitive propositions are necessarily true, they hold for any possible universe; and there is thus no particular reason to suppose that the metaphysics derived from them will be suited to the purpose of integrating a common sense and a science which have a specific reference to this universe. Also, it is worth asking what kind of proposition it is that can be both universal and necessary. Analytic propositions are so, presupposing as they do nothing but the definition of their terms. Provided you do not affirm the existence of any thing or state of affairs corresponding to the terms, you have at your disposal an indefinitely large number of universal truths valid in every possible world, since there is no limit to the number of definitions which may be proposed. Let us isolate for attention those analytic propositions whose terms do refer to what actually exists, and call them *analytic principles*.[47] (Thus 'all bachelors are unmarried persons' and 'oxygen is a chemical element' will be analytic principles, since not only are both propositions true in virtue of the meanings of their constituent terms, but there happen to exist bachelors, unmarried persons, oxygen, and chemical elements.) Someone might propose, then, that the analytic propositions which are the primitive propositions of the correct metaphysical system should all be analytic principles. But the difficulty here is that one can only find out which analytic propositions are analytic principles by way of concrete judgements of fact. (The proposition 'oxygen is a chemical element' may be true by definition, but the meaning of each of its constituent terms has been fixed only by virtue of a huge number of particular verified judgements of fact.) Thus the abstract metaphysics of all possible worlds turns out to be very empty indeed, its only restriction being the principle of non-contradiction. Furthermore, this abstract metaphysics ran counter to the intuition by Scotus and Ockham of the existing and present world *as* existing and present. After all, it is conceivable that we might have an *intuition* of immediately existing and present states of affairs without there really *being* any such; and this possibility, as Nicholas of Autrecourt pointed out, might, on these general premises, be realised in the present world.[48]

An alternative to abstract deduction is concrete deduction; here the primitive propositions are analytic principles whose terms have reference to what really exists. But 'a concrete deduction is possible only if an objective necessity binds the existent that is concluded to the existent referred to in the premises. For without this objective necessity logically impeccable inferences would arrive at possibly false conclusions'. (For concrete deduction to be possible, in fact, world-process must be systematic in the sense described above.)[49] There are many metaphysical systems which consist of concrete deductions; examples are Spinoza's single reality with necessary attributes and modes, emanationist doctrines about a necessary being from which proceed necessarily all other beings, and theories to the effect that God exists necessarily and is morally bound to create the best of all possible worlds. But it must be asked on what grounds such a method is chosen by the metaphysician in the first place. *If* you choose concrete deduction, certainly you will be forced into monism or emanationism or optimism or mechanistic determinism. But 'the real issue is to determine, not what follows once the method of concrete deduction is assumed, but whether or not that method is to be employed... If abstract deduction is empty, concrete deduction sets a prior question'. Since the question is about the general structure of the universe, the prior question must, it seems, regard the mind that is to know the universe. Now the premisses for any concrete deduction, for example that presented by Newton's *Principia*, must be synthetic — so as not to be empty of content (like the premisses of the abstract deduction we have just discussed) — and *a priori* — since they are not to be known by taking a look at what is to be seen, which is irreducibly particular. (We do not perceive tree-hood as such; we see particular objects which we subsume under a concept and call 'trees'.) If it possess such synthetic and *a priori* principles, the mind cannot just be as it were a mirror of the world, but must be a sort of factory which synthesises materials provided by outer and inner sense.[50] (This, of course, is Kant's insight, which, however, that philosopher did not apply thoroughly or consistently enough.)

But there are a number of difficulties in the way of deduction of concrete deduction from the principles governing the operation of the human mind itself, chief among them being that what is to be accounted for is not just Newton's or Einstein's concrete deduction, but a whole series of concrete deductions, none of them certain, but each merely the best available in its time. Apparently the human mind is not so much a factory with a determinate set of processes (as would appear, for instance, from Kant's list of categories), as 'a universal machine tool that erects all kinds of factories, keeps adjusting and improving them, and eventually scraps them in favour of radically new designs'. There is no one fixed set of *a priori* syntheses, since every insight (as may be seen from the discussion in the first chapter) constitutes such an *a priori*. Some say that Kant's oversight derives from the fact that he overlooked the medieval theory of abstraction.[51] But there are several medieval theories of abstraction (of how we come by knowledge of universals like 'man', 'horse' and 'triangle' from experience of particular men, horses and triangles). Scotus would have rejected Kant's theory of the *a priori* for the same reason that he rejected the view of Aristotle and Aquinas (practically identical with our own) as outlined above, 'that intellect apprehends the intelligible in the sensible and grasps the universal in the particular'.[52] For Scotus, knowing is fundamentally a matter of taking a look at what is *there*, either in external sense or in internal imagination; and thus the Aristotelian and Thomist account is, for him, one of seeing what is not there to be seen. (However long you stare at a cartwheel, or however vividly and persistently you imagine one, you will never see or imagine a circle in it; conception is not a matter either of an external or an internal look.) Therefore, as Scotus sees it, a series of steps must be invoked: (1) an 'abstraction' occurs, in which, unconsciously, a universal conceptual content is impressed upon intellect when one observes a particular thing; (2) intellect takes a look at the conceptual content; (3) the intellect compares different conceptual contents, and sees which are necessarily connected and which are incompatible. Once this is done, the thinker may proceed to deduce the abstract metaphysics of all possible worlds, from the necessarily connected concepts, and add to this an intuition of the actually existing and present world as actually existing and present.[53]

Aristotle and Aquinas, on the other hand, 'both affirmed the fact of insight as clearly and effectively as can be expected. As they considered the sensible as seen to be only potentially in the object, so they considered the intelligible as understood to be only potentially in the image'. (As the physical object does not become seen just by virtue of existing, but needs the presence of some being capable of sight actually to be seen; so neither the mere perception of that object, nor any memory-image of that perception, can include the intelligible aspect of the object, which can be attained only by the insight of an intelligent being.) Now both Aquinas and Aristotle affirmed self-evident principles, such as result necessarily from the definition of their terms (analytic propositions), as relevant to our knowledge of the world; but Aquinas at least added the requirement (equivalent to our statement of the conditions in which analytic propositions amount to analytic principles) that the terms be validated by the habit or virtue he called 'wisdom'. Aquinas considered two forms of wisdom, a higher form granted by the Holy Spirit, and a lower form concerned with knowledge of all things in relation to their ultimate causes. But evidently a third form of wisdom is needed, since we cannot solve the problem we have set ourselves by presupposing theology or mystical experience on the one hand, or enough metaphysics on the other to justify talk in terms of 'ultimate causes'; what is required is precisely the 'wisdom' to generate the principles on which a valid metaphysics is to rest.[54]

As it happens, Aquinas did not treat explicitly of this form of wisdom; though, as has been argued at length elsewhere,[55] an adequate account of this wisdom in cognitional terms can be pieced together from his writings. However, the polymorphism of human consciousness has had its effect in this field as everywhere else, producing strangely varied interpretations of the master's opinions on the theory of knowledge. 'G. van Riet needed over six hundred pages to outline the various types of Thomist epistemology that have been put forward in the last century and a half.' In fine, what we have called 'concrete deduction' would need a prior inquiry into theory of knowledge (in order that its method might be justified and its premisses supplied). This inquiry was conducted with insufficient generality by Kant, and with insufficient discrimination by Scotus; however, its possibility at least was implied by Thomas Aquinas, though 'the varieties of Thomist interpretation are as much in need of a prior inquiry as anything else'.[55]

So it is that we are compelled, after considering metaphysical methods which leave the inquiring subject out of account, to turn to those which aim to direct the metaphysical enterprise by guiding the subject which undertakes it. First to be considered is Descartes' prescription of doubting everything that can be doubted, and so starting from the indubitable. Within the range of what can be doubted, evidently, are concrete judgements of fact (which might always be otherwise than they are). Thus the deliverances of common sense and empirical science, which consist in just such judgements of fact, are excluded. Further, the meaning of all judgements whatever, quite apart from the question of their truth and falsity, becomes obscure and unsettled, since it becomes clear and precise only so far as such terms as 'reality', 'knowledge' and 'objectivity' can be made clear and precise; and *that* depends on an analysis and clarification of the facts of human cognitional activity. 'But if one excludes all concrete judgments of fact, one excludes the clarification.' The systematic doubter might draw momentary comfort from the fact that all mere suppositions satisfy the criterion of indubitability; but this is simply because doubt only arises at the level of reflection, when you wonder, about what you suppose, whether it is so. Analytic propositions are indubitable, just because in effect they are mere suppositions. (An analytic proposition is true by virtue of whatever meaning those who propound it suppose its terms to have, and not by virtue of any matter of fact.) As Descartes observed, the existential subject survives the exercise of systematic doubt, since something has to do the doubting; it merely is doomed to perpetual frustration, as can easily be shown. It so happens that the criterion of indubitability itself (that the truth is to be had by doubting everything which can be doubted) is a judgement of fact, and so not itself indubitable; so the frustrated existential subject cannot consistently even console himself with the reflection that there is anything rational about his doubting. Every assignable reason for practising universal doubt (that one ought to because something is so or not so, because of some matter of fact) is eliminated by its coherent exercise; if someone adopts it in the hope of being left with premises from which he may deduce the nature of the universe, he is bound to be disappointed, for the reasons we have given. One might adopt it on the ground that philosophical disagreements demand a violent remedy; only to be left as a result of its consistent exercise with nothing for philosophers to disagree about. (One cannot disagree about a mere supposition given only that it is self-consistent.) Descartes' programme of understanding the universe, assigning a reason for everything, and excluding the influence of unacknowledged suppositions, is thoroughly praiseworthy. This programme should, however, be dissociated from his universal doubt, which 'leads the philosopher to reject what he is not equipped to restore'; one can, after all, test the hypotheses and reach the conclusions of science only by scientific methods, of common sense only by the methods of common sense.[57]

Again, one may try to guide the inquirer by issuing the precept to observe the relevant facts. But the trouble with this precept is that the object of mere *observation* is simply a datum; 'without the combination of data and correct insights that together form a virtually unconditioned, there are no facts'. (The facts, as is rightly insisted by the most influential schools in the contemporary philosophy of science, don't just lie out there to be inspected, but are intrinsically conditioned by the framework of theory which we bring to bear on observed data.) This seems to be the truth of the matter; but it is a highly paradoxical truth. The whole previous argument has been directed to clarifying insight and judgement, and to accounting for 'the confusion, so natural to man, between extroversion and objectivity. For man observes, understands, and judges, but he fancies that what he knows in judgment is not known in judgment and does not suppose an exercise of understanding but simply is attained by taking a good look at the "real" that is "already out there now". Empiricism, then, is a bundle of blunders, and its history is their successive clarification.' There is an empiricism not only at the level of critical reflection, but also at the level of understanding; on the Scotist theory of knowledge, for instance (as we outlined it above), the intellect takes a look at a conceptual concept which has somehow unconsciously been impressed upon the soul. Of course, the assumption underlying this view goes far beyond Scotism; the objective universals of Platonism owe their origin to the idea that, as the physical eye looks on colours and shapes, so the eye of the soul looks on, or at least one recalls its having looked on, universals. And the Aristotelian and Thomist traditions are not without their ambiguities, since Thomist commentators have almost universally ignored Aquinas' affirmation of insight. As to the history of philosophy since Descartes – it may be understood largely as a tussle between the assumption that knowledge essentially consists in taking a good look, if not at external objects then at spiritual ideas, and the adumbration of the truth that it is to be had by the operation of inquiring intelligence and reflecting reasonableness on the data of experience. Descartes' dualism juxtaposes the rational affirmation, *cogito, ergo sum*, with the already-out-there-now-real stripped of secondary qualities. Spinoza and Malebranche tried to swallow the dualism from the rationalist end, while Hobbes, on the contrary, reduced thinking to matter in motion. Berkeley shifted reality to the cognitional order by refusing to attribute it to 'bodies', asserting as he did that the 'primary qualities' of matter in motion were even more certainly mere appearance than were the 'secondary qualities' of colour, taste and so on. Hume finally declared that our knowledge is not only of perceived elements but of unities within them and relations between them; but that the unities and relations have no better foundation than our mental habits, and so cannot lay claim to philosophical validity, whatever their practical usefulness.[58]

As to Kant, 'if it is merely confusion of thought that interprets objectivity in terms of extroversion', his 'Copernican revolution was a half-hearted affair'. Primary and secondary qualities, according to Kant, are alike appearances, and space and time *a priori* forms of outer and inner sense. And yet he will have it that things in themselves, although unknowable, are somehow known to produce impressions on our senses. It seems that Kant, for all the impressiveness of his achievement, could not break cleanly from the basic

conviction characteristic of animal extroversion that the real
is the 'already out there now'. However, 'once extroversion is
questioned, it is only through man's reflective grasp of the
unconditioned that the objectivity and validity of human
knowing can be established. Kant rightly saw that animal
knowing is not human knowing; but he failed to see what
human knowing is. The combination of that truth and that
failure is the essence of the principle of immanence that was
to dominate subsequent thought'. (The difficulty is that
objectivity as extroversion and rampant subjectivism may
seem straight alternatives; unless thought can be checked by
taking a look at reality, it would seem to be bound by
nothing but the immanent laws of its own development. The
latter assumption receives its classical exposition in the
philosophy of Hegel.) 'Cartesian dualism had been a twofold
realism, and both the realisms were correct; for the realism of
the extroverted animal is no mistake, and the realism of
affirmation is no mistake.' The difficulty is that, unless one
recognises two types of knowing, the realisms are incompatible with one another; the attempt to fuse them issues in
the destruction of each by the other. (How could the laws of
matter in motion, which evidently governed the human brain,
and the principles of rational thought, according to which the
human mind was able to direct itself, ever be reconciled? The
so-called 'two clocks' theory of the 'Occasionalist' successors
of Descartes, and the 'pre-established harmony' postulated by
Leibniz, are among the most instructive and amusing of the
attempts at reconciliation. According to these theories,
matter and mind are totally independent of one another from
a causal point of view; but the Creator of the universe has
wonderfully arranged things from the beginning of time such
that, for instance, whenever I decide to raise my arm, it will
actually move as a result of the operation of purely physical
laws. But my decision, being a mental event, can have no
influence whatever on the physical event of my arm's
movement.) After Kant, 'the older materialism and sensism
were discredited, but there was room for positivism and
pragmatism to uphold the same viewpoint in a more cultured
tone. German idealism swung through its magnificent arc of
dazzling systems to come to terms with reality in relativism

and neo-Kantian analysis. But if a century and a half have brought forth no solution, it would seem necessary to revert to the beginning and distinguish two radically different types of knowing in the polymorphic consciousness of man.' For Husserl's phenomenology has not broken the deadlock; instead of regarding description as preliminary to explanation, it moves from experience to a contemplation of abstract essences. It is scarcely surprising that it has rapidly succumbed to an existentialism which describes living and acting men as they are. The effect of phenomenology is that of a purified empiricism (in which a crude taking a look at the external world has been replaced by a subtle taking a look at ideas and concepts). 'In brief, empiricism as a method rests on an elementary confusion. What is obvious in knowing is, indeed, looking. Compared to looking, insight is obscure, and grasp of the unconditioned doubly obscure. But empiricism amounts to the assumption that what is obvious in knowing is what knowing obviously is.'[59]

Common-sense eclecticism remains the inertial centre of the process of doing philosophy, though it is seldom adopted by original thinkers.[60] Many who engage in philosophical activity never wander far from a set of unquestioned assumptions. These are a matter of 'common sense' – but unfortunately common sense varies with age, country, and religious denomination. Quite commonly a distinction is drawn between theoretical understanding on the one hand, which according to this view is to be distrusted; and on the other hand 'the pronouncements of pre-philosophic reflection, which ground human sanity and human cooperation and therefore must be retained'. Of course, it is very important to distinguish between this kind of common-sense eclecticism in philosophy, and common sense operating within its proper field. Common sense, just as surely as science, has its role to play; but only as subject to the kind of metaphysical criticism and reorientation that we have outlined. The trouble with common-sense eclecticism in philosophy is simply that its basic assumptions are exempt from such criticism and reorientation, and so remain vulnerable to the individual and group prejudices which have just been mentioned.[61]

As a result of contemplating the defects of empiricism and common-sense eclecticism, one might very well conclude that the proper method of philosophy lies in the very process that turns positions into their opposites, only to discover a new position that in turn begets its opposite, and so on. This is Hegel's conception of the matter. The five hundred years of philosophy between Scotus and Hegel were 'largely devoted to working out in a variety of manners the possibilities of the assumption that knowing consists in taking a look. The ultimate conclusion is that it did not and could not'. (Hegel, who understood clearly that Kant's 'things in themselves' were an excrescence in the latter's critical philosophy, no longer was able to identify knowing with any form of looking. However, since he did not go on to discover the virtually unconditioned that grounds particular judgements of fact, he could only conclude that what was at issue was successive stages of pure thought thinking itself, with no reality distinct from it in relation to which its concepts and judgements might be validated or invalidated.) Now we ourselves are to use the term 'dialectical', borrowed from Hegel, to describe the manner in which human thought and the institutions based on it develop; so it will be as well to distinguish our position clearly from that of Hegel. The whole Hegelian dialectic is contained in the field defined by the concepts and their interrelations. (There is in Hegel nothing corresponding to our 'virtually unconditioned', outside the conceptual field, which consists of particular matters of fact that render judgements true or false, and thus indirectly determines whether the concepts are instantiated in reality or not.)[62] Our dialectic awaits tentative solutions from nature and history to fix the concepts which will meet the anticipations of intelligent inquiry and reasonable reflection. Its succession follows a path which is neither unique nor necessary, since identical results may be reached by different routes, and there are aberrations as well as valid developments. The source of these various differences is clear; we, unlike Hegel, regard concepts not simply as related to one another, but in an intermediate role between experience and critical reflection. Hegel's dialectical opposition is within the conceptual field, but ours is a conflict between the pure desire to know and those other aspects of human consciousness which may distort its operation. Again, 'Hegel's absolute is a terminal concept that generates no antithesis to be sublated in a higher synthesis; we recognize a manifold of instances of the virtually unconditioned, and through them attain a knowledge of proportionate being in its distinctions and relations.' (For Hegel, the goal of thought is the attainment of the absolute; for us, it is knowledge of a world of facts and their interrelations.) Hegel's dialectic operates everywhere, even within nature; ours is a matter merely of the succession of ideas, opinions and actions in thinking subjects, and the effects of these in the world, and so has no relevance to purely natural process. As a matter of historical fact, Hegel's dialectic took its origin from Kant's reappraisal of the relation between Descartes' *res extensa* and his *res cogitans*; but whereas Kant did not totally free himself from the notion of extroversion as objectivity, Hegel 'took the more forthright position that extroverted consciousness was but an elementary state in the coming-to-be of mind . . . In contrast, we affirm the reality of the *res cogitans* for human knowing and that of the *res extensa* for elementary knowing'. There is no denying that Hegel's range of vision is enormous; but it has one crucial limitation. Its neglect of the virtually unconditioned leads to a view of rality as it would be if there were no virtually unconditioned, or, to put it bluntly, no facts. Anyone who grasps the virtually unconditioned transcends Hegel's position — which is consequently bound to topple over, as happened as a matter of historical fact, into the materialistic factualness of Marx or the subjective factualness of Kierkegaard.[63]

(The claims made for the method of metaphysics outlined here are certainly ambitious. But one may plead they are no more so than those implicit in every systematic treatise of metaphysics or epistemology, or in any point of view which assumes, for example, that the present achievements of science or the convictions of a particular variety of common sense are the ultimate arbiters of truth.) Our own analysis of human knowledge eliminates the rigidity of the Kantian *a priori*; it conceives philosophy as universal knowledge without infringing the domains of common sense and science;[64] it yields a metaphysics which brings to contemporary thought the wisdom of the Greeks and the medieval Schoolmen, to integrate them with future as well as present scientific discovery;[65] and it is 'elaborated in accord with a method that makes it possible to reduce every dispute in the field of metaphysical speculation to a question of concrete psychological fact'.[66] (Roughly, what the inquirer has to do is to ask himself: 'Am I a being who understands *how* and *what* things are and judges *that* they are so on the basis of experience? If so, what follows about the nature of the reality which is the object of my actual and potential experience, understanding, and judgement – i.e. the world as a whole?')

It is worth asking how far the state of mind conducive to scientific investigation is also conducive to philosophical reflection. A scientist's dedication to truth, and his habituation to the relevant pattern of experience[67] (where the mind is applied neither to day-dreaming, nor to indulging or expressing emotions, nor to influencing other persons, nor to the tasks of day-to-day living, but to the propounding and testing of hypotheses), ought to suit him to be a philosopher. However, in the past, the philosophical appetite of scientists has been too apt to be satisfied by a scientific monism which regards philosophies as misguided attempts to obtain knowledge which could in fact only be reached by science. The unification of knowledge would be brought about by a conception of objectivity as extroversion, and of knowledge as taking a look. 'It followed that the universe consisted of imaginable elements linked together in space and time by natural laws; because the elements were imaginable, the universe was mechanist;[68] because the laws were necessary, the mechanism was determinist.' Mechanics was thus the one true science, and the various actual branches of science, from chemistry through biology right up to human history, were just macroscopic ways of talking about a microscopic reality. 'It was unsuspected that there was involved an extra-scientific supposition in the pronouncement on the meaning of objectivity, knowledge and reality. That was far too obvious to be questioned. It followed that to doubt mechanist determinism was to doubt the validity of the sciences, and so doubters were summoned to explain which of the methods or conclusions of the sciences they thought to be mistaken.'[69]

But recent science has been making this position more and more implausible. Darwinian explanation depends, as has been indicated above, not on necessary laws but on the realisation of probabilities; Freud established the notion of psychogenic disease (which at first sight at least is not reducible to chemical or physical explanation), in spite of his own personal espousal of mechanistic determinism; Einstein got rid of the absolute space and time in which the imaginable elements postulated by mechanism were supposed to reside; quantum mechanics showed the dispensability of images of particles, waves, or continuous process. 'No less than his predecessors, the contemporary scientist can observe and experiment, inquire and understand, form hypotheses and verify them. But unlike his predecessors, he has to think of knowledge, not as taking a look, but as experiencing, understanding, and judging; . . . he has to think of the real, not as a part of the "already out there now", but as the verifiable.' St. Augustine of Hippo remarks that it took him years to make the discovery that to be real is not necessarily the same as to be a material object. 'Similarly, one might say that it has taken modern science four centuries to make the discovery that the objects of its inquiry need not be imaginable entities moving through imaginable processes in an imaginable space-time.'[70]

The breakdown of the premiss of scientific monism, unfortunately, leaves intact for a while long-ingrained habits of mind. It appears, too (from what we argued earlier), that there is a difference between scientific method and the method to be followed if one is to gain an integrated view of the universe as a whole and of man's place within it. And there are a number of reasons why scientists tend to find philosophy baffling or repellent. For one thing, while there is a scientific method prior to particular scientific work and results, philosophical method is coincident with particular philosophical work and stands or falls with the success or failure of particular philosophies. (Scientists who disagree usually at least have applied more or less the same method to arrive at their different conclusions; but there are as many philosophical methods as there are types of philosophy.) So the scientist is apt to conclude that philosophers have no method at all. The scientist is also annoyed by the failure of philosophers to agree on a single, precise, universally accepted technical language. The trouble here, of course, is just that each philosophy has its characteristic view of the fundamental elements of the subject, and so is bound to express these fundamentals in its own way. Conceptions of knowledge, reality, and objectivity vary in accordance with the polymorphism of human consciousness, and all other relevant conceptions vary in consequence.[71]

Another difficulty is psychological; there is a necessary element of *belief* (which involves deference to authority) in science, such as is quite inappropriate in philosophy.[72] 'Knowing is affirming what one correctly understands in one's own experience. Belief is accepting what we are told by others on whom we reasonably rely.' But no scientist knows every conclusion of science; his training brings him abreast of the knowledge in his subject and enables him to carry on its work, but does not attempt to make him recapitulate the whole history of science. 'The extent, to which belief is essential in the scientific tradition, disposes and conditions the minds of scientists in a manner that ill equips them for philosophy.' You cannot settle philosophical questions by looking the answers up in a handbook, or by appealing to someone else's marshalling of the evidence, or to an authoritative set of experiments. 'Philosophic evidence is within the philosopher himself. It is his own inability to avoid experience, to renounce intelligence in inquiry, to desert reasonableness in reflection... Philosophy is the flowering of the individual's rational consciousness in coming to know and take possession of itself.' To this end schools, treatises and text-books are merely contributions. The scientist will tend to be strongly attracted to those branches of philosophy which rely extensively on symbolic logic, and thus seem to offer the security of an impersonal and automatically expanded position. He also is liable to hope for an integration of the sciences by scientists, and hence for a philosophy which will be able to go by the name of science. In the light of his antecedents — he is conditioned by training to believe what scientists say — this attitude can easily be explained, even readily excused; but this does not make it any more reasonable. Scientists, like other men, are subject to the polymorphism of human consciousness, especially outside the borders of their speciality.[73]

3.5. *Elements of Metaphysics*

It remains actually to sketch the elements of metaphysics. The function of metaphysics is to outline what can be understood here and now of what will (or could) be understood in the indefinite future, when all proportionate being is understood. 'Though full explanation may never be reached, at least the structure of that explanatory knowledge can be known at once.' Now knowing becomes complete through the three stages of experience, understanding, and judgement. 'Experience is of things as potentially intelligible, but through experience alone we do not know what the things are. Understanding is of things as formally intelligible, but through understanding we do not know whether things are what we understand them to be. Judgment is of things as actually intelligible but through judgment alone we would not know either the nature or the merely empirical differences of what we affirm to be.' Let us distinguish those aspects of the knowable apprehended respectively in experience, understanding and judgement as *potency, form* and *act*. These three together constitute a unity, since it is one thing that is experienced, understood, and judged of. You don't know one thing or state of affairs in experience, another in understanding, and yet another in judgement. (I can observe the planet Neptune, come to an understanding of it, and make true judgements about the constitution of its atmosphere, its mean distance from the sun, and so on. But there is only one planet Neptune that is the object of my experience, my understanding, and my judgement.) The account of potency, form and act given here will cover all possible scientific explanations. 'For a scientific theory is a theory verified in instances; as verified, it refers to act; as theory, it refers to form; as in instances, it refers to potency. Again, as a theory of the classical type, it refers to forms as forms; as a theory of the statistical type, it refers to forms as setting ideal frequencies from which acts do not diverge systematically.' The terminology is derived from Aristotle, and the use of it here is fairly closely related to his; however, he was concerned, as was shown above, with merely descriptive knowledge, whereas we insist on explanation. Aristotle considered colours, sounds, heat, and so on, to be forms; on our theory, they are only ambiguously so, since they are so not *as experienced*, but only *as explained*.[74] The conflict between Aristotelianism and emerging science at the time of the Renaissance was almost inevitable, partly because of the ambiguity in Aristotle's theory itself, partly because of the Aristotelians' misunderstanding of that theory, and partly because the new scientists were entangled in that misapprehension as to the nature of explanation, that it was a matter of replacing talk about secondary qualities with talk about primary qualities, which has already been described.[75]

Exactly what the forms of proportionate being are will be known only when full explanation is reached. Still, heuristic techniques reveal two types of forms which we will label *conjugate forms* and *central forms*. (Roughly, central forms are things, conjugate forms are properties.) 'One reaches explanatory conjugates by considering data as similar to other data; but the data, which are similar, also are concrete and individual; and as concrete and individual, they are understood inasmuch as one grasps in them a concrete and intelligible unity, identity, whole.' Nor, as we have already argued (in the discussion of the concept of a thing),[76] is there any possibility of dispensing with this grasp or transcending it as our understanding of the world increases. (Apart from the concept of thing, or central form, it will be remembered, we have argued that no sense can be made either of the phenomenon of change or of the advance of science in explanation of the world.) The difference between our 'central form' and Aristotle's 'substantial form' is merely nominal (both terms designate concrete particular things as understood). But the alteration in terminology seems appropriate, since the meaning of 'substance' in English has been profoundly affected both by Locke's philosophy,[77] and by the common confusion of what is substantial with what can be seen or felt. Thus the word 'substantial' is better avoided in this context. The word 'conjugate', in the phrase 'conjugate form', brings out that the essence of conjugate form is intelligible *relations* between things. 'Central act is existence, for what exists is the intelligible unity. Conjugate act is occurrence, for what occurs is defined explanatorily by appealing to conjugate form.' So also with potency; central potency and conjugate potency are the aspects of things and events which are merely experienced or imagined. 'To illustrate the meaning of the terms, central and conjugate potency, form, and act, let us suppose that mass-velocity is a notion that survives in fully explanatory science. Then the mass-velocity will be a conjugate act; the mass, defined by its intelligible relations to other masses, will be a conjugate form; the space-time continuum of the trajectory will be a conjugate potency; what has the mass will be individual by its central potency, a unity by its central form, and existing by its central act.'[78]

(It may be asked how this metaphysics of central and conjugate potencies, forms and acts, corresponds to the concrete world as investigated by the sciences. Roughly, proportionate being consists of a series of levels, each characterised by its own set of conjugate forms, and therefore each investigated by its own autonomous science. Each level (A) differs from the one directly below it (B) in that what was merely a coincidental manifold at the level of B becomes systematic, or able to be grasped by a direct insight, at the level of A. Each level is further constituted by its own central forms or things, every one of which is differentiated by conjugate forms of that level and of all lower levels. Thus every plant has physical, chemical and specifically biological properties; every man has physical, chemical, biological, sensitive psychological, and intellectual properties; and there is, of course, a department of science corresponding to each of these levels. Since each level is characterised by a systematisation of states of affairs which were unsystematic at the next lower level, there is no question of the reduction of all sciences to the science which deals with the lowest level — of 'physicalism' as postulated by some philosophers of science).[79] 'If there is any explanatory science, then there is a set of conjugate forms, say C_i, defined implicitly by their empirically established and explanatory correlations.' Different combinations of forms from the set define the unities or things which differ from one another but belong to the same explanatory genus. Different combinations of the empirically established correlations yield a range of schemes of recurrence, and such schemes, so far as they are realised, make systematic the occurrence of certain conjugate acts. (For example, so far as there is life on earth, certain kinds of events characteristic of a state of affairs where there are living beings occur there with regularity.) Now it seems at first sight obvious that either all such acts are systematic, or some are coincidental and random. But there is in fact a third possibility; that events may occur which are coincidental from one point of view but systematic from a higher viewpoint. 'Besides occurring systematically in virtue of the schemes, S_i, and occurring at random, conjugate acts of the type, A_i, may occur quite regularly but in a manner which cannot be accounted for by any of the schemes, S_i. In that case, there is the evidence that is necessary and sufficient to affirm the existence of another set of conjugates, C_j, defining another genus of things, T_j, and yielding another range of schemes, S_j, that make systematic another type of conjugate acts, A_j.'[80] (An example which might be used to illustrate the point is the description in C.S. Lewis' *Out of the Silent Planet* of the hero's encounter, after he has reached the planet Mars, with a strange animal, which he suddenly realises to be a rational creature. Here a series of actions by the animal which would have been simply coincidental from the point of view of mere animality — a set of schemes of recurrence which make systematic intussusception, excretion, sexual activity, and so on — are realised, by a sudden direct insight on the part of the hero, to be indicative of rationality. The rationality of the animal was expressed in acts which followed a certain regularity, but a regularity which could not be accounted for on the basis of its merely animal nature.)

At each level of proportionate being, there are coincidental conjugate acts which provide a potency to be systematised by forms of the next higher genus. (Only where there are electrons and protons can there be chemical elements; only where there are the chemical elements carbon, hydrogen and oxygen can there be living organisms, and so on.) This gives us a series of *genera*, each of which contains different *species*. Now in things of each higher genus, there survive conjugate forms, potencies and acts of lower genera. However things, or intelligible unities, at lower levels, do not survive as such within things of higher levels. Of course there can, for example, be foreign bodies within the tissue of an animal or plant; but these will not be part of it as are the organs of the animal, and the organs are not separate things or intelligible unities, but are what they are only in relation to the rest of the organism. From what has been said, it is clear that there will have to be a separate and autonomous science for each genus. For investigations at each level will lead to the discovery of sets of conjugates; but there will be no *logical* connection between sets of conjugates at different levels. Suppose C_i and C_j are sets of conjugates at successive levels. 'All the terms of the set, C_i, will be defined by their internal relations; all the terms of the set, C_j, will be defined by their internal relations; and since the two sets have no terms in common, there will be no logical process from one set to the other.' It will be seen that the structure of successive genera runs parallel to that succession of higher viewpoints which has already been described.[81] The coincidental manifolds of the lower of any two successive sets of conjugate acts can be imagined symbolically; and as the coincidental manifolds provide the conjugate potency for the higher conjugate forms, so the symbolic images provide the materials for insight into the laws relating the higher forms.[82]

What we have just said may be expressed in terms either of a position or a counter-position. On the position, the symbolic images have a merely heuristic value; they facilitate the transition from one science to another. On the counter-position, the images will be not simply heuristic symbols, but representations of things as they really are; and the successive intelligible systems of the sciences will be merely subjective arrangements of thought, since the intelligible cannot be imagined; and so finally 'one is left with unverifiable images of the lowest genus as one's extra-scientific and pseudo-metaphysical account of reality'. The whole conception of explanatory genera and species which we have outlined rests, it must be insisted, not on the present state of the sciences, but on the constitutive properties of insight as such. The complementarity of classical and statistical laws at each level leaves room for the coincidental manifolds which provide the potency for the forms at the next higher level. It may be asked what degree of certainty can be attributed to our account of explanatory genera and species. That there are in fact explanatory genera and species as described may be said to be uniquely probable, as the hypothesis meets the issue fairly and squarely, and seems to have no serious rivals. And such unique probability is all that can be expected of a metaphysics whose task is to integrate the data of common sense and empirical science, not to lay down the nature of any possible world. Such a metaphysics 'is bound to be nuanced; it may have no doubt about central and conjugate potencies, forms, and acts; yet it can be content with unique probability when it comes to differentiating the explanatory genera and species of forms'.[83]

The method of metaphysics outlined here provides a means of liberating the sciences from the whirligig of philosophic dialectic; for the counter-positions spread to scientific thought, and infect the formulation of scientific conclusions, even when they do not derive, 'like Cartesian dualism in Galileo and Kantian criticism in Newton', from the failure of science to reach an adequate account of its own presuppositions. But it is in the human sciences in particular that this method of metaphysics may be expected to demonstrate is point and usefulness, since the human sciences have the additional complication that not only the inquiry, but what is inquired into, is liable to be involved in the aberrations of the polymorphic consciousness of man. It is important, moreover, that metaphysics should keep in touch with the sciences, not only for their good, but for its own; that the metaphysician should not talk about 'forms' or 'quiddities' or whatever while forgetting that these are simply what is to be known through the process of scientific investigation. 'Just as the scientist has to raise ultimate questions and seek the answer from a metaphysics, so the metaphysician has to raise proximate questions and seek their answers from scientists.'[84]

4 The Problem of Interpretation.

4.1 *Myth and Mystery*

'If Descartes has imposed on subsequent philosophers a requirement of rigorous method, Hegel has obliged them not only to account for their own views but also to explain the existence of contrary convictions and opinions.'[2] It seems that all philosophies, both actual and possible, rest on cognitional activity either as correctly conceived or as distorted by oversights and mistaken orientations. We ask the question whether there is a single basis from which any philosophical theory or system can be interpreted rightly, and we argue that our cognitional analysis provides such a basis. 'In this fashion, the *a priori* element of cognitional analysis joins hands with the *a posteriori* element of historical data.'[3]

The inquiry so far as we have already undertaken it forces us to reckon with a paradoxical *known unknown*. Human questions outnumber human answers; as well as what we know, there is what we know we do not yet know. Now it is evident that man's mind has an emotional and sensitive as well as a merely intellectual aspect to it, and the known unknown will appear from this point of view as the strange, the unexplored and momentous as opposed to the familiar and as it were domesticated. The field of *myth* and *mystery*, which we now consider, consists of the emotion-laden images connected in the human mind with the known unknown. Now it would seem from what we have said that mystery and myth must be quite universal and permanent, so long as there is a known unknown of unanswered questions, and so long as man's mind consists of an emotional as well as an intellectual component. Of course an account of particular mysteries and myths is a matter for the history of culture and religion. But a genetic account of their radical meaning, their significance, their emergence and their disappearance can hardly be omitted in a contemporary metaphysics. Of representative modern thinkers, Comte, Schelling, Cassirer, Tillich and Bultmann have all paid particular attention to myth, and Gabriel Marcel to mystery. We have already given in some detail an account of explicit metaphysics, and have alluded to latent and problematic metaphysics as its prior stages. There arises the question of how far myth and mystery correspond to these prior stages, and whether they may be expected to vanish when men have passed beyond them. 'An explicit and adequate metaphysics is a corollary to explicit and adequate self-knowledge.' But this involves a clear conception of insight; which in turn presupposes the detailed investigation of mathematics, science, and common sense; which itself would not be possible without a prior evolution of language and literature and the security and leisure provided by economic and political progress. But that an explicit metaphysics cannot be *achieved* prior to a definite stage in human development does not mean that it may not be *attempted*. The genesis of man's self-knowledge and thus of the metaphysics consequent upon it has extended over a long period of history; and as metaphysics must give an account of its own genesis, so it cannot entirely prescind from the phenomena of myths and mysteries.[4]

Just as an adequate metaphysics is to be attained by means of an accurate analysis of the structure of human knowing and so of the world which is known and remains to be known, so the introduction of blind spots into the structure reveals the categories of inadequate philosophies and, at the limit, of mythic consciousness. It is of the essence of mythic consciousness that it operates entirely without the benefit of critical reflection. 'For it, the real is the object of a sufficiently integrated and intense flow of sensitive representations, feelings, words, and actions.' (Sufficient criteria of truth are correspondence with immediate appearance, and satisfaction of an emotional or dramatic kind.) Judgements to break the integration occur, but only in the sphere of domesticated and familiar reality, where trial and error operate as an effective pragmatic criterion of truth; but such judgements can have no ground when unanalysed consciousness is directed towards the known unknown. 'As the uncritical scientist builds for himself a universe constituted by tiny, imaginable knobs or by a sponge-vortex aether, so the myth-maker builds for himself a more vital and more impressive world.' If we confuse experience and the experienced with explanation and the explained, as is almost inevitable before philosophy has become fully critical, we will inevitably become confused by anthropomorphic projections. Since we feel the force of gravity to be directed from above downwards, we infer that men at the antipodes must walk about like flies on the ceiling. Causality for us cannot be an intelligible relationship of dependence, but has to be envisaged in terms of the sensation of muscular effort and transmission of motion through contact.[5] Things have properties, but these cannot be intelligible conjugates but merely objects of sensation. The things themselves are constituted as such not by their intelligible unity, but merely by a capacity to occupy space and endure through time; thus things must be 'bodies', and cannot be anything else. (Materialism, for all the appeals which it makes to science, is fundamentally just as uncritical as the ancient myths; it differs from them only in being less interesting.)[6]

Now there is a complementary fallacy at the level of interpretation. 'Just as anthropomorphic projection results from the addition of our feelings to the content of our insights into things, so subjective projection results when we interpret the words and deeds of other men by reconstructing in ourselves their experience and uncritically adding our intellectual viewpoints which they do not share.' This leads to misunderstandings of the words and deeds of men who acted and wrote and spoke at times and places widely different from our own. There is apparently no escape from relativism so long as we stick to the descriptive viewpoint. (One can only achieve more or less stimulating and ingenious hunches as to what Confucius or Genghis Khan or Ernst Haeckel meant or intended by their words or acts.) Of course, there can be no history without documents and monuments from the past. But even if one supposes a cinema of past actions and a sound-track of past words, one still has before one the question of the insights, judgements and decisions which make the words and deeds those of more or less intelligent and reasonable beings. 'Interpretation of the past is the recovery of the viewpoint of the past; and that recovery, as opposed to mere subjective projections, can be reached only by grasping exactly what a viewpoint is, how viewpoints develop, what dialectical laws govern their historical unfolding.' At present, the explanatory viewpoint is by no means established in the human sciences,[7] and it is rather optimistic to claim that it is so even in the natural sciences. Our own incomplete victory over subjective and anthropomorphic projections should make us realise how ubiquitous these are bound to be before the advance of science and philosophy have given a concrete meaning to the explanatory viewpoint. Thus the primitive cannot but understand nature in an anthropomorphic way, and must be unable to conceive of other men with a mentality very different from his own.[8]

'As the foregoing analysis implies, mythic consciousness is the absence of self-knowledge, and myth is a consequence of mythic consciousness as metaphysics is a corollary of self-knowledge.' Myth, being 'the product of an untutored desire to understand and formulate the nature of things', recedes as metaphysics advances. By its dialectical relationship with metaphysics, myth looks forward to its own negation, and to a metaphysics the more consciously true because conscious and rational in its rejection of error. The task of overcoming myth by metaphysics is, however, a permanent one. For each new generation of men must develop intellectually, and so be liable to the counter-positions by the way; and this makes it easy for unscrupulous men to get their way by an appeal to the senses and emotions which would make no impression on developed intelligence and reason. 'Power in its highest form is power over men, and the successful maker of myths has that power within his reach and grasp.' Metaphysics thus has to be extended into a philosophy of education, so that there can be cut out at the root the danger of adventurers climbing to power by clever

myth-making. There is a gap between the heuristic anticipation of understanding and understanding itself, and between
verbal fluency and the understanding of the realities to which
the words refer. The speculative gnostic and the practical
magician take advantage of this gap. The danger here is due
to the fact that partial insights have the same subjective
characteristics as complete understanding, and 'the satisfaction of understanding can be mimicked by an air of
profundity, a glow of self-importance, a power to command
respectful attention'. So the gnostic and magician have their
day.[9]

But for all the intrinsic instability of myth which has just
been described and accounted for, we have, as has also been
shown, a relationship with the known unknown which
cannot be either escaped or superseded. 'Man by nature is
oriented into mystery.' Though metaphysics may grasp the
structure of proportionate being, there remains ever more
clearly and distinctly, as we shall see, the question of
transcendent being.[10] Mere explanation, moreover, does not
content the human mind, since the world of pure science and
metaphysics is very different from the world of poetry or of
common sense. In any case, man's explanatory self-
knowledge can only be effective in practical living to the
extent that he is provided with 'images that release feeling
and emotion and flow spontaneously into deeds no less than
words'. Even full understanding does not remove the need for
mystery, which has its basis in the very nature of man, who is
essentially sensitive and emotional as well as intellectual and
rational. And 'even adequate self-knowledge and explicit
metaphysics may contract but cannot eliminate a "known
unknown", and . . . they cannot issue into a control of
human living without being transposed into dynamic images
which make sensible to human sensitivity what human
intelligence reaches for or grasps.' (In other words, there is a
permanent need for something which relates to the sensitive
and emotional side of man as myths do, but which is not
based as they are on illusion. Whether such a need can in fact
be met is of course another matter, and remains to be
considered in a later chapter.) Every myth is sooner or later
discredited, since the counter-positions on which it is

founded invite their own reversal because men cannot in the long run renounce the thorough exercise of their intelligence and reasonableness. But, men being what they are (more or less ignorant and prone to self-deception, and with emotional needs such as can be met only by myth or by mystery), the elimination of one myth is usually succeeded by the genesis of another, and the advances of science and of philosophy merely bring it about that the later myth is defended by a more sophisticated philosophy, and made effective through more impressive technological invention, than was the earlier. Hence the profound disillusion of contemporary man, who hoped through knowledge to ensure a development which was always progress and never decline. Knowledge, he has discovered, is ambivalent; it increases power without necessarily increasing virtue. He is too proud to accept mystery, only to be put at the mercy of the myths which are its sole alternative.[11]

4.2 *Objectivity in Interpretation*

There remains the problem of how one may achieve an objective interpretation of the meanings of the words, actions and writings of men at other times and places, with their expression of the successive stages in the evolution of man's knowledge of himself and his world. The object of any interpretation is to communicate the principal insight or insights expressed in a document; and the difference between an interpretation and its original will depend upon the interpreter's understanding both of the habitual insights and deficiencies of insight characteristic of his own audience, and of the difference between these and those of the audience of the original as envisaged by the author. Reflective interpretations, which deliberately take into account the difference between different audiences at different places and times, are subject to obvious difficulties. First, audiences are an ever-shifting manifold, varying with culture, orientation of interest and the innumerable possible degrees of intellectual development. Of course, one may just happen to hit off a right interpretation and thus communicate to one's audience the principal insights expressed in an original document. But this does not entail that a truly reflective interpretation,

amenable to scientific criteria, is really feasible. It is true that
there is a historical sense which has the same relation to other
times and places as common sense has to one's own. The
experienced historian can thus come to know instinctively
how typical people in typical situations in his period spoke
and acted. But this historical sense is just as liable as is
common sense to the bias due to one's personal point of view
and that of one's class or group; like common sense again, the
historical sense is more likely to hit off a right answer than to
be able to give good reason for it. 'But if interpretation is to
be scientific, then the grounds for the interpretation have to
be assignable'; and the scientific interpreter cannot rest
content with a mere range of possible interpretations of an
original differing from one another according to the different
biases of the interpreters. It must on the contrary 'discover
some method of conceiving and determining the habitual
development of all audiences and it has to invent some
technique by which its expression escapes relativity to
particular audiences.'[12]

In order to cope with this problem, we shall introduce the
notion of a *universal viewpoint*. 'By a universal viewpoint will
be meant a potential totality of genetically and dialectically
ordered viewpoints.'[13] (In other words, it is a viewpoint from
which the interpreter may see at least in principle how all
other viewpoints develop, and what are their merits and
limitations.) One gets to the universal viewpoint by directing
attention to the experience, understanding and critical
reflection of the interpreter. It differs from any aspect of
phonetics, comparative grammar, lexicography, and so on, by
being concerned directly with the interpreter's ability to
grasp *meanings* rather than with the verbal *expression* of
these meanings. (It seems typical of the counter-positions
persistently to direct attention away from the meaning as
such, which cannot be the direct object of experience, to the
expression, which is so.) The universal viewpoint is what
enables the thinker to transpose his thinking to the level of
other cultures and epochs. It is based on adequate self-
knowledge and the metaphysics which is a consequence of it;
it 'has a retrospective expansion in the various genetic series
of discoveries through which man could advance to his

present knowledge. It has a dialectical expansion in the many formulations of discoveries due to the polymorphic consciousness of man, in the invitations issued by positions to their own development and in the implication in counter-positions of their own reversal. Finally, it can reach a concrete presentation of any formulation of any discovery through the identifications in personal experience of the elements that, as confused or as distinguished and related, as related under this or that orientation of polymorphic consciousness, could combine to make the position or counter-position humanly convincing.' The four dimensions, as it were, of the universe of meanings, are the full range of possible combinations of experience and lack of it, of insight and absence of it, of judgement and failure to judge, and of 'the various orientations of the polymorphic consciousness of man'. (The self-conscious and critical interpreter sees how his own knowledge has been reached, and how each stage could be presented or more or less misrepresented. In understanding thoroughly the basis of his own understanding, he has a reliable basis for understanding the expression of all other understandings and failures to understand.) 'In the measure that one explores human experience, human insights, human reflections, and human polymorphic consciousness, one becomes capable, when provided with the appropriate data, of approximating to the content and context of the meaning of any given expression.' Someone might retort that what has been presented as a universal viewpoint is not really such, but simply a corollary of our own peculiar brand of philosophy. But the answer is that a viewpoint which takes its stand on human cognitional activity itself can *ipso facto* account in principle for whatever arises from that activity. An accurate analysis of the process of perception, understanding, and judgement can ground an understanding of one's own and all others' perceptions, insights, judgements, misperceptions, failures of insight, and omissions of judgement. Of course, it is not implied that this particular account of the matter will not be vastly improved in detail by more exact accounts of experience, insight, judgement, and the polymorphic consciousness of man; what are at issue here are questions of principle rather than of detail.[14]

Ways of expression may be distinguished from one another according to the manner in which they are intended to affect the cognitional activity of an audience. Advertising agencies and ministries of propaganda do not at all desire to stimulate people to the exercise of intelligence, or detached reflection, or rational choice; on the contrary, what they want to do is to secure an automatic response which dispenses with critical questioning.[15] Again, novels, plays and poems convey insights and stimulate reflection, but by an indirect mode of operation, in which the immediate effect of the words is to evoke images, memories and feelings. 'If there is no frontal attack on the reader's intelligence, there is the insinuation of insights through the images from which they subtly emerge.' (Dickens' *Our Mutual Friend* brings to its reader a profound understanding of a certain kind of social corruption and sickness, not however directly by a sociological analysis, but indirectly by the telling of a story.) In the scientific treatise, there is a direct concern with the reader's understanding; in philosophical writing, with his judgement. 'As the scientist is indifferent to the images, as long as the insights are attained, so the philosopher is indifferent to the insights, as long as the reader is made to mount to the level of critical reflection.' Advanced philosophical writing does not so much submit ordered materials to a reader's judgement, as 'reveal to that judgment the immanent controls to which ineluctably it is subjected'. So much for some of the most significant aims of expression. The expression itself will be a flow of sensible events originating in the thoughts and wishes of a speaker or writer, and terminating (if all goes well) in a reproduction of these in a hearer or reader. 'To recognize the existence of levels of expression is to eliminate the crude assumptions of the interpreters and still more of their critics that take it for granted that all expression lies on a single level, namely, the psychological, literary, scientific, or philosophic level with which they happen to be most familiar.'[16] (One is reminded of the mathematician induced to read a classic epic poem, who asked, having done so, 'what does *that* prove?')

In treating of the succession of modes of expression, it is to be remembered that development in general is from the relatively undifferentiated to the differentiated, 'from the global and awkward to the expert and precise'. The specialised modes of expression which we have outlined have not always existed or been recognised; this makes things somewhat complicated for the interpreter (who thus cannot assume that any document from any time or place falls at all neatly within any of the categories we have mentioned). Philosophical style and manner, to take one example, have evidently altered a good deal with the passage of time; and scientific and literary modes of expression have been more or less fused or confused at various periods with it and with one another. (As late as the eighteenth century, Erasmus Darwin could write what was in effect a scientific treatise in verse.) The main point here is that specialised modes of expression have gradually to be evolved; that they do not spring ready made into being. Nowadays, a literary composition which begins with the phrase 'Once upon a time' may be expected to be a fairy-story — that is, 'to offer a certain stimulus to imagination and feeling, and to be exempt from reasonable criticism on the part of scientific intelligence and of philosophic reflection'. Since the relation between aims of communication and means of expression is itself variable, one cannot provide a table which correlates the two in a manner which will be valid for all places and times. The problem of relating them can thus be met only 'by determining the operators[17] that relate the classifications relevant to one level of development to the classifications relevant to the next'. (One has to determine the laws according to which literary modes of expression and aims of communication develop and influence one another in doing so.) The greatest difficulties of interpretation arise when the new wine of literary, scientific or philosophical meaning has to be poured into the old bottles of established forms of expression. In cases like this, the modes of expression are bound to be misleading signposts to the unwary reader. Now the scientific or logical treatise undertakes to define all its terms rigorously and to prove all its conclusions. It stands unambiguously on a single level of expression, its object being primarily 'to present clearly, exactly, and fully the content and implications of a determinate and coherent set of insights'. It mercilessly disregards possible deficiencies in its readers' intellectual development. But this sort of rigour has its limitations. The introduction of and first approximation to one's definitions and rules cannot but be expressed in ordinary and non-technical language, if they are to be understood by anyone at all. Again, in a science, the given state of knowledge can be cast very usefully in the form of such a treatise; but this is no way to set out tentative solutions and unsolved problems. When one moves from study of the static systems which are the province of the physicist and chemist, to the systems on the move which are the concern of the biologist and psychologist (where genetic method, in addition to classical and statistical methods, is applicable), the limitations of this kind of treatise are still more evident; since here not only thought about the matter in hand, but the matter in hand itself, consists not in static system but in system on the move. Each biological species, and each human psyche, is such a system. And there is no question of a more developed and subtle logic arising to handle these exactly and rigorously, just because the organism and the psyche both develop tentatively and in response to a non-systematic manifold of circumstance. (Thus accurate description and explanation of such matters cannot be amenable to the kind of rigour which is achieved by the sort of treatise we have described.) 'Still further limitations of the treatise make their appearance when one turns to the human level.' To the complexities of genetic method there have now to be added the graver complexities of dialectical method. (Individual and social insights, and in consequence the whole gamut of events and things which rely on them, do not occur systematically.) Human minds are ambivalent between the intellectual and the elementary pattern of experience, and display every degree of compromise between them. Logic is of course well established as a science, but it owes its universality and rigour to the fact that it deals with unspecified concepts and problems. On the supposition that some department of human knowledge at a given stage is quite determinate and coherent, logic as a technique can be successfully applied to it. But in fact the departments of human knowledge are commonly in process of development, and many of the objects of that knowledge are so as well. 'As long as they are developing, they are heading for the determinacy and coherence that will legitimate the application of logic as a technique.'[18]

The structure of classical empirical method, it will be remembered, operates like a pair of scissors, the upper blade of which consists in a series of generalities demanding specific determination, and the lower blade of working hypotheses, deductions, testings, revisions of hypotheses, and so on. With appropriate modifications, the same model is applicable to the method of interpretation. 'The possibility of any interpretation whatever implies an upper blade of generalities; and the existing techniques of scholars supply a lower blade by which the generalities can be determined with ever greater accuracy.' There is no real trouble about the lower blade; there exist any number of useful techniques for deciphering documents and monuments. What has been lacking so far in interpretation is the upper blade; and the inevitable consequence of this lack is the relativism and subjective bias with which hermeneutics has up to now been afflicted. The upper blade has two components, which 'regard the potential totality of meanings and the potential totality of modes of expression'. In order to clarify the matter, let us introduce the conception of the *protean notion of being*, by which we mean whatever can possibly be judged to exist or to be the case in the light of any possible understanding of any possible experience. 'For the totality of meanings the upper blade is the assertion that the protean notion of being is differentiated by a series of genetically and dialectically related unknowns. For the totality of modes of expression the upper blade is the assertion that there is a genetic process in which modes of expression move towards specialization and differentiation on sharply distinguishable levels.' The spatially ordered series of marks found in a document is no more than one determinant of its meaning; to achieve a correct interpretation, interpreters must use their own experience, understanding and judgement to get at the possible meanings of the document, and then go on to determine its actual meaning. 'Unless they can envisage the range of possible meanings, they will exclude *a priori* some meanings that are possible.' The possibility of envisaging the full range of possible meanings lies in the universal viewpoint, and 'the possibility of connecting possible meanings with particular documents lies in the genetic sequence that extrapolates from present to past correlation between meaning and mode of expression'.[19]

Some sketch of how the method just described would be implemented now seems desirable, so that its principles may be made clearer. All monuments and many documents which are to be interpreted are artistic; that is to say, they provide images from which one can reach insights, rather than formulating the insights explicitly in the manner of a scientific treatise. Also, of course, there exist innumerable gradations between these two extremes. Let us define as the *pure formulation* of anyone's meaning that which proceeds from the universal viewpoint and is addressed to it. If you transpose this pure formulation of meaning to Q's viewpoint, and to the resources of language and expression available to Q, this gives you Q's hypothetical expression, which may then be checked against his actual expression in the document or on the monument for which he was responsible. This account, sketchy and summary as it is, brings out two things of importance; first, how the interpreter's own experience, understanding and judgement are involved in finding out the meaning of whatever he is trying to interpret; and second, a systematic procedure for circumventing merely relative interpretation with all its pitfalls. 'It calls for a clear distinction between the interpreter's account of Q's context, his assumptions regarding Q's sources of expression, his inferred account of the manner in which Q would express his content in the light of his context through his resources of expression, and finally Q's actual expression. It introduces multiple verifications; not only must hypothetical expression square with actual expression, but the totality of assumptions regarding sources of expression have to satisfy the genetic sequence, and the totality of pure formulations of contexts have to satisfy a genetic and dialectical unfolding of human intelligence.'[20]

The introduction of really advanced mathematics into physics resulted in a division between experts in theory and experts in experimentation within the subject. Similarly, if the proposals here are accepted and implemented, one may expect a minor bewilderment from authors of learned monographs that they should be expected to collaborate in an intellectual enterprise which can be explicated only in terms of rather abstruse principles. More serious and articulate will be resistance based upon the counter-positions. According to them, the aim of interpretation could be nothing but to get as it were a cinema of what was done in the past, a sound-track of what was said, and what Aldous Huxley would have called a 'feelie' of past emotions and sensations. 'Fortunately, counter-positions bring about their own reversal. Just as Descartes' vortices[21] violated the canon of relevance that obliges the scientist to add nothing to the data except the content of verifiable insights, so the ideal of the cinema and the sound-track is the ideal not of historical science but of historical fiction. There is no verifiable cinema of the past nor any verifiable sound-track of its speech.[22] The available evidence lies in spatially ordered marks in documents and on monuments, and the interpreter's business is not to create non-existent evidence but to understand the evidence that exists.' The artist or the teacher may, no doubt, reconstitute for us the sights and sounds of the past, and thus perhaps prepare us for understanding it. But their role is subsidiary, and must not be misunderstood or exaggerated.[23]

As well as leading to misconceptions of the goal of interpretation, the counter-positions promote blunders in procedure. If objectivity were a matter of extroversion, then the meaning that one was trying to discover as well as the marks on the paper would have in some way to be 'out there', and the objective interpreter would manage to observe this out-there meaning, as opposed to the subjective interpreter who merely read his own ideas into the document. But the plain fact is that there is nothing whatever 'out there' but spatially ordered marks; to appeal to dictionaries and grammars, to studies of language and style, is merely to direct attention to more spatially ordered marks, so far as the criterion of the objective is really the observable.[24] It must be concluded that both objective interpreters (who more or less succeed in getting at the meaning of the documents which they interpret) and subjective interpreters (who are apt to read their own bias into them) inevitably make use of their own experience, understanding and judgement in the prosecution of their work. If the criterion of objectivity were really exclusive faithfulness to what is observable 'out there', there could be no interpretation, but only gaping at what is visible or tangible or subject to sensation of some other kind. (One cannot literally 'see' the meaning of a document; but that does not mean that one can hear or taste or smell it instead.) From the viewpoint of the counter-positions, the idea of a universal viewpoint (on which our account depends) will be dismissed as the product of vain and empty theorising; but from the positions it is quite clear that, short of the possibility of such a viewpoint, there could be no objective interpretation by one man of the meaning of what another man has said or written, since there would be 'no general possibility of rising above one's personal views and reaching without bias what the personal views of another are'.[25]

It is often maintained that an author ought to be interpreted in his own terms, and this dictum does express an important truth. But of course Plato, Aquinas or Kant cannot literally speak for themselves; and even if a re-incarnation of Plato were to arrive and recite to us the whole corpus of the *Dialogues*, the understanding of them, apart from the solution of a textual problem or two, would be left just where it was. A methodical hermeneutics demands an explicit acknowledgement by the interpreter of his own immanent sources of interpretation (in other words, of his own experience, understanding and judgement, which are what enable him to construe a document as the expression of what another has understood and judged on the basis of his experience). From the positions, 'one can acknowledge the reality of the various blends and mixtures of the patterns of human experience[26] and one can grasp how these blends and mixtures generate confusion and error on the notions of reality, objectivity, and knowledge. Through that grasp one reaches the protean notion of being; just as being is the intelligently grasped and reasonably affirmed, so what anyone happens to think is grasped intelligently and affirmed reasonably, will be coincident with what he happens to think is being; and as human utterance, as distinct from gibberish, proceeds from putative intelligence and reasonableness, a grasp of the protean notion of being gives access to the universe of possible meanings'. The counter-positions, on the other hand, lead to systematic distortions of the authors to be interpreted. They prevent the identification of the real with what is intelligently grasped and reasonably affirmed, and thus of the protean notion of being with the objects of putative intelligent grasp and reasonable affirmation. If one starts from the logical positivist premiss that a meaningful statement is either an analytic proposition or one that refers to sensible data, one must inevitably conclude that the majority of philosophers have been talking nonsense, and that the history of philosophy is a matter of cataloguing different brands of nonsense. If one is a radical existentialist, one cannot but accept Bultmann's programme of singling out the elements of, for example, the New Testament which can be re-expressed in existentialist terms, and dismissing the rest as insignificant and confused. Again, on the basis of common sense or even of historical sense, one can do no more than hit off more or less imaginative and emotionally-toned reconstructions of Nature Religions, Greek Mysteries, the primitive Christian community, and so on.[27]

4.3 *Canons of Interpretation*

An interpretation is an expression of the meaning of another expression; and a distinction must be made between those interpretations which are literary and those which are scientific. A literary interpretation offers the reader images through which he can grasp the insights and judgements which the interpreter thinks to be those of the original author. A scientific interpretation is concerned with formulating these insights and judgements in a manner consonant with the collaboration and control which are the hallmark of science. A methodical hermeneutics treats of such scientific interpretation. We propose a number of canons here, by way of summarising and tabulating the conclusions we have already reached. According, firstly, to the *canon of relevance*, one must begin from the universal viewpoint, and one's interpretation must convey some differentiation of the protean notion of being. Recourse to the universal viewpoint will eliminate the bias of the interpreter and of his audience. One may then exactly state opposed interpretations, with a reasonable hope that the oppositions may be eliminated by appeal to the data. The second canon, the *canon of explanation*, lays down that the interpreter's differentiation of the protean notion of being must be explanatory rather than descriptive, relating to one another rather than to us[28] the contents and contexts of possible documents and interpretations. 'The explanatory different-iation of the protean notion of being involves three elements. First, there is the genetic sequence in which insights gradually are accumulated by man. Secondly, there are the dialectical alternatives in which accumulated insights are formulated with positions inviting further development and counter-positions shifting their ground to avoid the reversal they demand. Thirdly, with the advance of culture and of effective education, there arises the possibility of the differentiation and specialization of modes of expression.'[29]

Third, we distinguish a *canon of successive approxi-mations*. The totality of documents cannot be interpreted by a single interpreter, nor yet by a single generation of interpreters; there must be a division of labour, and one must try to ensure that the labour is cumulative. For this to be possible, there must be reliable principles in accordance with which satisfactory interpretations may be selected and unsatisfactory ones corrected. With such principles, the end of a colossal task is already, however distantly, somehow in sight; without them, immense labour may result simply in movement round in a circle. Four such principles will now be outlined. The first is the demand for the universal viewpoint; if a contributor fails to present his results in terms of the protean notion of being, a critic can do this for him. A second principle relates to the qualities requisite in an interpreter, if he is to be able to extrapolate sufficiently from his own point of view to be able to grasp and convey that of another. The interpreter must have adequate self-knowledge, so as properly to apprehend the nature of human experience in general, the way insights accumulate, and the phenomena of reflection and judgement. Since every stage of human development is connected genetically and dialectically with every other, it must be possible in principle to retrace the steps that led from the past to the present. A third principle 'results from the genetic sequence of modes of expression and the recurrent gap between meaning and expression'; this gap is proportional to the greatness in the novelty of an author's meaning, the unpreparedness of his audience, and the lack of malleability in the means of expression available to him. A fourth principle is derived from the goal of interpretation, that of truth. Every proposed interpretation starts as a mere hypothesis; and the question then is not the number or authority of the persons who say that the interpretation is obviously correct, but what the evidence is for it. 'Nor is evidence some peculiar sheen or convincing glamour. It supposes the coherence of the hypothesis with the universal viewpoint, with the genetic and dialectical relations between successive stages of meaning, with the genetic sequence of modes of expression and the recurrent gaps between meaning and expression. It consists in the fulfilment offered by the data of documents and monuments for this wide-ranging and interlocked coherence.'[30]

A fourth canon for interpretation will be the *canon of parsimony*. On its negative side, this will exclude the bogus aim of interpreters at the unverifiable though imaginable cinema and sound-track of what was said and done in the past. On its positive side, it will exclude the scepticism of the relativist, and counter the claim that you cannot explain anything until you have explained everything.[31] Very radical surprises at least are excluded so far as the universal viewpoint is reached, since the whole range of possible meanings will then at least in principle be envisaged. Fifthly and lastly, scientific interpretations must observe a *canon of residues*. The interpreter, like the physicist, must be prepared for inverse as well as direct insights, so as to deal with the inevitable residue of mere matters of fact.[32] (It would be absurd for an interpreter to expect his interpretation to establish that his author could not have but written exactly as he did.)

It is important not to confuse dialectical development with genetic at the level of meaning. An intelligent writer is liable to advance in insight as he writes, and, at times, his fresh insights will be so basic as to make it appropriate for him to scrap what he has already written and begin afresh. But since there is a limit to human endurance, the re-writing may be done inadequately, or not at all. In these cases, there is a risk that the interpreter may misapply the principles of logic; and regard an author who has written in the light of a moving accumulation of insights as not so much intelligent as incoherent. And if the identity of the author is not beyond question, he is liable to be divided up by the interpreter into a number of different people. Similar problems arise when one turns from the problems of the progress of insight to that of the development of expression. There is an absence of genetic system in such development when new ideas have to be expressed through a gradual transformation of prior means of expression. At first, old words and images appear in new collocations; these pass out of currency to be succeeded by yet another set; and, provided the initial collection of ideas endures, 'the transformations do not end until a technical vocabulary on an explanatory basis is established'.[33] It is the nature of allegory to display through images and feelings the known unknown to be grasped by intellect; but while the basic content of the allegory may be authentic mystery, this is apt very soon to give way to myth. One may take as an example the Iranian conception of a cosmic struggle between light and darkness. On the level of mystery, this may be taken as expressing the conflict between the detached and disinterested desire to know with other desires; but, as a matter of historical fact, it has been expanded into a mythic cosmic dualism with a pantheon to match.[34]

The aim of interpretation is to gain and impart insight into the insights of others. The setting-out of criteria by which disputes may be resolved, and conclusions tested, in this area of investigation, should be of some importance at the present time, when differences derived from philosophical preconceptions so often give rise to differences in interpretation of the same document by competent investigators.[35]

5 Practical Reasoning

5.1. *Patterns of Experience*

As has already been said, insight is as significant in practical living and the area covered by common sense as it is in philosophy and the sciences. In the affairs of daily life as well as in abstruse theoretical matters, one may get the point or fail to get it. It is in practical matters too, particularly those pertaining to the individual's moral character and the place in the human community at large of his class and group, that a more or less deliberate *flight from insight* is apt to occur. (Self-knowledge is a difficult and painful business; there are some truths, particularly about myself, of which I would much rather be ignorant. I may indeed be prepared to misrepresent plain facts, and bully and persecute my fellow men, rather than be brought to acknowledge these truths.) As well as insights there are oversights — which occur with especial frequency when understanding is wilfully being evaded. The flight from insight blocks the occurrence of those insights which would upset its comfortable equilibrium. Nor is it content with a merely passive resistance. Though covert and devious, it is highly resourceful, inventive and plausible. (The more ingenious rationalisations of neurotic individuals, and of corrupt political regimes and oppressive social classes, provide notorious examples.) The intellectual enterprise represented by *Insight* may be regarded not only as a study of human understanding, and an unfolding of its philosophical implications, but also as a campaign against the flight from understanding.[2]

As will be shown, there appears to be a connection between the flight from understanding on the one hand and repression, inhibition, memory-slips, screening-memories, psychological abnormality, and psychotherapy on the other. Now mere sensation is an abstraction; as a matter of fact, sensation always occurs in the context of one of a range of *patterns of experience*. It has a bodily basis and is linked to bodily movements, and both sensations and movements are subject to organisation and control. 'The notion of a pattern takes us beyond behaviourism, inasmuch as attention is not confined to external data; it takes us beyond a narrow positivism, inasmuch as the canon of relevance[3] leads us to acknowledge that there is a content to insight; but it observes the canon of parsimony by adding no more than a set of intelligible relations to elements of experience.' Various such patterns are to be distinguished. Firstly, there is a *biological pattern*, a set of intelligible relations that link together sequences of sensations, memories, images, and bodily movements, to realize the purely biological ends of intussusception, reproduction, and self-preservation. In the *aesthetic pattern*, experience occurs for the sake of experience, beyond the limits set by biological purpose. It is the function of art to liberate experience from its merely biological function, and intelligence from the constraint of mathematical proof, scientific verification, and common-sense factualness.[4] Art expresses a wonder which is prior to the neatly-formulated questions of systematising intelligence. Also, it may provide attractive or repellent answers to the question of what man may be or become and why. 'Animals, safely sheathed in biological routines, are not questions to themselves.'[5]

The control achieved by the artist over sensations, images and emotions not only breaks the bonds of biological drives, but generates in experience a flexibility which makes it a ready tool for intellectual inquiry. In the specifically *intellectual pattern* of experience, the stream of consciousness collaborates with the spirit of inquiry; memory ferrets out instances which support or run counter to prospective judgement, and imagination anticipates possibilities which, if realised, would verify or falsify a theory. The intellectual pattern is subject to great variation from person to person; its 'frequency, intensity, duration and purity' depend both on native aptitude and on training. 'To learn thoroughly is a vast undertaking that calls for relentless perseverance. To strike out on a new line and become more than a week-end celebrity calls for years in which one's living is more or less constantly absorbed in the effort to understand, in which one's understanding gradually works round and up a spiral of viewpoints with each complementing its predecessor and only the last embracing the whole field to be mastered.' Fourthly and lastly, there is to be distinguished a *dramatic pattern* of experience. The biological aspect of man, his eating, sexual activity and so on, cannot be ignored, but it can be and is transformed. Men work as hard as they do not just to live, but to make living dignified. We need approval, moreover, from other people. Each individual develops insights into the roles he might play, and works out his own peculiar selection and adaptation of these. In the case of animals, each species seems to have a particular kind of complexity of response native to it.[6] In man, an initial plasticity and detachment grounds later variety.[7]

5.2. The Flight from Insight: (A) Mental Health and Disease
Neural patterns and processes demand psychic represen-tation and conscious integration; one selects and arranges, rejects and excludes. Now there is evidently a huge number of possibilities of habitual feeling and behaviour open to man, which vary with locality, period, and social context. 'Still, there are limits to this versatility and flexibility. The demand functions of neural patterns and processes constitute the exigence of the organism for its conscious complement; and to violate that exigence is to invite the anguish of abnormality.' When consciousness is directed in a manner which conflicts with the underlying neural possibilities, psychic aberration is the result. Now acknowledgement of the real as the verified, in accordance with the theory of knowledge outlined earlier, makes it possible to affirm the reality of the higher system, in this case of irreducibly psychical events and of laws relating them, no less than of the underlying manifold. There is thus no reason to hold that 'psychogenic' disease is really invariably caused by physio-logical factors not yet discovered; since on our view the psychic is a 'real source of organization that controls

underlying manifolds in a manner beyond the reach of their laws'. Again, things can go wrong not only at the psychic but at the intellectual level; one can fail to want insight, and be prejudiced in relation not only to theoretical but to practical and personal matters. This is apt to bring about withdrawal from living into the private world of fantasy, and the resulting isolation prevents the healthy development of the insights of common sense; so it is that *scotosis*[8] arises in the censorship governing the emergence of psychic contents. Rationalisation tends to accumulate evidence in favour of itself, and to brush aside in horror any intrusive contrary insight. The desire for insight gives rise to images from which the relevant insight may be grasped; similarly, fear of an insight represses from consciousness anything liable to evoke it. Primarily, the selective mechanism of the mind, alluded to by Freud as the censor, is constructive in its selection of material relevant to insight and dismissal of material irrelevant to it; only in aberration does it lead to repression. Since insights arise from images rather than from the affects associated with them,[9] it is only to be expected that images and affects will not get blocked from consciousness in quite the same way; and, sure enough, there is a phenomenon well known to psychoanalysts, in which an affect becomes conscious in association with an image other than that to which it was originally attached. One of the effects of scotosis is to defeat the effort to achieve smooth performance. To speak or play a musical instrument fluently, you have to concentrate on higher controls, rather than giving your mind to each requisite action; and so needs and desires which are inconsistent with conscious intention may succeed in slipping through. (When the polite young woman told her mother that her prospective husband was 'well-bed', in an important sense she said what she really meant, though not what she intended to convey to her mother.) It is the function of sleep to restore the organism, and in dreams, the psychic equivalents of neural demands rejected by the censor during the day find expression. Now we imagine as we please; but our emotions and feelings are quite another matter. Thus the dream as a safety-valve is liable to appear as a wish-fulfilment, and more likely than not, since the censor is still half-heartedly in operation, attached to some incongruous object.[10]

To penetrate from the surface to the latent content of a dream is thus to get at what is, so to speak, purposefully hidden. The disreputable dispositions or possibilities in mankind at large, in my relations, my immediate family, above all in myself, are very unpleasant to contemplate. I am likely to preclude the occurrence of insights into such things, and if my unconscious patterns are so stimulated as to demand them, the demand can be met indirectly in a dream. It is important not to be misled into the belief that the latent content of one's dream, as distinct from one's conscious desires and projects, is constitutive of the 'real' self. It consists merely of possibilities rejected both by the waking and by the dreaming consciousness. Parricide, cannibalism, incest, and suicide, are after all genuine possibilities; they do occur. But at least the spectre of a *real* monster underlying the superficial veneer of civilised man may be laid to rest, if the matter is rightly understood. The 'screening memories' of early childhood, (where we 'remember' a fiction which is in some way related to a real event which we don't wish to remember), perform a rather similar function to that of the dream. The peculiarities of sexual development are what make it the ordinary source of materials for scotosis. Hunger is present from birth, and its nature and manifestations do not change much in the course of growth. But the sexual instinct has a long development, with successive changes in neural demands and exigencies. There is thus any amount of room here for waywardness, accident, incomprehension, and blunder. Now adverse situations occurring at random can be offset by dreams, by a healthy environment, or by instruction. But one adverse situation may be followed by others, and each instance of waywardness may make the next more probable. So it is that a scotosis becomes established, and expert analysis of the psyche is needed to remove it.[11]

When adverse situations become the rule rather than the exception for most of a society, that society is able to survive only by providing for itself the public equivalent of a dream.[12] Aristotle in ancient times, and Stekel and others in the present century, have rightly seen the theatre as a means of mass therapy. Constraints of social organisation give rise to corresponding dreams; the relief afforded by the dreams may be noticed, and given dramatic expression. In myths, of course, it is well known that there may readily be seen the reflection of social and sexual realities.[13] The same factors give rise to taboos, but there is a vital distinction to be drawn, though it is often overlooked, between the sensitive mechanism which enforces taboo, and the rational reflection which, as will be shown in detail later, is at the basis of moral obligation.[14]

It is of the essence of the account presented here that psychic illness is closely associated with the flight from insight, recovery from it with intellectual illumination. It is characteristic of the work of Stekel, in particular, that he consistently envisages analytic treatment as retrospective education. Once somatic disorder and psychosis are excluded, the working hypothesis on Stekel's theory is that the patient who is mentally ill is suffering from a scotosis.[15] The analysand devises means to prevent the coming revelation and to repress the insights which will constitute it. The love or hatred which has been repressed, when it emerges, is apt to get directed onto the analyst; thus arises the well-known phenomenon of the 'transference'. The cure consists in a series of insights, or flashes of illumination. The analyst's task consists in helping the patient at least to the principal insights constitutive of his cure. For this, the analyst himself must have a large stock of the relevant insights, and also special knowledge of the patient. It may be asked what is the evidence for the view that suspension of understanding is a regular feature in psychogenic disturbance. In general, 'one may say that there exists empirical evidence for a psychotherapeutic notion in the measure that the notion is operative in actual treatment of all types of disorder rather than in a partial selection of types, that it survives prolonged and varied experience, that the survival contrasts with a readiness to drop unverified notions, that failures cannot be traced to the notion in question'. All these requirements seem to be fulfilled by Stekel's conception. What is at issue here, it must be emphasised, is not Stekel's psychological theory as a whole, but only a particular facet of it. To similar effect,

H.S. Sullivan alludes to 'selective inattention' on the part of analysands, and describes what it is like when a patient suddenly sees the point of one of his dreams.[16] The fact that determinism is no longer as fashionable as it once was among scientists has the greatest significance for depth psychology. 'Were mechanist determinism correct, then neither normality nor disorder could be psychogenic.' Freud would have introduced a new technique, not discovered an autonomous science. Freud himself was professedly a determinist. But so far as the assumption of determinism has any actual effect on the working of his theory, it seems to amount only to an insistence that everything is explicable. But this last, though true enough on our own view, does not entail determinism; it would only do so on the supposition – which we have already found reason to disbelieve[17] – that all scientific explanation is in terms of classical laws. Again Freud often evinces the scientific outlook of his time, and talks as though psychic events were mere appearance and unobservable entities the reality. What, one might ask, is Freud's libido? 'Is it what is known either by observing psychic events or by correlating these observables or by verifying these correlations? Or is it a construct that stands to Freud's verified correlations in much the same manner as the sponge-vortex aether once stood to electro-magnetic equations? To resolve this ambiguity, if it can be resolved, would call for an investigation by a trained expert in the history of science.'[18] (At all events, its postulation was a genuine scientific discovery so far as it conforms to the former description, the consequence of a counter-position so far as it conforms to the latter.)

5.3. *The Flight from Insight: (B) Social Progress and Decline*

So much for insight and the flight from insight in the private life of the individual. It is time to look at their effects in human actions and products, and in the life of communities and states. It is of the essence of practical common sense to use knowledge once acquired for making and doing. The fruits of this use are technology, politics, and culture. Even at the most elementary stages of civilisation, hunters and fishermen take time off hunting and fishing to make such equipment as spears and nets. Such pieces of gear, relatively permanent yet useful for acquiring the basic necessities of life, make possible a kind of primitive capital formation. (An ambitious man in a primitive fishing community might gain power and influence by making a corner in nets, just as a man of the present day can be accumulating money.) Also the concrete realisation of novel practical ideas needs some human co-operation, and a division of labour.[19] (If two men make nets and go fishing with them, and each devotes about the same time to both activities, their combined efforts will probably be more effective if they pool resources, and one specialises in making and repairing nets, the other in catching fish.)

The more sophisticated technology becomes, the more elaborate is the social co-operation needed to sustain it. Moreover, 'most men get ideas, but the ideas reside in different minds, and the different minds do not quite agree'. Communication and discussion may lead to agreement, but often they only serve to reveal the disparity more clearly for what it is. So persuasion becomes necessary, and the most effective · persuader becomes a leader. Each step in technological and economic development exposes new differences, and yet a common policy has to be reached. At the very basis of the social order, of course, stand relationships of more or less affection between person and person. Each one of us 'was born of his parents' love', and 'grew and developed in the gravitational field of their affection'. The sense of belonging together so derived is at the very basis of the social structure. Because of this sense, in spite of the immediacy of each man's individual needs and desires, social order is not achieved merely (as Hobbes thought) as a result of external constraint. However, only in prosperous times, and then with an effort, do inter-subjective groups fit in harmoniously with the larger social order. In times of crisis, at least, they fall to bickering with one another.[20]

Now the individual's intelligence and reasonableness enable him to conceive a general good, in which the fulfilment of his own needs and desires has some place, though not a unique or exclusive one.[21] However, *individual bias* leads a man to pursue his own needs and desires at the expense of this general good. *Group bias*, as opposed to individual bias, is supported by normal inter-subjective feeling. Group spontaneity (when feelings are not tempered by intelligence and reasonableness) fails to regard all changes in the light of the general good of society. The group, like the individual egoist, tends to have a blind spot for 'insights that reveal its well-being to be excessive or its usefulness at an end'.[22] Thus only those practical insights are liable to be put into effect which either meet with no group resistance, or find favour with groups powerful enough to overcome what resistance there is. Now the advantage of one group is commonly the disadvantage of another, and so there arise feelings of frustration and bitterness, and offensive and defensive psychic mechanisms further obstruct the thoroughgoing application of intelligence and reasonableness. But at least this form of aberration contains the principles of its own reversal. What started as a mere neglected possibility issues ultimately in a grossly distorted reality. (An inconspicuous failure by a statesman to legislate wisely, due to laziness, thoughtlessness, or class prejudice, may ultimately cause, and be seen to cause, suffering and injustice which is widespread and intense.) The bias generates unsuccessful classes, full of the communal bitterness and frustration to which we have alluded; and a revolutionary can readily turn this frustration into a militant force. In the ensuing conflict, the attitude of the dominant group naturally strongly affects that of the depressed groups. 'Reactionaries are opposed by revolutionaries. Progressives are met by liberals. In the former case the situation heads towards violence. In the latter case there is a general agreement about ends with disagreement about the pace of change and the mode and measure of its execution.'[23] (Thus, at any rate in the long run and at great cost, group bias is apt to generate its own antidote.)

General bias is due to the lack of self-analysis inherent in common sense. (The man of common sense is apt to have an overall distrust of the exercise and implementation of sustained intelligence and reasonableness, particularly when they bring his own basic assumptions up for questioning.) It has already been described how 'at each turn of the wheel of insight, proposal, action, new situation, and fresh insight, the tendency of group bias is to exclude some fruitful ideas and mutilate others by compromise'. Dominant groups are not so liable to veto technical and material ideas for improvement, as they are proposed changes in political and economic institutions (which changes are liable, after all, to lessen the dominance of these groups). A *shorter cycle* of events, due to group bias, has just been sketched; but there is also a *longer cycle*, which is caused by the neglect of fruitful ideas as a result of the general bias of common sense. (The limitation of common sense is that it is constitutionally incapable of taking the long view, that it cannot properly evaluate practical ideas with no fairly immediate application. Mere common sense has never issued and can never issue in far reaching social and political reforms; for these, there is needed a much more radical application of intelligence and reasonableness.) 'So far from granting common sense a hegemony in practical affairs, the foregoing analysis leads to the strange conclusion that common sense has to aim at being subordinated to a human science that is concerned, to adapt a phrase from Marx, not only with knowing history but also with directing it.' The limitations of common sense are that it cannot cope with the long view, or with intricate or disputed issues. Also, 'the general bias of common sense involves sins of refusal as well as of mere omission. Its complacent practicality easily twists to the view that, as insistent desires and contrasting fears necessitate and justify the realization of ideas, so ideas without that warrant are a matter of indifference'.[24]

The succession of higher viewpoints characteristic of science and mathematics has already been described; but in practical affairs, the general bias of common sense seems to lead to something like a reversal of this process, in which each successive viewpoint is *less* comprehensive than the last. The disregarding of timely and fruitful ideas leads to increasing social deterioration, to greater departure from rationality and coherence. The detached and disinterested intelligence and reason seem to have less and less relevance to the situation as it is. So it comes about that 'the general bias of common sense generates an increasingly significant residue that (1) is immanent in the social facts (2) is not intelligible

(3) cannot be abstracted from if one is to understand the facts as in fact they are'. This residue may be called *the social surd*. Just as the neurotic mounts an ingenious resistence to the analyst, so men of practical common sense become warped by the situation and regard as silly and impractical any proposal which lays an axe to the root of the social surd. From the surrender of detached and disinterested intelligence and reason there derives inevitably a major reversal on the speculative level. In the place of any former culture, philosophy and religion, which are likely to have been implicitly or explicitly critical of the *status quo*, there arise new varieties which pride themselves on being 'realistic', on starting from the facts as they are, on being averse to wishful thinking.[25] The central defect of this point of view is its lack of any basically critical attitude, which might enable it fairly to distinguish between social progress and social surd. From this incapacity there results an insecurity. Each new arrival in the field of ideas bolsters its own convictions by attacking and denouncing its predecessors. There are any number of such arrivals, because the further the surd expands, the more demand there is for justification of further contractions of the claims of intelligence and reason.[26]

Evidently the course of human development has not been a smoothly mounting curve of progress. The shorter cycle goes on manifesting itself, with social groups becoming factions, and nations going to war. So it is with the longer cycle. There are wars of religion, so men must live by reason; reasonable men have to tolerate disagreement; toleration is helpless to provide solutions to social problems; and so the final resort is to totalitarianism. Totalitarianism needs deliberately to create and propagate a myth, which will subordinate men to 'reality';[27] the reality being the economic development, military equipment, and political dominance of the all-inclusive State. The ends of this State will justify any means — of indoctrination, economic pressure, the breaking-down of moral conscience, torture, and total war. The totalitarian has uncovered a secret of power; to defeat him, if one is lucky enough to do so, is not to eliminate the temptation to try once more his methods of coercion and deception. 'Those not subjected to the temptation by their

ambitions or by their needs, will be subjected to it by their
fears of danger and their insistence on self-protection.' So, in
an uneasy peace, one totalitarian system begets another to
oppose it. Sooner or later, the gamble of war is bound to
seem worthwhile to one of the parties. Such a war might be
totally destructive — there would be the end of the longer
cycle. But it may be indecisive, in which case the basic
situation will remain unchanged. If a single world-empire is
the result of the war, it will be characterised by 'both the
objective stagnation of the social surd and the warped
mentality of totalitarian practicality'. Such a social organism,
with no enemy to fight, and no goal to attain, cannot cohere
indefinitely within itself. Common sense will desert the
empire for the individual and group interests which it
understands; this centrifugal tendency will be augmented by
the resentments and hatreds characteristic of each little
group, and by the tendency of each to overstate both the
case in its own favour and the case against its rivals. So in the
long run disintegration and decay set in.[28]

Fortunately, on the assumption of emergent probability,[29]
nothing is inevitable. The long cycle which has just been
described is so long, and the havoc it causes is so complete,
because of the difficulty of the lesson which it has to teach.
This is, that the general bias of common sense, whose fruit
the longer cycle is, cannot be corrected by common sense.
But it remains possible that man may use insight in some
measure to direct and control his future history. Thus the
long cycle invites attention to theories of history, such as
have been propounded by Vico, Hegel and Marx. The notion
of a theory of history has exercised widespread influence
through the liberal doctrine of automatic progress, the
Marxian theory and practice of the class war, and the various
myths of nationalist totalitarianism. A higher viewpoint is
needed, if one is to do justice to the virtues and limitations of
each of these positions. This higher viewpoint may be
summed up as recognition and implementation of the
principle 'that intelligence contains its own immanent norms
and that these norms are equipped with sanctions which man
does not have to invent or impose'.[30] (The systematic
implementation of intelligent insight and reasonable reflec-

tion will issue in a normative social and political science, which will provide at once an analysis and a critique of human institutions. The flight from insight, even on the general plea of common sense practicality, will in the long run bring about its own nemesis.)

On the one hand, there is progress, whose principle is liberty (and the consequent implementation in theoretical and practical matters of the unrestricted and unbiassed desire to understand); on the other hand there is decline, whose principle is bias (either individual, or group, or general, with the kind of flight from understanding typical of each). 'To ignore the fact of decline was the error of the old liberal views of automatic progress. The far more confusing error of Marx was to lump together both progress and the two principles of decline' (group and general bias) 'under the impressive name of dialectical materialism, to grasp that the minor principle of decline would correct itself more rapidly through class war, and then to leap gaily to the sweeping conclusion that class war would accelerate progress.' What is needed to correct the oversights and implement the insights of both schools is a human science which can distinguish between the liberty that generates progress and the bias that generates decline, and hence will be critical as well as empirical. Only thus can it aid man to understand himself, and guide him in the implementation of that understanding.[31]

Now man's culture is his capacity to reflect on his situation; only through such reflection, and hence through culture, can man meet the challenge of decline. As the social surd advances, culture is liable to be forced more and more to justify itself in terms of the dominant technology, economics and politics, rather than being allowed to bring a critical scrutiny to bear on them.[32] General bias must thus be counterbalanced by a detached intelligence which will neither be forced into an ivory tower nor capitulate to the social surd. Now practical intelligence demands a division of labour and differentiation of functions; hence there cannot be an absolutely classless society.[33] There have to be classes, and there have to be states; all that is disastrous is their disproportion. What is needed, to cope with the principles of decline in human society, is a *cosmopolis* which demands men's first loyalty, which cuts classes and states down to size, which 'is founded on the native detachment and disinterestedness of every intelligence', and which 'is too universal to be bribed, too impalpable to be forced, too effective to be ignored'.[34]

It may be asked how far this 'cosmopolis', which has been introduced as a theoretical answer to the practical problem of social decline, can further be delineated. It cannot be a police force; since ideas must come first, if they are to be really operative and not merely a façade, and force should at most be incidental. It would by no means rule out the existence of such institutions as the United Nations or a world government, but it would tend to be a curb on any disposition to merely short-sighted practicality in these organisations. Cosmopolis would be particularly concerned with putting into effect timely and fruitful ideas which otherwise, through the general bias of common sense, would be passed over. While being supremely practical in the long run, it would not waste time and energy on matters of short-term practicality, by being a busybody in the affairs of particular classes and states. It would not trouble much to condemn individual egoism, since this is already sufficiently disapproved of by human society at large. Nor would it pay a great deal of attention to group egoism, which inevitably generates its own reversal after a certain period of time. But cosmopolis would make it its business to explode and ridicule those rationalisations of the sins of dominant groups which contribute so much to the longer cycle of decline. It would not be much concerned with particular shifts of power among classes and nations. But the myths and the falsifications of history which attend these shifts of power would be very much its concern. It would 'prevent the formation of the screening memories with which an ascent to power hides its nastiness', and encourage the simple truth when this is out of fashion. It is of course essential that cosmopolis itself be purged of the rationalisations and myths which were the heritage of mankind before it came on the scene; since 'if the analyst suffers from a scotoma, he will communicate it to the analysand'. Cosmopolis as a dimension of consciousness is not altogether new, since the liberals have been already filling people's heads with the idea of progress, and the Marxists activating class-consciousness. 'It is the higher synthesis of the liberal thesis and the Marxist antitheses. It comes at a time when the totalitarian fact and threat have refuted the liberals and discredited the Marxists.'[35]

5.4. *The Nature of Good*

The nature of good and bad as such, and our knowledge of them, is now to be considered. (The general idea here is that good at the level of experience is the satisfaction of particular desires and needs; but that men can conceive and will states of affairs such as tend to realise systematically these satisfactions, and which are constitutive of the good at the level of understanding and judgement.) On an elementary level, the good is the object of desire, and its attainment pleasant or satisfying. The good of order – of a well-run city, or household, or economic system — stands to the satisfactions of particular desires and needs as system to what is to be systematised, (as scientific law to the instances in which it is verified). Hence it is the object of insight and judgement, rather than of experience. Now social order finds in the desires and aversions of individuals both a permanent ally, and a constant source of egoistic and group deviation. Fortunately the good or order, while it lies outside the field of sensitive appetite, is none the less itself an object of devotion; one may feel, for example, at least as emotional about socialism as about food or clothes. Such orders 'are constructions of human intelligence, possible systems for ordering the satisfaction of human desires'. Now, human willing is related to human reasoning in that we may grasp intelligently and reasonably not only facts, but also practical possibilities. Among these possibilities are the transformation of our own spontaneous dispositions to feel and to act; we may achieve this transformation by understanding ourselves, and making deliberate choices on the basis of this understanding. (A man, for instance, might upset his wife by almost invariably spending his evenings in the pub. His decision not to go out by himself quite so often, taken as a result of knowing the effects of this, may alter his habit, and so sooner or later his spontaneous desires and feelings on the matter.) We are agents as well as mere knowing subjects; and we have a spontaneous drive to suit our action to our knowledge.[36]

However, we may evade the implications of this in various ways, either through cowardice or through laziness. First, we may try to avoid the self-consciousness which consists in acknowledgement of the motives underlying our words and deeds.[37] A second kind of evasion is rationalisation, in which we revise our beliefs not so much in the light of intelligence and reason, as in deference to how it suits our wishes and prejudices for us to act and speak. This playing fast and loose with intelligence and reason is a more sinister business than merely lying, or alleging extenuating circumstances for oneself which are a judicious blend of acknowledged truth and unacknowledged falsity. This kind of flight from insight provides a ready market for myths and for some brands of philosophy. (It may suit me, for instance, to hold the emotivist theory of ethics, if my conscience convicts me of behaving rather badly. I can argue somewhat as follows: 'It's not as though there were anything more to morality than feelings of scruple. Therefore, if I can get away without being punished for this action of mine, and if I can get rid of my feelings of scruple, that will end the matter so far as I am concerned'. The suggestion here is *not* that there are not some grounds for holding that the emotivist theory of moral utterances is valid; only that there are some situations into which a man might get himself which would tend to make him exaggerate the arguments in favour of this theory, and to neglect those that tell against it. Again, someone might convince himself that he was validly arguing his way into a political fraternity which justified his feelings of aggression, or a religious system which compensated for his feelings of inadequacy and timidity.) A third way out may be called that of moral renunciation. A man who takes this path does not either fail to advert to his motives, or cook his arguments in deference to his wishes and desires. He is content instead with a merely speculative rather than a practical acknowledgement of the aspiration to make his living intelligent and reasonable.[38] (One might summarise the three types of evasion respectively in the slogans 'I don't want to know what I ought to do'; 'If that is what I ought to do, I had better tinker with my reasoning faculties until I can come to "know" that I "ought" to do something different'; and 'I know what I ought to do, but I'm not going to do it'.)

It will be evident that our analysis of 'good' and 'ought' in terms of intelligence and reasonableness runs counter to those analyses of these conceptions according to which their essence is simply to evince emotion and to commend practical attitudes. Admittedly these activities are concomitants of moral self-consciousness; but it is a blunder to confuse them with moral self-consciousness itself. (A morally self-conscious agent does what he deems to be intelligent and reasonable, rather than simply riding the current of his desires and aversions). The view of morality according to which it is simply a matter of emotion is at least popularly attributed to Freud; but Freud's own admirable practice would seem to belie this. 'When Freud decided eventually to publish his *Traumdeutung*, he was overcoming emotions and sentiments and following what he considered the only intelligent and reasonable course of action; and such following is what we mean by obeying moral conscience.' We now have the means of making a distinction between *true* and *false values*. True values are the object of fully intelligent and rational choice, while false values are those chosen as a result either of flight from self-consciousness, or of rationalisation, or of moral renunciation. Each choice that we make, whether of a true value or of a false, modifies our habitual willing and our effective orientation in the world, and so our contribution to progress or to decline. It may be seen that false values in the ethical order, being due to an incomplete and truncated development of understanding and reason, and so ultimately inviting their own destruction or reversal, are analogous to counter-positions in the metaphysical order. It may also be seen that metaphysics and ethics are closely interrelated on our view, since the root of both is the dynamic structure of the intelligent and rational self-consciousness (which puts questions to experience and gets answers both about what is the case, and what ought to be done). The application of our method to ethics, as in the case of metaphysics, at once sets forth correct precepts and provides a radical criticism of mistaken ones.[39]

Up to now we have talked of 'good' as not only the satisfaction of human desires and needs, but also the orders, grasped by human intelligence and reasonableness, which systematise these satisfactions of desire and need. Let us now talk of it in a sense which includes but goes beyond both of these.[40] (Good then will be the realisation of intelligible order, evil the failure to realise it.) 'If the intelligible orders of human invention are a good because they systematically assure the satisfaction of desires, then so are the intelligible orders' (in the natural world) 'that underlie, condition, precede, and include man's invention.' The hedonistic idea of the good as merely the object of desire does not do justice to the place of intelligence and reason in man's conception and implementation of the good. Good as experienced and evil as experienced are not the end of the story; both of them are either aspects of a potential good, or by-products of its realisation. This conception of good does not deny or minimise pain and suffering at the level of experience, or overlook the reality of disorder and false values at the level of understanding and judgement. The intelligibility of the universe, as has already been argued,[41] is partly statistical — that is to imply, to be grasped by inverse as well as by direct insights. As so understood the goodness of the universe 'consists potentially in unordered manifolds, formally in the effective probability of the emergence of order, and actually in the eventual emergence'. As for that aspect of the universe which consists in human beings and their affairs, 'its goodness consists potentially in the failures and refusals of autonomous self-consciousness to be consistently reasonable, formally in the inner and outer tensions through which such failures and refusals bring about either the choice of their own reversal or the elimination of those that obstinately refuse the reversal, and actually in the consequent removal of disorders and false values'.[42] (Evil occurs, in other words, either as a potential good, or as a by-product of the realisation of the actual good.)

Human freedom has still to be discussed, with its actual limitations and the conditions for its realisation. The significance of the canon of statistical residues is *not* that it establishes freedom; it is true, however, that it makes it easier to dispose of arguments against the very possibility of freedom. (Freedom is not mere indeterminism, though indeterminism is a necessary condition of freedom.) That the free human act is not determined does not imply that it is arbitrary; 'what is intelligible, intelligent and reasonable is not arbitrary'. For free human acts are necessarily more or less intelligent and reasonable ones. Thus those acts are not free which occur according to the mere routines of sensation and feeling whose laws may be discovered by the student of sensitive psychology. As to the psychologist himself, 'if his statement of his results is intelligent and reasonable, it consists in the imposition of higher integrations upon what is merely coincidental as far as the laws and schemes of his psyche go'. And other people can be intelligent and reasonable, both in their factual beliefs and in their practical living, besides sensitive psychologists. The main point to be borne in mind here is that freedom only arises in the context of insight and judgement (where one can conceive or fail to conceive of a possibility of action, and once it is conceived decide or fail to decide to put it into effect).[43]

Not only do we have insights into what is or might be the case; we also have *practical insights* into what is to be done. Here, too, there is need of subsequent reflection by which we decide that a course of action conceived as possible should actually be put into effect — according to whether it is pleasant, or useful if unpleasant, and so on. Of course, we would never do what has to be done if our every action was fully weighed, if we did not act largely out of habit. But the question often arises of whether my habits of action might not be improved, and to what extent the values to which my habits are geared are false rather than true in the sense we have just outlined. 'I become rationally self-conscious inasmuch as I am concerned with the reasons for my own acts, and this occurs when I scrutinize the object and investigate the motives of a possible course of action.' The term of such reflection is *decision*. The nature of decision is best described by comparison with judgement. Both select one member of a pair of contradictories; 'as judgment either affirms or denies, so decision either consents or refuses'. Both are rational, as dealing with states of affairs apprehended by insight, and both occur as a result of a reflective grasp of reasons. However, they differ in that judgement is concerned to complete one's knowledge of what exists or is the case, whereas decision is concerned to put into effect what would not otherwise be the case. The fully self-conscious human subject is not only intelligent and reasonable in forming his opinions about what is the case; he also conforms his willing to his knowing by making reasonable decisions.[44] To know one's obligations is of course one thing, to decide to fulfil them another. Instead one may, as has previously been said, surrender consistency between knowing and doing (for instance, out of idleness or timidity). The act of will is not, after all, coerced by knowledge of the obligation. If the act of will is absent, one may be a rational knower in a particular instance without being a rational doer.[45]

A distinction of fundamental importance is to be made between material and spiritual reality. The material reality within which men live is merely *subject to* intelligible laws which the scientist may discover. But human intelligence and decision can *impose* law or intelligible order on otherwise coincidental manifolds. (A man may impose order merely upon the objects in his living-room, or he may implement more impressive intelligible orders in the manner of Beethoven or Kandinsky.) We distinguish the *spiritual* from the *material* as that which is intelligible as an intelligence, as opposed to that which is intelligible without being an intelligence.[46] (To understand the movements and gestures of a conscious man, as opposed to the movements of a raindrop on a window-pane or a frog in a pond, I have to take his understanding into account.)[47]

One has to distinguish between *essential freedom* — to inquire, to judge, to decide — and the *effective freedom* to implement one's decisions. There are various restrictions on effective freedom. Firstly, there are those of external circumstance. 'Just as the prisoner is not free to go and come as he pleases, so the Eskimo is not free to mount a camel or the desert nomad to go fishing in a kayak. Whatever one's external circumstances may be, they offer only a limited range of concretely possible alternatives and only limited resources for bringing about the enlargement of that range.' A second restriction on freedom is one's psychoneural state. Even perfect psychic adjustment does not dispense me from acquiring skills and habits if, for instance, I am to play a musical instrument competently or speak a foreign language. And such adjustment may be lacking owing to the effects of scotosis. A third limitation on effective freedom is that of intellectual development. The same principles hold good for the occurrence of practical insights as for that of insights generally; and 'the less the development of one's practical intelligence, the less the range of possible courses of action that here and now will occur to one'. Fourthly, there are limitations of antecedent willingness. Where willingness is lacking, persuasion may be possible; but persuasion takes time (and opportunities may be missed meanwhile). Again, one may be at first willing to implement an intelligent and reasonable scheme which occurs to one; but on second thoughts, settle back into the routine dictated by one's habitual activities, emotions, and general cast of mind. In spite of these difficulties, effective freedom may be won, though it is not to be won easily. Most people seem neither consistently intelligent and reasonable nor consistently animal in practical matters; though it is true that 'they tend to the positions in enouncing their principles and to the counter-positions in living their lives'. The central practical difficulty is that we develop biologically prior to developing psychically, and psychically before intellectually and rationally. 'Complete self-development is a long and difficult process. During that process one has to live and make decisions in the light of one's undeveloped intelligence and under the guidance of one's incomplete willingness. And the less developed one is, the less one appreciates the need of development and the less one is willing to take time out for one's intellectual and moral education.' The significance of satire for such development is that it breaks in upon pretence and upon stupid and inept routine; even where men are afraid to think, they may not be afraid to laugh. The milder form of humour which laughs with rather than at its victims has the use of adverting to the gap between the ideal on the one hand, and human beings as they are, myself as I am, on the other.[48]

By moral impotence we mean here the limitation of effective freedom not by the barriers of external circumstance or psychic abnormality, but by the ultimately graver defect of incomplete development of intellect and will. The effect on men of consciousness of their moral impotence is very ambivalent. While it may spur one man to learn from his failures and make new efforts, it will be regarded by another as evidence that there is no point in trying, that he must simply put up with himself as he is.[49]

What applies to the individual and his decisions applies also to the policies of a group or community. The result is one that we have previously described, of social situations which are a compound of the rational and the irrational, to be :.derstood only by a parallel structure of direct and inverse insights. (The point about many of the products of bureaucratic muddle and compromise, for instance in local government or university or business administration, is precisely that they have no point.) But the difficulty in applying a remedy for such situations is that even a subtle, accurate and protracted analysis of the situation will enlighten only those who are already sufficiently intelligent and reasonable to profit from it. (And those who are sufficiently favoured by the inequities consequent on the social surd will have every motive to engage in flight from an understanding which will be such as to subvert it, and to implement that flight by the publication of lies and if necessary by persecution.) The problem of how to remedy this situation is at once radical and permanent. It is radical, since it relates to the very structure of human understanding, will and activity; it is permanent, since the development of intelligence, rationality and good will in the teeth of conflicting interests, motives and distractions belongs to the very essence of man. Thus the social context, though it intensifies the problem, does not create it.[50] The problem is not even to be solved by discovery of the correct principles of philosophy, ethics or human science; since their very correctness will only make them seem wrong to disoriented minds. Again, force is no solution, since the development of intelligence, rationality and good will can be in the last resort nothing but the willing achievement of the human subject himself.[51]

What general characteristics, it will be asked, must the solution have, if it is none of those already described? 'If it is to be a solution and not a mere suppression of the problem, it has to acknowledge and respect and work through man's intelligence, and reasonableness, and freedom. It may eliminate neither development nor tension yet it must be able to replace incapacity by capacity for sustained development. Only a still higher integration can meet such requirements. For only a higher integration leaves underlying manifolds with their autonomy yet succeeds in introducing a higher systematization into their non-systematic coincidences. And only a still higher integration than any that has so far been considered can deal with the dialectical manifold immanent in human subjects and the human situation.' The question whether such a higher integration has actually emerged will be considered in the next chapter.[52]

6 God and Philosophy[1]

6.1 *Summary of the Argument*

We have seen how the 'self-appropriation of one's own intellectual and rational self-consciousness begins as cognitional theory', and 'expands into a metaphysics and an ethics'. It remains to be seen how it 'mounts to a conception and an affirmation of God, only to be confronted with a problem of evil that demands the transformation of self-reliant intelligence into an *intellectus quaerens fidem*' (an understanding seeking for faith).[2]

An analysis of the nature of human understanding, and so of the world of existing things that confronts that understanding and is gradually mastered by it, leads to the conception of an 'unrestricted act of understanding' which understands itself, and through itself everything else that exists or could exist. The complete intelligibility of the world, and the non-existence of any unintelligible mere 'brute' fact, is only possible (it will be argued) on the assumption of the real existence of such an unrestricted act of understanding, which understands all possible worlds and wills the one which actually exists, and which can be shown to possess the attributes generally ascribed to God. Now the reflection on the nature of the world which leads us to conceive and to affirm God leads us also to acknowledge the existence of evil within human individuals and society, and to the conviction that men by themselves cannot remedy this evil. That God is good and omnipotent is reliable ground for the belief that he has provided a solution to the problem, a solution which both really meets the problem and respects the freedom of man which gave rise to it in the first place. Examination of history and culture brings us to the actual solution, which not only repairs the ills in man, but brings him to superhuman perfection. So much for a brief summary of the main line of argument in Lonergan's natural theology. I shall in the following paragraphs describe it in rather more detail.

6.2. *The Existence of God* .

The human mind is characterised by an unrestricted desire to understand, which is never to be entirely satisfied until no more questions remain to be asked. But in fact further questions always confront the human mind and its understanding, which as a consequence are in a perpetual state of development. 'It is only on the assumption of an unrestricted act (of understanding) that everything about everything is understood.' Now by material nature we mean either what is constituted by the empirical residue,[3] or is conditioned intrinsically by it. But the spiritual, or that which understands as well as being capable of being understood, is not so constituted or intrinsically conditioned; for it is of the essence of understanding in men to *abstract* from the merely empirical, to form universal judgements on the basis of particular instances.[4] Our own inquiries, and the insights which are achieved by means of them, are initially, and commonly, into what is given in sense-experience. But though sense-experience certainly conditions inquiry and insight, it does not do so intrinsically; since, as we have been arguing throughout, understanding is sufficiently independent of the flux of experience to frame general laws on the basis of the particular instances given in that experience, and to judge whether these correspond to what is actually the case or not. Seeing is seeing colour, and the coloured is necessarily spatially extended; thus seeing *is* conditioned intrinsically by the empirical residue. But the understanding, which frames theories and judgements on the basis of such perception, is not so. If we ourselves as spiritual beings transcend the empirical to the extent described,[5] so *a fortiori* would the unrestricted act of understanding, which 'would understand all beings, including those that are material', but would itself be 'the immaterial, non-temporal, non-spatial unity such that, if it is grasped, everything about everything else is grasped'. The unrestricted act of understanding could not deduce or predict events. It could deduce only if it advanced in knowledge by transforming one abstract premiss into another (as in mathematics and formal logic, and sometimes in science), or by combining abstract premisses with concrete information (as often in science); but it could not so advance, because it would already know everything. It could predict only if some events were present and others future relative to it. But, since it transcends the empirical residue in the way that has already been described, it is non-temporal; the totality of temporal sequences 'is part of the everything about everything else that it grasps in understanding itself'.[6]

Now Lonergan would admit (in agreement with Aquinas, Kant, and other opponents of the ontological argument)[7] that, even in the case of God, the fact that we have a coherent concept of such a being does not entail that such a being exists. By appropriate definitions, no doubt one can make 'God exists' into an analytic proposition.[8] 'But one asks for the evidence that the terms as defined occur in concrete judgments of fact.' Descartes' argument from the fact that we have a concept of God directly to his existence 'would be valid if conceiving were looking and looking were knowing' (in other words, if simply to conceive an object were equivalent to having a perception of it, and if having a perception of it were equivalent to making an adequately grounded judgement that such an object existed in reality). But if the ontological argument (from the concept of God directly to God's existence) is fallacious, it may seem that 'there is no possibility of affirming rationally the existence of God . . . There seems no possibility of verifying an unrestricted act of understanding either in our external or our internal experience'. But there are compelling reasons, which we have already advanced, for disbelieving the principle that verification is necessarily a matter of the experience of sense-contents. There are abundant and clear counter-instances to this assumption, of which the law of falling bodies may provide an example. In this case, 'all that is experienced is a large aggregate of contents of acts of observing. It is not experience but understanding that unifies the aggregate by referring them to a hypothetical law of falling bodies. It is not experience but critical reflection that asks whether the data correspond to the law and whether the correspondence suffices for an affirmation of the law.'[9] The existence of God is verified not in experience, but as the conclusion of an argument. There are many such arguments, but they all seem to have the following general form. 'If the real is completely intelligible, then God exists. But the real is completely intelligible. Therefore, God exists.'[10]

An inquiry into the nature of causality will reveal that an unrestricted act of understanding must exist in order for the existence of the world to be accountable. 'In general, causality denotes the objective and real counterpart of the questions and further questions raised by the . . . unrestricted desire to know.' There are as many types of cause as there are types of question which can be asked. A distinction is to be drawn between the internal and external causes of anything (roughly, between what it is in all its aspects, and what are the preconditions for its existence or occurrence). Internal causes have already been discussed at some length; external causes are what are at issue in the present discussion.[11] There are three types of external cause; the efficient, the final, and the exemplary. These types of cause are the answers to the questions of what brought anything into existence, and in accordance with what model, and for what purpose, it did so. The nature of each kind of cause can best be brought out by means of an example. In the case of a bridge, the final cause is its use by a human community, the efficient cause the work of building it, and the exemplary cause the design conceived by the engineer. Of course, the universe at large is not particularly like a bridge; consequently, it is necessary to go to the root of these notions to see how far they are of general application. If they were found to apply generally, one would be led to affirm 'a first agent, a last end, a primary exemplar of the universe of proportionate being'.[12] The first step in the argument is to affirm the intelligibility of whatever exists or is the case; the next step is the acknowledgement that when inquiring into the things and events which constitute the universe one goes on meeting matters of fact which one cannot explain, which in turn give rise to further questions. The only possible term of such an inquiry is a being or beings[13] in which there is no element of mere matter of fact, and which is 'capable of grounding the explanation about everything else'.[14] (And this could only be at least one unrestricted act of understanding that understands all possible worlds, and wills that which actually exists.)

It remains to be shown that the unrestricted understanding whose will grounds the world is one, free, eternal, and creator and conserver of all else that exists. If there were several unrestricted acts of understanding, 'they would differ merely empirically; and the merely empirical is not self-explanatory'. Accordingly, there can be only one. Moreover, the ground of the universe cannot be necessitated in founding a contingent universe, for what follows necessarily from the necessary is itself necessary. But it cannot be arbitrary either, since what resulted arbitrarily from the necessary would be mere matter of fact without explanation. 'But what is neither necessary nor arbitrary yet intelligible and a value, is what proceeds freely from the choice of a rational consciousness.' This last sentence may tend to confirm the doubter in his suspicion that the idea of causality which has provided the basis for this argument for the existence of God has by no means been freed from merely anthropomorphic associations; since it leads 'rather obviously to the affirmation of an unconditioned intelligent and rational consciousness that freely grounds the universe in much the same fashion as the conditioned intelligent and rational consciousness of man grounds freely his own actions and products'. But of course the specifically human type of consciousness is not purely intelligent and rational; it is rather in tension between the pure desire to know and other desires. 'On the other hand, in so far as one considers in man solely his intelligent and rational consciousness, one cannot but deal with what is related intimately to the universe and to its ultimate ground. For what is the universe and its ground but the objective of man's detached, disinterested, unrestricted desire to know?' The unrestricted act of understanding is timeless, for if it were in time it would either be involved in material nature (like physical objects) or develop (like human understanding). It brings about what is in space and time without being spatial or temporal, is the agent of change without being subject to change. God *eternally* wills Bucephalus to exist *for the short period* that he does exist; thus the changes involved in Bucephalus coming into existence and passing out of existence are not changes in God. The unrestricted act of understanding is creator, in that it makes everything else out of nothing; since the pre-existence of any matter which God merely ordered or fashioned would be unexplained, so 'the alleged matter would prove to be nothing'. It is personal, for like man it is a rational self-consciousness, but 'as unrestricted act' what man is 'through restricted desire and limited attainment'. Such a being, however clearly and in a manner free from anthropomorphic projection it is conceived, 'clearly satisfies all that is meant by the subject, the person, the other with an intelligence and a reasonableness and a willing that is his own'. God's causality must be exercised so long as the world or any of its parts exist, for the world and all its parts are dependent for their existence on God; and for God to be cause of the world, whatever some thinkers may have supposed, is nothing else than for it to be dependent for its existence on him.[15]

Lonergan's argument for the existence of God may be summarised as follows: that the existent is as such intelligible, that there are no matters of merely brute fact; and that this is possible only on the assumption of the existence of an unrestricted act of understanding, which understands all that could exist or be the case, and wills what actually does exist or is the case.

6.3. *The Practical Problem of Evil*[16]

Given that there is no matter pre-existing creation, and hence that God's will and intention are completely efficacious, it would appear that God is responsible for all the evils and sins of the world. But before one leaps to this conclusion, it is necessary to make certain distinctions. Evil is to be divided into three categories, physical evil, moral evil, and basic sin. By basic sin is meant the failure of free-will to choose an obligatory course of action, or to reject a reprehensible one. In the case of basic sin, the rational creature's 'attention remains on illicit proposals; the incompleteness of their intelligibility and the incoherence of their apparent reasonableness are disregarded'. The morally evil action which results from this 'constriction of consciousness' is more conspicuous, but in fact derivative from basic sin and so ultimately of less significance. The result of morally evil action is increase in tension and temptation in the agent himself and in his social environment. In the category of physical evil are to be included 'all the shortcomings of a world order that consists, so far as we can understand it, in a generalized emergent probability'.[17] Such a world-order entails a relatively undeveloped state of affairs occurring before a developed, with advance only at the price of risk. There will be breakdowns and failures in development, and security may be had only along with sterility. In particular, a man's intelligence has to develop, and his good will to be acquired, for him to live and act as he should.[18]

Thus besides what God absolutely wills and hence exists or is the case, and what he absolutely does not will and therefore neither exists nor is the case, there is a third category constituted by 'the basic sins that he neither wills nor does not will but forbids'. It may be wondered how even the permission by God of basic sin is to be explained. The answer is that 'it is not evil but good to create a being so excellent that it possesses rational self-consciousness whence freedom naturally follows . . . ; to leave that freedom intact, to command good indeed and to forbid evil, but to refrain from an interference that would reduce freedom to an illusory appearance. Consequently, it is not evil but good to conceive and choose and effect a world order, even though basic sins will and do occur'. Physical and moral evils would indeed be absolutely evil if the ultimate criterion of good and evil were sensitive pleasure and pain. But if the criterion of good is intelligibility,[19] this is not the case; for everything in the universe can be understood but basic sin (since this is a matter of defect in the intelligibility proper to the actions of an intelligent and rational being). 'For the imperfection of the lower is the potentiality for the higher; the undeveloped is for the developed; and even moral evils through the dialectical tension they generate head either to their own elimination or to reinforcement of the moral good.'[20] (The main point of this rather abstract argument is that all such evils may be understood as either brought about or permitted *for* states of affairs which could not be brought about without them, or at least without the real possibility of them.)

6.4 *Understanding in Search of Faith*

The nature of the problem of evil, and also of the world order within which it occurs, provides us with a heuristic structure[21] through which we may reach a general account of the characteristics of any solution which will be such as both to meet the problem and to conform to the world order. Once this general account of possible solutions has been reached, we may appeal to the facts to find where the solution in fact lies. First, the solution will be one, since there is one God, one world order, and one individual and social problem of sin. Secondly, 'the solution will be universally accessible and permanent. For the problem is not restricted to men of a particular class or of a particular time; and the solution has to meet the problem'. Thirdly, the solution will not disrupt but continue harmoniously the order of the universe. 'For there are no divine afterthoughts.' It will not involve introducing into the world a new species or genus of being, since the solution is to be for a specifically human problem. New conjugate forms (qualities and dispositions) have to be introduced to man's intellect, will, and sensitivity, since sin is a matter of the misdirection and consequent disorientation of these. Human badness arises from the fact that 'man's living is prior to learning and being persuaded . . . The solution . . . must reverse the priority, and it does so inasmuch as it provides intellect, will and sensitivity with forms or habits that are operative throughout living'. The forms will be in some sense supernatural, in that nature is what presents the problem which is to be solved. Now the present world order is one in which higher forms which evolve always systematise non-systematic elements in lower forms of existence;[22] thus one would expect that the new qualities and dispositions provided for man's intellect, will and sensitivity would solve the problem by controlling elements in them which otherwise are non-systematic or irrational. 'Since higher integrations leave intact the natures and laws of the underlying manifold and since man is intelligent and rational, free and responsible, it follows that the solution will come to men through their apprehension and with their consent.'[23]

For human intellect there must be provided basic truths about man and God, not because men are intrinsically incapable of reasoning these out for themselves, but because they in fact never reach unanimity on them. To human will, there must be added dispositions powerful enough to counteract the effects of one's own waywardness and of the social surd, to fight evil by means of a stronger and more persistent good. As has already been shown, mankind has a permanent emotional and practical need for mystery, which, when it is not satisfied, will express itself in the formation of myths. 'Inasmuch as intelligence and reasonableness and will issue into human words matched with deeds, they need at their disposal images so charged with affects that they succeed both in guiding and in propelling action . . . Since mystery is a permanent need of man's sensitivity and intersubjectivity, while myth is an aberration not only of mystery but also of intellect and will, the mystery that is the solution as sensible must be not fiction but fact, not a story but history. It follows, then, that the emergent trend and the full realization of the solution must include the sensible data that are demanded by man's sensitive nature and that will command his attention, nourish his imagination, stimulate his intelligence and will, release his affectivity (and) control his aggressivity.' (Meditation on the history, and participation in it by ritual and recitation, will control men's emotions and make them amenable to pursuit of the good, and gradually purge away their tendency to break out in aggression and violence.) To the extent that the solution goes beyond the minimum requirements specified, there will be revealed truths which men could never discover for themselves or, even if they did discover, adequately comprehend. Those who know of the existence of the solution and its nature will have the duty to collaborate in making known the good news of it, and since human nature varies according to culture and environment, of 'recasting the expression of the solution into the equivalent expressions of different places, times, classes, and cultures'.[24] (They will also have particularly at heart that critique of the social surd, and destruction of its protective carapace of myth, which we have ascribed to our hypothetical 'cosmopolis'.)[25]

(Where the shape of the hat is as closely specified as this, the identity of the rabbit which is concealed under it scarcely needs to be added. The actual 'emergent trend and full realization of the solution' are to be found, when the facts of history are scrutinised, in the history of the ancient Israelite nation and its culmination in the words and deeds of Jesus Christ.)

6.5 *Faith and Humanism*

Of conceivable solutions, some would be such as simply to solve the problem of evil, others such as both to solve it and in addition to alter human qualities and dispositions in other ways. In the latter case, they would be liable to include aspects whose nature and existence could not be concluded merely from scrutiny of the problem of evil and analysis of what would be a solution to it. If the solution is of this kind (and scrutiny of human history and culture shows that in fact it is), it will go beyond any form of humanism, and will be a means of bringing men not so much to a human as a superhuman perfection. Let us call this kind of solution 'supernatural'. On the supposition that such a supernatural solution exists, men being as they are will be apt to grasp and apply it imperfectly; and 'the imperfect realization of the supernatural solution is apt to oscillate between an emphasis on the supernatural and an emphasis on the solution'. For instance, faith will preserve a sterile purity which makes no real difference to human living; or it will become nothing but a means to material or social improvements.[26] (The recent history of Christianity may be felt to provide abundant justification of this contention.)

A humanism which is fully consistent with itself, if our argument is right, will ultimately be led to embrace the solution which actually exists to the problem of evil, and if that solution happens to be supernatural, will in consequence become something more than humanism. But because of the

imperfection both of men's understanding of the supernatural solution and of their implementation of it, it may
well be expected that there should be a humanism in revolt
against the supernatural solution; a humanism which is such
as to condemn mystery as myth, and to exalt reason in such a
way as to exclude faith.[27] 'For a time, it may base its case
upon the shortcomings of those that profess the supernatural
solution but live it imperfectly or intermittently or not at all.
But this incidental argument sooner or later will give place to
its real basis. For it rests on man's proud content to be just a
man, and its tragedy is that, on the present supposition of a
supernatural solution, to be just a man is what man cannot
be. If he would be truly a man, he would submit to the
unrestricted desire' to know and to find out the truth, 'and
discover the problem of evil and affirm the existence of a
solution and accept the solution that exists. But if he would
be only a man, he has to be less. He has to forsake the
openness of the pure desire; he has to take refuge in the
counter-positions; he has to develop what counter-
philosophies he can to save his dwindling humanism from
further losses; and there will not be lacking men clear-sighted
enough to grasp that the issue is between God and man,
logical enough to grant that intelligence and reason are
orientated towards God, ruthless enough to summon to their
aid the dark forces of passion and of violence'.[28]

Lonergan and the
Problems of
Contemporary Philosophy

Lonergan's work is concerned with the central philosophical issues of ontology and epistemology, and consequently has relevance to most of the questions with which philosophers are characteristically concerned. To avoid inordinate length, this chapter will amount to little more than a series of notes and suggestions. It will be convenient to divide it into comments on (*a*) Lonergan's theory of science, (*b*) his epistemology and metaphysics, (*c*) his moral philosophy, and (*d*) his philosophy of religion.

Lonergan's philosophy as a whole might be summarised as a thorough working-out of the following maxim. Reality, or the concrete universe, is the goal aimed at by the whole process of experience, understanding, and judgement, engaged in by the inquiring human subject. Lonergan's theory of knowledge thus seems to be a version of the 'logic of question and answer' recommended by Collingwood;[1] one comes to know the truth by the repeated process of putting questions to experience, arriving at theories which are answers to these questions, and then making reasonably-grounded judgements in terms of these theories. So much perhaps is obvious; what may not be so obvious are the implications of this thesis for the whole range of actual and potential human knowing, and therefore for the nature of the world which is the object of that actual or potential knowledge.

(*a*) A large section of *Insight* is devoted to problems in the philosophy of science and in scientific method.[2] Three main points of view in the philosophy of science may usefully be distinguished; that which stresses the role of experience; that which draws attention rather to the role of theories and their testing; and that which emphasises what is to be learned from the actual historical development of science. It is worth giving a brief sketch of each of these points of view, in order that the nature of what Lonergan has to contribute may be seen in relation to them. The first view is particularly concerned with the importance of unbiased gathering of data, of assembling facts, of making and recording observations. Accredited theories and authorities should never be allowed, on this view, to predetermine one's selection of facts, let alone the interpretation one places upon them. Theories should be allowed to arise, as in fact they will arise, as a result of patient and unprejudiced amassing and scrutiny of observable facts. This view is associated, and in the main rightly so, with Francis Bacon. Its watchword is induction; one observes a series of instances of a thing of type A having a quality of type x or an effect of type y, and no instances of such a thing not having such a quality or effect; and so one concludes that all A's have quality x or effect y. The main virtue of this account of the matter is generally said to be the way in which it safeguards objectivity against authority and prejudice; however, though in the ascendant in nineteenth-century theories of science, it is not now fashionable. This is because it appears to underestimate both the importance of hypotheses in science, and the vigour and originality of thought that is necessary to come by such hypotheses. No man ever came to a hypothesis just by letting observable facts somehow impress their pattern upon his mind. Also, as was argued most forcibly by Hume, and has been underlined by modern developments in logic, induction simply is not a formally valid procedure of argument. However many things of type A you encounter which happen to have quality x, it is always possible that the next A you run into will fail to have it.

The role of theory, and of its testing and consequent change, in the advancement of science, is emphasised particularly by Karl Popper, the most famous and articulate exponent of the second view which I have mentioned. Popper is impressed, firstly, by the fact that no-one has ever shown how 'induction' could be valid. The whole question of how one *comes by* theories, indeed, is for Popper a matter only of interest to psychologists; the crucial question for the investigator of scientific method is not how theories are arrived at, but how they are and should be validated. Secondly, he draws attention to the unfortunate manner in which a theory may often be complicated and modified in such a way that any conceivable evidence might *verify* it. Psychoanalysts and Marxists, in particular, are notorious for their ability to fit any conceivable event into their theoretical systems; but unless conceivable states of affairs are excluded by a form of explanation, it can have no predictive power, and so cannot be properly scientific. The stress in the validation of theories, then, should be on their *falsification*; and the best theories are those which, while they might well have been falsified by many observations and experiments, in fact survive sustained and reiterated testing of this kind. The ideal scientist would be constantly seeking to falsify the theory in which he believed, and would always be willing to scrap it as soon as the relevant evidence turned up. (It is important that the result of no single token-experiment would suffice as a falsification; the experiment would have to be repeatable.)[3]

The greatest difficulty with Popper's account is not that scientists have failed as a matter of fact to act as on his view they should; after all, Popper could easily insist that whether scientists have actually proceeded in such a way or not, they ought to have done so. It is rather that, had the great pioneers of science discarded their theories the moment any contrary evidence turned up, many of the most important discoveries of science would not have been made when or as they were, and possibly would never have been made at all. For example, in the dispute between Lavoisier and Priestley as to whether the oxygen or the phlogiston theory of combustion was correct, each side could appeal to evidence which told against the other. Hence, on the criteria suggested by Popper, not only the erroneous phlogiston theory, but the ultimately successful oxygen theory as well, should have been rejected. In fact, the phenomena which were apparently inconsistent with the oxygen theory were later explained, quite satisfactorily, by an extension of it.[4] At first sight at least, this is an example of just the kind of tinkering with a falsified theory to make it accommodate the facts which

Popper deplores. An account which is consistent with this and similar episodes which have in fact characterised the successful progress of science has been advanced by Thomas Kuhn. As Kuhn sees it, during normal periods in the development of the sciences their conceptual schemes and general basis of theory is uniformly accepted by competent practitioners. At such times there is no question of trying to falsify the dominant theories; the working scientist will be concerned only to elaborate them and to extend their application. Occasionally, however, the sciences go through a period of crisis, when theorists can no longer accept the previous conceptual scheme as satisfactory, and seek for a new one. Such a time of crisis occurred in physics at the beginning of the present century, when Newton's physics and cosmology seemed no longer universally acceptable, but before Einstein's theories had succeeded in establishing themselves.[5]

What is disquieting about Kuhn's account is that it apparently makes wholly insoluble the problem of what it is for a received scientific theory to be *true*. What it seems to come to is that the general theories acceptance of which characterises periods of 'normal science' are somehow *true for* those who hold them, and suddenly become no longer *true for* a body of scientists. But it seems repugnant to our normal ideas of truth and falsity to say, for example, that the Ptolemaic system of cosmology was true so long as it was universally accepted as true, and became false only when the Copernican system replaced it in scholarly esteem. And one wonders by what token some deviations from an accepted general theory, like Copernicus's and Einstein's, are strokes of genius, while most others are mere manifestations of crankiness. The Baconian and Popperian accounts of science, for all their differences, have in common at least that they each give some account of what it is for the authoritative pronouncements of scientists to be more or less worthy of provisional acceptance as true, what it is for them to be likely to be false. After all, except perhaps on a very queer view of truth, the consensus of learned men has certainly been wrong in the past.

Perhaps the solution to this puzzle might be along the

following lines: that arguments against the possibility of knock-down falsification do not affect the possibility of what one might call cumulative falsification. On the theory of cumulative falsification, the more facts there are which *tend* to falsify a theory, the *less* rational it is to hold it; on the other hand, this does not imply that any single repeatable result of observation or experiment will be itself sufficient conclusively to falsify the theory. Thus Lavoisier, in favour of whose theory of combustion so many experimental results seemed to tell, could rationally entertain the expectation that his theory would ultimately be seen to accommodate the few facts which apparently told against it. This would appear to be quite in accordance with Lonergan's theory in *Insight*, which has features in common with all three of the views I summarised on the nature of scientific method, though perhaps most with the second. In agreement with the first view, Lonergan insists that the empirical inquirer is confined to insights into the data of sensible experience, and may add to these only the laws verified in them.[6] On the other hand, his insistence on the creative role of the thinking subject in propounding the relevant insights, and in judging whether or not these are verified in the data, is more reminiscent of Popper. However, his acceptance of the need for co-operation and consequent deference to authority in prosecution of the scientific enterprise is in the spirit of Kuhn.[7] Like Popper again, Lonergan holds that no scientific hypothesis, however well confirmed, can be regarded as absolutely certain. In any given case, there always remains open the possibility that more relevant questions may be asked, and more evidence adduced, such as will make a new theory seem preferable. However, while we may not be certain that any particular *theory* evolved by scientists may not be confronted with evidence which will demand its revision, we can at least be certain that the *method* of science is valid, since it is impossible to conceive of any manner in which an empirical hypothesis could be valid except by being empirically and rationally grounded.[8]

(*b*) One may say, roughly, that for Lonergan scientific knowledge is what is derived from inquiry into and reflection on experience, and metaphysical knowledge is what is derived from inquiry into and reflection on the fact that this is so. However, there is knowledge of another kind from that which is fully scientific or metaphysical, that is, that resulting from the naive extroversion which spontaneously and unreflectively affirms the reality of what it immediately confronts. Properly scientific or metaphysical knowledge, on the other hand, results from a comprehensively critical attitude, where the subject has questioned his experience and his consciousness, has formulated theories, and has tested in experience and consciousness judgements expressed in terms of those theories. The babel of conflicting philosophies, both past and present, is due to the infinite degrees of compromise possible between naive extroversion and the fully critical attitude. In materialism, we find the compromise at its most elementary stage. 'Matter' is in effect the intentional object of simple extroversion, that is to say, that towards which naive extroversion is directed. A materialist is just critical enough to see the reason for saying that sensation pertains to the perceiver rather than the object perceived; what really exists, consequently, must be a 'matter' which is not the direct object of sensation, but which somehow gives rise to sensations in us. Phenomenalism is more sophisticated; British philosophers at least should realise how hard it is to argue from the premises of Locke without reaching the conclusions of Hume.[9] Phenomenalism is the inevitable result of consistent application of the principle that the real world is the object simply of sensation; but unfortunately neither causality, nor other minds, nor scientific laws, nor indeed one's own self over and above the stream of impressions and ideas, can be the object of sensation. But if the real world is nothing more or less than what is to be known by the three-fold process of sensation, of the understanding of what is presented to sensation, and judgement in terms of that understanding, phenomenalism is clearly due to mistaking one part of the process of knowing for the whole. And there would appear to be a fundamental incoherence about phenomenalism, so far as those philosophers who have reached the view that reality is nothing but the flux of sensations, or sense-data or sense-contents,[10] have come to this view by an exercise of that understanding and judgement whose significance in the apprehension of truth about the world their theory implicitly rejects. If the real and the true are what one comes to know by the exercise of understanding and judgement on the data of sensation and consciousness, this is at once inconsistent with phenomenalism, and presupposed in any argument to the effect that phenomenalism is true.[11]

Materialism, quite apart from its conformity with the natural prejudice already mentioned, is fostered by an incompletely critical understanding of the nature and presuppositions of science. The work of Galileo and Locke made it clear enough that 'secondary qualities', of colour, taste, and so on, could not be the objects of mere extroversion; but their oversight was to treat the 'primary qualities' of mass, movement and extension as though they were so. Now evidently it is of the essence of science to move from a merely descriptive to an explanatory account of things and their properties (central forms and conjugate forms). One rises from the level of mere observation and description to that of explanation, in which things and their properties are envisaged in terms of the mechanics of Newton or Einstein, the periodic table of the elements, the theory of evolution, and so on. This is a fact which is hardly in dispute; Lonergan's importance lies in what he makes of it. Now it is plain enough, when one thinks about the matter, that these forms of explanation have not been achieved simply by glancing at the external world, or even by staring at it; they have been achieved by reiterated putting of questions to experience, and by verification or falsification of judgements couched in terms of theories arrived at by this questioning. Explanation can be in terms of physical, chemical, and biological laws, and the concepts and terminology based upon them; it can also (*pace* the behaviourists and materialists) be in terms of the experiences, insights, judgements and decisions, as the expression of which human behaviour is to be understood. This last is the kind of explanation which is appropriate in the case of the subjects dealing specifically with man, such as psychology, sociology, history, and the interpretation of documents and monuments.

At each level of reality — the subatomic, the chemical, the

biological, and the specifically human — there are things and properties *judgements about which may be more or less verified* in experience, but *which are not themselves mere objects of experience.* The presence of a particular kind of fundamental particle may be verified by a series of streaks on a photographic plate; but the particle itself is something with a characteristic mass, velocity, electrical charge and so on, judgement about whose presence is verified by the streaks. Again, that Augustus Caesar understood, judged, deliberated and acted in certain ways is something which I may discover by consulting documents or deciphering monuments; but Augustus's thoughts and actions are not to be derived by me from the document by looking at it only, or even putting it under a microscope; I must concoct a theory, make particular judgements in terms of it, and then see whether these judgements are or are not supported by what I see in the document or on the monument concerned. Facts like this have led to sophistications of empiricism; but what is needed, according to Lonergan, is a clean break with empiricism, which always boils down in the long run to mistaking what is a part of the process of knowing for the whole.

At each level of reality, (the subatomic, the chemical, the biological, and so on), the intelligible laws constitutive of that level render systematic patterns of events which are only coincidental from the point of view of the laws governing the level below. Thus, things at each higher level cannot properly be claimed to be 'nothing but' aggregates of things at the next level below; since they are characterised by properties constitutive of that level but not of lower ones. Thus the argument underlying 'physicalism', to the effect that human beings are nothing but biological organisms, biological organisms nothing but parcels of chemical compounds, chemical compounds nothing but aggregates of atoms, atoms nothing but conglomerations of elementary particles, can be refuted.[12] After all, the fundamental particles are not direct objects of experience and cannot even accurately be imagined, but are asserted to exist only as a result of the verification in experience of judgements couched in terms of theories which postulate such particles; but if *that* is the index of the real, human thoughts and animal sensations are every bit as real as protons and electrons.[13]

Behaviourism in psychology and the social sciences is another result of the mistaken doctrine that the real is nothing other than the publicly observable. The fundamental confusion which makes this doctrine humanly plausible is between the true principle that scientific hypotheses must be verifiable in experience, and the erroneous one that the things and properties asserted to exist by the theory must themselves be direct objects of experience. That the reductionist ambitions of some behaviourist psychologists are based upon error does not imply, of course, that behaviourists have not found many important correlations, such as the conditioned reflex, and the laws of operant conditioning.[14] This last point illustrates one of the most important functions of epistemology and metaphysics as Lonergan conceives them; to liberate scientific discoveries from the shackles of the erroneous theories of knowledge in terms of which they are often formulated, and which these discoveries are mistakenly supposed to confirm. This may be expected to be particularly relevant to the human sciences, where not only the scientist himself, but the human beliefs and values and actions which he is studying, are liable to be influenced by misunderstandings of this kind.

The well-known paradoxes of Hume — that causal laws have no firmer basis than our habits of mind, that we have no knowledge of any self over and above the stream of sense-impressions — constitute one of several examples in the history of philosophy of what happens when a great thinker pushes through the premises of an erroneous theory of knowledge to their logical conclusion. Neither the self nor the causal nexus are to be apprehended by *experience*; but experience is not the only component of the cognitional process. Kant tried to show how human knowledge remained possible, in spite of the difficulties raised by Hume; but he could never quite break through to the true view that reality is nothing else than that which comes to be known through the whole cognitional process of experience, understanding, and judgement, engaged in by the conscious human subject. As Kant saw it, since experience does not get us into direct touch with things in themselves, the latter must remain for ever inscrutable to us; the phenomenal world of common sense and of science is a compound of the raw material of sensation with the *a priori* forms of our thought. Reality for Kant was not the direct object of experience, as it was for the empiricists; its nature was irreducibly problematic, except as regards the merely phenomenal world part investigated, part constructed, by the processes of human cognition. From the incompleteness of Kant's criticism there results the arbitrariness of the categories, the inscrutability of the human subject, the total mysteriousness of things in themselves (ghosts of the intentional objects of extroverted consciousness), and agnosticism on the transcendental issues of the existence of God, freedom, and immortality. A comprehensively critical rationalism has no business to stop before these issues, but is likely to be at least in a fair way to clearing them up once and for all.

The successors of Kant got rid of his shadowy things in themselves — only to conclude that the real world does not exist at all independently of thought, but is simply created by it. If things and facts are not direct objects of either naive extroversion or perception, it might be asked, what consistent alternative is there to saying that they are simply evolved by thought in the process of coming to a clearer and clearer conception of its own nature? This, in effect, is Hegel's solution to the central epistemological and ontological problem of the relation of human thought to reality. But if empiricism puts too exclusive stress on the first element in the cognitional process, experience, Hegelian idealism overemphasises the second, the evolving by creative intelligence of concepts and ideas. Hegel overlooked the significance of the third element, of judgement whether one's ideas, or the propositions framed in terms of them, are adequately grounded by the evidence which exists independently of them. It is one thing for me to conceive a hippogryphon; it is another thing for me to judge on sufficient grounds that such an animal exists in reality.

It is often assumed that realism and idealism are simply antithetical to one another. But if Lonergan's account of the matter is basically correct, there are two kinds of realism, that of the uncritical extrovert on the one hand, and that of the fully critical philosopher, for whom real things and facts are what are gradually revealed by the human cognitional process as a whole, on the other. Between these two forms of realism, idealism would appear to be a half-way house. Its criticism goes far enough to establish the inadequacy of mere extroverted awareness as the criterion for reality and objectivity, but not far enough to determine the true criterion. One might put it that naive realism plays thesis, and idealism antithesis, to fully critical realism as synthesis.

Another common attempt to deal with the central problems of epistemology and metaphysics, and one very common among contemporary philosophers, is to treat them as though they did not exist. To raise such problems at all, it is argued, language must 'go on holiday',[15] be taken out of its normal and proper situations in life. On this view, Plato, Aristotle, Locke, Hume, Kant, and the early Wittgenstein all erred by posing at all the general question of the relation of human thinking to the real world. The business of philosophy will then be simply to describe both ordinary language, and the specialised languages of science, poetry, religion and so on. But it is to be objected that ordinary language, as it actually exists and has existed, involves oversights as well as insights, is bound up with assumptions about the world which turn out to be muddled or mistaken. From the point of view of common language and the common sense which it enshrines, Einstein's conceptions as to time, space and absolute rest are nonsensical; yet it would be a bold or stupid man who argued that they were erroneous merely for that reason. In fact, the presuppositions of common sense are frequently exposed and corrected by science; and in any case, the deliverances of common sense vary notoriously from place to place and from time to time, and what passes for common sense in a New Guinea swamp is not what passes for common sense in an English suburban living-room. To assume that the basic presuppositions of ordinary language are all right, as many philosophers appear to do, is to neglect the extent to which the advance of science may change and has actually changed these presuppositions. As Bertrand Russell remarks somewhere, common sense leads to science, and science shows that common sense is at least quite often wrong. If the perennial issue between common sense and science is to be resolved in any other way than by one party shouting down the other, one has to get a viewpoint from which the scope and limits of each can be assessed.[16] But a rational investigation of the scope and limits of science on the one hand and common sense on the other, and of the languages which characterise each of them, leads straight to the central issue of metaphysics, the general problem of knowledge and its relation to reality.

Lonergan's philosophy provides no brief for the characteristic neglect of the human subject by contemporary empiricists and philosophers of science — a neglect not unreasonably stigmatised by a recent author as an unempirical feature of the usual kinds of empiricism.[17] In opposition to the apparent tendency of science, of course, phenomenology and existentialism have been particularly concerned with the human subject, and with the anxiety, hopefulness and bewilderment with which he confronts the worlds of inanimate objects and other persons.[18] Indeed, while the points of view of the two most influential varieties of contemporary philosophy, the analytic and the existentialist, would appear to be mutually destructive, Lonergan's philosophy provides a vantage-point from which both may be seen to have an important role to play, and each to have characteristic virtues and limitations. The human subject is capable of understanding or failing to understand not only the material world; he may also more or less fail to understand himself, his desires and the motives of his actions. Fear or cowardice may lead to a more or less deliberate flight from understanding, not only by the individuals but by communities. Many of the phenomena of mental illness become intelligible when understood in terms of such a flight from understanding, as does the sudden rush of enlightenment which frequently signifies a neurotic's return to mental health.[19]

In the case of communities, a very similar kind of flight from understanding renders intelligible the disposition of political and ecclesiastical authorities to falsify the history of their own rise to power, and to find scapegoats for their own wickedness and incompetence.[20] The social sciences, whose essential concern is with individuals and groups acting each in accordance with a certain mixture of understanding, misunderstanding, and avoidance of understanding of itself and its situation, may be every bit as rigorous as natural science, without the slightest tendency to reductionism. For their hypotheses may certainly be *verifiable by reference to* observable behaviour, without the *meaning of the terms in which they are expressed* being reducible to what is merely observable. By an application of the epistemological principles laid down by Lonergan, a new psychiatry (for example) would be able to combine the speculative insights of the existentialists and psychoanalysts with the experimental techniques of the behaviourists, and reveal the present war to the knife between these two parties as due to opposite misunderstandings of the actual exigences and metaphysical implications of scientific method. (What seems to be involved, to be exact, is a neglect of the canon of parsimony on the one side, and its misunderstanding on the other.[21]) In inquiries concerned with history and interpretation, Lonergan shows the way out of that recurrent and depressing dilemma; whether we should be content with an 'objective' account of the 'facts', which eschews considerations of motive and meaning, on the one hand; or whether we should aspire to an empathy with the minds of men of other times and cultures, of which the deliverances are unfortunately quite impossible to verify, on the other.[22]

It seems worthy of remark that Noam Chomsky's account of the nature of human language is just what one would expect on Lonergan's view of the relation of human knowledge and inquiry to the world. According to Chomsky, all grammatical sentences in a language can be derived, by the application of certain rules of transformation, from 'simple, declarative, active sentences' consisting of a noun-phrase and a verb-phrase.[23] This is presumably what is liable to happen if each man's linguistic behaviour is to be accounted for as resulting from an understanding orientated towards a world of things and their properties (central and conjugate forms) which exist and occur (by central and conjugate acts). In such basic sentences the things may be said to have the properties, the things to exist and the properties to occur.

Chomsky's brilliant analysis of the defects of the behaviourist account of language is also quite consistent with the principles arrived at by Lonergan, though I do not believe that either scholar has been influenced by the other.[24]

My account of these applications of Lonergan's metaphysical principles has necessarily been very brief and sketchy; but I hope it gives some idea of their relevance to a number of important fields of inquiry.

(c) The basic premiss of Lonergan's moral theory is that the fully intelligent and reasonable subject may grasp a possible state of affairs in which the needs and desires of people in general, and not only those of himself or his group, will tend to be satisfied. To conceive and will such a state of affairs is to conceive and will the good. This highly objectivist view of ethics is not the least controversial of Lonergan's views. However, philosophers may be less predisposed against it now than they would have been a few years ago.[25]

The objections to treating value-judgements as though they were statements of fact, which objections underlie emotivism and prescriptivism, depend on well-known arguments of Hume and G.E. Moore. Hume, in a famous and much-quoted passage, said that philosophical authors were inclined to prove, or to purport to prove, some matter of fact, such as the existence of a Deity; and then to proceed to infer that one *ought* to perform one kind of action rather than another. However, he himself could not see how such an inference, from what is the case to what one ought to do, could possibly be valid.[26] (Hume himself cannot be said to apply this principle very consistently in his own works; certain observations later in the *Treatise* appear to be inconsistent with it.)[27] A more detailed argument that such inferences were invalid was propounded by Moore in *Principia Ethica*; and it is to Moore's argument that, when the fact-value dichotomy is challenged, its supporters will often appeal. Moore remarks that philosophers have often defined 'good' in terms of other properties — for instance, contribution to the greatest happiness of the greatest number, or furthering of the evolution of the human race to an overall state of greater happiness and intelligence, or conformity with the revealed will of God. But all such definitions, Moore held, involve the same fallacy, which he called the 'naturalistic fallacy'. This is shown as follows. Let us suppose that by 'good' is meant 'contributing to the greatest happiness of the greatest number'. In that case, to affirm that something is good, and at the same time to deny that it contributes to the greatest happiness of the greatest number, is a contradiction. But now suppose that someone declares that a particular action (say) is *not* good, though admitting that it *does* contribute to the greatest happiness of the greatest number. We may say that he is wrong as a matter of fact; but we can hardly deny that his claim *makes sense*, or say that he is simply contradicting himself. But if 'good' were really properly *definable* as 'contributing to the greatest happiness of the greatest number', then he *would* be contradicting himself. From the correctness of the definition, it would follow that the proposition in question was a contradiction. But the proposition is not a contradiction, since it makes perfectly good sense to say at once that an action is good, and that it does not contribute to the greatest happiness of the greatest number. Therefore, since a false conclusion can be deduced from it, the definition cannot be correct. It may easily be seen that just the same form of argument invalidates the two other definitions of 'good' cited, or indeed any other that can be suggested. It might always be false, for instance, as a matter of fact, that any action was good, and at the same time contrary to the will of God; but if someone claimed that an action was both of these things, he would not be talking nonsense. By the same pattern of argument, all attempts to define 'good' in terms of other qualities and effects can be refuted.[28]

Moore believed that 'good' is a simple and indefinable property, in this respect like 'yellow'.[29] But since it is very difficult to see what experience, or reasoning based upon experience, could enable one to discover whether this simple and indefinable property did or did not belong to anything, it was hardly to be expected that philosophers of more empiricist tendency than Moore, who accepted that the above argument was valid, would agree with him in this. In the section on ethics in *Language, Truth and Logic*, A.J. Ayer supplemented Moore's argument with the well-known 'verification principle' in establishing his own conclusions. This principle is to the effect that all meaningful non-analytic propositions are such that some experience or other would tend to verify or to falsify them. Moore had shown that 'good' could not be defined in terms of other properties or effects; and there was no assignable type of experience which would tend to verify or to falsify the claim that something had this simple and indefinable property of goodness. Therefore, since, by the verification principle, all genuine non-analytic propositions were such that experience would tend to verify or falsify them, it followed that no sentence of the form 'X is good' could express a genuine non-analytic proposition. The upshot of Ayer's argument is that to call anything good is not really to ascribe a property to it at all. Indeed, Ayer admitted, in some cases to call something good *is* to ascribe a property to it; but such ascriptions are always distinct from the evaluative element which is the central function of the statement that something is good. And any attempt to define this evaluative element in terms of descriptive properties would fall foul of Moore's argument. It followed that to call anything 'good', except in so far as it was incidentally to ascribe certain properties and effects to it which were nothing to do with the essence of goodness, could not really be to describe it at all. Ayer concluded that it was to evince a certain emotion about the thing in question, and to demand that others should share one's attitude towards it.[30]

The doctrine that moral judgements are rather a matter of commending or prescribing than of describing anything has been much favoured by analytical philosophers since the nineteen-forties.[31] Yet, while it makes some sense to commend or prescribe things, persons and actions of any kind whatever, it is more than doubtful whether all kinds of things, persons and actions can intelligibly be described as good, or, in the case of actions, such that one ought to do them. It may indeed make sense to hold that an action (say) is good, while admitting that it does not tend to promote the greatest happiness of the greatest number – when, for instance, it is in obedience to a law the general effect of which is thus beneficial, or when the agent is keeping a promise in performing it. But, in spite of such cases, it is surely true to say that the *less* a man is admitted to be concerned with meeting the needs and desires of his fellows, and the *more* he is admitted to set himself to frustrate them, the *less* sense there is in saying that he is a good man, or that his actions in general tend to be good actions.[32]

I conclude that Moore and his successors have not shown that the goodness of persons and actions is not at least largely a matter of how far they tend to add to the sum of human happiness or fulfilment, and intend or are intended to do so. If this is the case, Lonergan's ethical theory cannot properly be dismissed on the ground that it involves the 'naturalistic fallacy', or that it does not take into account the dichotomy between statements of fact and judgements of value.

(*d*) I have summarised three aspects of Lonergan's natural theology, that is to say, of his account of God's nature and activity in as far as these can be apprehended by human reason without special divine revelation. These aspects concern (1) the existence and nature of God, (2) the problem of evil and (3) the Christian revelation as the practical solution to the problem of evil. I shall now make comments on and mention objections to each aspect in turn.

(1) The whole enterprise of constructing rational arguments for the existence of God has been subjected to heavy attack, by theologians as well as by unbelieving philosophers. The attitude on the part of theologians appears to me difficult to justify. Of course in a sense Christian dogmatic theology as such *presupposes* that there is a God, that he has revealed himself in Jesus Christ, and that this revelation in Christ is mediated to men through Scripture and the Christian community. But it may, on the face of it, be intelligently questioned whether there is a God, and, if there is, whether he has revealed himself at all, and, if he has done so, whether it is in the way that Christians claim. The burden of proof would appear to lie, to say the least, on those who say that one cannot reason about these matters or ought not to do so.

Karl Barth, owing to whose great theological achievement the negative attitude to such 'natural theology' may be said to have become fashionable, was concerned particularly to preserve properly dogmatic theology from contamination by methods and principles which were alien to it. He considered that any attempt to argue to the existence and nature of God from general philosophical reflection on the nature of the world, or of man, could ultimately result only in the 'God' derived from such reflection usurping the place of the true God revealed in Christ.[33] But one may surely insist quite as strongly as Barth that Christian dogmatic theology must be based on the revelation of God in Christ, without conceding to him that there is not also a place for natural theology in the sense in which I have described it. Barth will have it that to the believer natural theology is superfluous, since he already accepts God's existence and his revelation of himself; while the unbeliever is in possession of no premises from which the existence of God and the fact of his revelation of himself can be shown to be certain or even probable. Consequently, belief can only preach to unbelief, and cannot argue with it on premises accepted by both parties.

Barth's reasons for rejecting natural theology seem to founder on the principle, *abusus non tollit usum*. That one *can* use philosophical argument, on the basis of general reflection on the world or on man, in such a way as effectively to supplant the revelation of God in Christ, does not entail that one may not also use it quite consistently to show the certainty, or the probability, or at least the possibility, that God exists and has revealed himself as Christians suppose.[34] If one cannot, indeed, is this not very good reason for holding Christianity to be false? But however this may be, the negative or contemptuous attitude to natural theology has been taken over from Barth by many who have not a tithe of the intellectual seriousness and sophistication of that great theologian. Barth's reasons for rejecting natural theology are at least clearly set out and rigorously argued.[35] But the effect of his influence in this matter on many of his successors seems to have been not so much to make them abstain from natural theology, as to induce them to do it very badly. For example, J.A.T. Robinson has impugned the traditional forms of attempted proof of God's existence on the ground that such attempts presuppose, 'psychologically if not logically', the possibility that there is no God.[36] He then says that since God is ultimate reality, and there must be an ultimate reality, then there must be God. But the question inevitably arises, in what sense this 'ultimate reality' is supposed to be ultimate. Two possible answers spring to mind; first, that 'X is ultimate reality' logically entails that "X does not exist" is a contradiction'; second, that 'X is ultimate reality' entails 'X is that on whose existence everything else depends for its existence'. In the first case, then, the appeal to 'ultimate reality' turns out to be a disguised citation of the ontological argument, and in the second case, of the cosmological or causal argument. Thus, Robinson has in fact made an ambiguous and ham-handed use of some of the very arguments which he purports to reject. More recently, T.F. Torrance has claimed that theological inquiry is necessary not because God is a problem, but because we are; the existence of perfection needs no argument.[37] But in fact it may very well be doubted, and frequently has been so, whether there actually exists, or could possibly exist, a perfect being; and so the case for its doing so at least seems to be worth arguing.

It has been suggested that, if there were a rationally compelling proof of the existence of God, this would impair that freedom of man to believe in God and to love him which is of the essence of the faith of a Christian.[38] But those arguments for the existence of God which have been historically influential have not purported to do more than demonstrate the existence of a being (or even at least one being) with *some* of the attributes which Christians have ascribed to God, thus leaving others to the assent of faith. This is also true of Lonergan's argument. And even a rationally compelling proof would convince only those who were both intelligent enough to understand it, and sufficiently submissive to the claims of intelligence and reason to follow them to the end, even in matters where they have motives for evading their consequences. If God exists, there are few men for whom the fact of his existence is entirely convenient. Thus the virtue of faith would hardly be lessened by the mere existence of a rational proof, particularly considering the number of evasions which can be suggested by the counter-positions, and have been underwritten by some of the most imposing figures in the history of human thought. In any case, if there are no good reasons for believing in God's existence, I do not see why belief in him is not rather a vice than a virtue.

So much for the theological objections. Far more serious, in my opinion, are those which are raised by philosophers. These may be divided into two categories: those which depend on assumptions about the relation of human knowledge to reality different from those of Lonergan, and those which argue differently from similar basic assumptions. The most well-known and perhaps the most impressive philosophical attack on proofs for the existence of God, that of Kant, evidently falls into the first category. According to Kant, every existing thing or state of affairs which can be an object of knowledge must also be capable of being an object of sensation. God cannot be an object of sensation; hence, if we are to assert his existence at all, it must be as a matter of faith, and not of knowledge.[39] According to Lonergan, we can know whatever we can intelligently and reasonably affirm in answer to questions put to the data of human experience and human consciousness. And many of these answers, not only the particular one to the effect that God exists, concern things and states of affairs such as cannot be objects of sensation. To the first category also would belong most of the objections which would be made by materialists and radical empiricists. Such objectors would have to impugn Lonergan's theory of knowledge as a whole, rather than treating the question of the existence of God as a separate issue.

Recently a philosophical apologetic for theism has appeared which, while apparently quite independent of Lonergan's, has interesting points of contact with it. In his *Philosophical Theology* J.F. Ross propounds what he calls Principle E or the Principle of Explicability, to the effect that every state of affairs is in principle explicable; this is evidently equivalent to Lonergan's thesis that there are no merely 'brute' facts. Ross's argument from Principle E to the existence of God runs as follows. Whatever state of affairs is explicable, is explicable either of itself alone, or by reference to something else. The first class of states of affairs Ross calls 'auto-explicable', the second class 'hetero-explicable'. Now suppose that God does not exist, when what is meant by 'God' is the omnipotent Cause, the unproduced producer, of all else that exists. Since nothing else could bring it about that such a being did not exist, it seems that God's non-existence cannot be hetero-explicable. Thus, given both Principle E, and that God's non-existence is not hetero-explicable, it must follow that, if God does not exist, the fact must be auto-explicable. But it can only be auto-explicable if 'God exists' is self-contradictory. Therefore, unless 'God exists' is self-contradictory, which will only be the case if the concept 'God' is incoherent, God must exist.[40]

It is clear that there is some similarity between Ross's argument and Lonergan's; perhaps the most salient difference is that, while for Lonergan the fully intelligible is an agent acting for good reason, for Ross it is an analytic proposition.[41] But critics are perhaps likely to question the truth of a thesis shared by both authors, that there is something incoherent in the notion that the term of all explanation is an absolutely brute fact or a set of absolutely brute facts, which, while being inexplicable in itself, is that by reference to which every other fact is ultimately to be explained. William Kneale has written that Aristotle's conviction that there is at least one sempiternal thing — that is to say, thing that has neither beginning nor end — has been something of a guiding principle in the history of science. He points out that the ancient atomists thought that all coming to be and passing away of things in the world was the result of the continual arrangement and re-arrangement of sempiternal particles.[42] Nowadays most physicists have given up the idea of the conservation of a sempiternal 'matter'; but they still retain that of the conservation of energy. There seems to be a persistent need for the human mind to think of the changes which take place in the world as ultimately dependent on the conservation of something. Even the proposition attributed to Heraclitus, that everything is in a state of flux, is in a sense itself an acknowledgement of this principle. 'For this slogan is the limiting case of cosmology, in which we commit ourselves to nothing sempiternal but flux itself.' Now, because the existence of such an entity or such entities has no beginning or end, there is a sense in which we may say that it or they do not merely happen to exist, since it is or they are the precondition for anything else happening to exist or to be the case.[43] This is as much as to say that such a being or beings is or constitute 'necessary' as opposed to 'contingent' being.

Now Lonergan will have it that explanation of the world can terminate only in the postulation of the real existence of an understanding which understands itself, and thereby everything else that exists or could exist. But I suppose someone might concede that the existence of such a being was conceivable and even highly plausible, but at the same time deny that there was anything absolutely self-contradictory about the existence of unconditioned brute facts of the kind described by Kneale. These would themselves be the unproduced producer of the things and states of affairs which constitute the world; but it would surely be more than questionable whether the sum of such brute facts would be worth calling 'God'. *If* God exists, then the basic states of affairs constitutive of the world will be *due to* his *fiat*, and *for* his purpose of bringing into being the universe as we find it to be; thus they will have an explanation. But it might be argued that there is nothing inconceivable about such states of affairs being merely brute-given, being the case without explanation of why they are the case. Someone might even agree with Lonergan's general theory of knowledge, but claim that the basic facts underlying the universe might be apprehended as brute-given as a result of an inverse insight; though Lonergan might reasonably attribute such a move to an unregenerate hankering after the counter-positions. Certainly, so far as human experience goes, a reasonable explanation of what is neither necessitated nor arbitrary (in the sense of having no assignable point or purpose) is that it is due to the rational choice of an agent.[44] And the facts concerned are *ex-hypothesi* not necessitated by other brute facts; and they have an assignable point and purpose in the existence and operation of the material universe. Thus the postulation of an intelligent being who wills them would appear to be highly plausible.[45] But I am not sure how far it is susceptible of conclusive proof.

(2) The relation of evil to the purposes of God has next briefly to be considered. In an ingenious discussion of the

problem of evil from an atheistic point of view, J.L. Mackie has argued that the *prima facie* contradiction which constitutes the problem of evil for the theist is in fact a real contradiction.[46] If there were an omnipotent and infinitely good being, he would neither perpetrate evil nor permit it to exist. But evil does exist. Therefore there cannot be a being who is both omnipotent and wholly good. Mackie is not concerned in his article with the type of theism which gives up either the doctrine of God's omnipotence or that of his absolute goodness; he complains that most theists are not honest or consistent enough to modify their position in this way. He concedes, for the sake of argument, that a theist might maintain without obvious absurdity that God brings about or permits one type of evil as logically necessary for the bringing about of another type of good. (To maintain that God was *causally* necessitated in this kind of way would plainly be to deny his omnipotence.) Thus, it might be argued, God brings about or allows the existence of such evils as pain and frustration in order that altruism and heroism may exist as well — in fact, that he uses physical evil as a necessary means to moral good. But, unfortunately for the theist, it is as clear that moral evil — cowardice, cruelty, selfishness and so on — is brought into existence by these means as that moral good is so. Thus to the theist's appeal to a second order good to justify a first order evil, the atheist may retort by pointing to the existence of a second order evil. And the same fate is liable to attend the theist's appeal to a third order good to justify a second order evil. Indeed, whenever the theist points to good of order n+1 to justify evil of order n, the atheist may refute him by pointing to an evil of order n+1. Thus theodicy along these lines is involved in an infinite regress.

But in fact the Christian theist may avoid Mackie's infinite regress, believing as he does in the real existence, in the future, of a permanent and great moral good, as a means to which he deems the physical and moral evils of the present to be temporarily permitted by God. He does not believe (whether through faith or reason or both does not matter, since the question immediately at issue is whether theistic belief is self-consistent, not whether it can be proved) that a moral evil will come to pass of the same degree and order as this permanent and great moral good. Thus, if this is third order good, the theist may claim that God brings about or permits first and second order evil in order that there may be third order good. This third order good, of victorious and stable goodness matched with happiness, is logically impossible, it may be argued, without the real existence of physical evil and at least the real possibility of the existence of moral evil. In effect, this is Lonergan's solution to the problem, set out in terms suggested by Mackie's objections.

Mackie would object that there is no valid distinction to be drawn between what God brings about and what he only permits; since he believes the idea of free-will to be at bottom incoherent. (He does not give his reasons for this in the article cited; so I will mention reasons which have been adduced by other philosophers.[47]) All events which are explicable, including human actions, are thereby necessitated; if there are events which are inexplicable, and not necessitated, they are merely arbitrary; and neither the necessity nor the arbitrariness of an action is consistent with the free-will of its agent in performing it. But this argument depends on the assumption that explicability implies necessitation, which is one which we have already found reason to doubt.[48] Thus the incoherence of the notion of free-will, and so of the belief dependent on it that God merely permits rather than directly causes some human actions, has not been shown. It has further been suggested that it would have been possible for an omnipotent being to arrange things in such a way that, though human agents could perform evil actions, they always *in fact* refrained from doing so. But surely it may reasonably be objected to this that if God really gives a man freedom to do or not to do a particular action, even God cannot at the same time, as a matter of logic, ensure that in fact the man does not do it.[49] Thus the proffered suggestion as to what the omnipotent might have done would appear, on analysis, to be self-contradictory.

I conclude that Lonergan's treatment of the problem of evil, and his attempt to demonstrate the consistency of the existence of an omnipotent and good God with the occurrence of evil, can be defended against those objections with which I am acquainted.

(3) There remains to be considered Lonergan's claim that in Christ God has provided the real solution to the practical problem of evil. The essence of the claim is that in the narrative of the bible, and supremely in its climax in the words and deeds of Jesus, we find a piece of history prolonged examination and contemplation of which can (1) fulfil the human emotional and imaginative needs which will otherwise induce men either to construct myths, or to distort truth to correspond with myth; and (2) draw away the emotions of men and societies from the need to express themselves in hatred and violence, and enlist them in the service of the moral and political ideal of universal justice, brotherhood and peace. Now if this claim is true, one would expect *a priori* a state of affairs which has proved embarrassing to many Christians, but which can easily be shown to be the case; that is, that the Gospel narratives can be closely paralleled in myths and legends from all over the world. One might also expect that however much the allegedly historical element in other myth-like stories tends to dissolve under objective and unbiassed critical scrutiny, that in the Gospels will not do so.

If this account of the matter is correct, one can also see why it is that the 'Christ-myth' theory, to the effect that there was no historical Jesus at all, has seemed so plausible to many; and also why it is that attempts to provide a coherent account of a *real* Jesus, to the story of whose life mythological trimmings were added by his immediate followers, have apparently so far always ended in failure. In addition it provides strong reasons for believing that the whole programme of 'demythologising' the Gospel, as advocated by Rudolf Bultmann and his disciples, is based on a series of false assumptions — for instance, that one can get closer to the Jesus of history by systematically removing from our accounts of him those features of them which are analogous to features of acknowledged myths and legends, and that the Gospel will be a more effective force in human life once these excisions have been carried out.[50]

The features of the story of Jesus which make it analogous to myths of heroes from all over the world have been succinctly summarised by C.G. Jung: 'improbable origin, divine father, hazardous birth, rescue in the nick of time, precocious development, conquest of the mother and of death, miraculous deeds, a tragic, early end, symbolically significant manner of death, post-mortem effects'.[51] Jung himself would agree with the 'demythologising' school that these elements have largely been added to the real facts about Jesus, while acknowledging, in explicit opposition to them, that it is precisely these features which give the Gospel its extraordinary power in human life. However, some recent studies of the Gospels, and particularly of the presumed transmission in oral form of their material when the contemporary background is taken into account, make it very difficult to believe that the postulated amount of elaboration of the original facts could really have taken place.[52]

The manner in which the Christian mystery may be said to 'control the aggressivity' of men as individuals and societies is clearly, though indirectly, indicated by the great ethologist Konrad Lorenz.[53] This author remarks that the aggression arising from militant enthusiasm is the greatest potential source at once of evil and of good within human society. He mentions four factors which foster and are fostered by militant enthusiasm: a cause, a large group of persons associated together, a leader, and an enemy. The need to discharge the emotion of militant enthusiasm is apparently so potent that where no adequate cause, or leader, or enemy, exist, people will find any excuse to create or invent them. Now it is fairly obvious that all of these conditions are fulfilled by the Christian Church, which consists in a large body of individuals spread over space and time, whose cause is the advancement of the ideal social, political and moral good of the Kingdom of God, whose enemy is the forces of evil as such (and not the men who are its slaves), and whose leader is Jesus Christ. (That the Church has not lived up to her task is obvious and notorious; but there is no space to discuss the matter here.[54]) It would seem that the Christian revelation meets our biological condition; and that the needs which can be met by acceptance of the incarnation of God in Jesus Christ, if they are not met there, are liable to express themselves in warped mythologico-political formations in modern as in ancient times, with results which are as much more fatal as man's technical power over his environment is more developed.

The view that the solution to the problem of evil must be *one*[55] is liable to be strongly disputed, particularly by those who are sympathetic to the non-Christian religions. Does not the concrete problem of evil vary, it might be asked, even on Lonergan's own account, according to geographical, historical, and social milieu? But the nature of the exclusive claim made for Christianity must not be misinterpreted; Lonergan has himself asserted that there are good theological grounds for the thesis that means of salvation are to be found in the non-Christian religions.[56] And there is some reason for holding, as a result of study of the history of religion, that Christianity combines in a unique way *both* the affirmation of a transcendent God, *and* the concreteness of myth or mystery, *and* a basis in historical fact. The history of religion does seem to exhibit a tension between acknowledgement of a unique Creator God on the one hand, and the need for the immediate emotional impact of myth or mystery on the other. It appears, for example, from the work of Mircea Eliade, that this dialectic is to be found in primitive religions all over the world.[57] Islam may be said to place particular stress on one side of the dialectic (the affirmation of a transcendent Creator), some aspects of Hinduism on the other (the concreteness of myth or mystery). Moreover, 'there is in man a craving for an incarnate God strong enough to force itself into the most unpromising religious systems ... Whereas Muhammad and the Buddha achieved deification in flat contradiction to what they claimed and wished, and whereas the incarnations of Vishnu have no basis in fact, Jesus Christ both lived and died and claimed to be the Son of God.'[58]

Such an argument for Christian theism as the most intelligent and reasonable world-view available for man is likely to strike many as a singularly bizarre conclusion to a study of human understanding. Yet the argument must be considered on its own merits; the intellectually conscientious man does not dismiss a course of reasoning simply because its conclusions appear inconvenient or repugnant to common sense.

Afterword

It may be wondered what the bearings of Lonergan's thought are on the most recent work in philosophy, of the kind which has held the centre of the stage over the late 1970s and the 1980s. Very characteristic of this philosophy has been scepticism about the possibility of providing foundations of a philosophical nature for knowledge, morality or culture in general. Indeed, the conviction that the search for such foundations rests on a mistake could be said to constitute the central conviction of what has been called 'postanalytic philosophy.'[1] In this respect, the trend of the style of philosophy which prevails in the 'Anglo-Saxon' world seems to be converging with that of the one practised on the continent of Europe, where the 'deconstruction' sponsored by Jacques Derrida, and Michel Foucault's accounts of the pervasive effects of the will to power in the establishment and maintenance of knowledge-claims, appear to lead to the same kind of scepticism as to the possibility of foundations of knowledge.

This *rapprochement* between two schools of thought usually supposed to be poles apart from one another – philosophical analysis on the one hand and phenomenology and existentialism on the other – has been noted by Richard Rorty,[2] whose work may be taken as admirably representative of current trends. As Rorty sees it, the older view, that it is the main business of philosophy to find out the foundations of knowledge and value and to set them out, was expounded early in the present century by Bertrand Russell in Britain and Edmund Husserl on the continent of Europe. In this respect, they were carrying on a venerable tradition which had been inaugurated by Descartes in the seventeenth century. But Martin Heidegger, Ludwig Wittgenstein and John Dewey have each in his different way called into question such attempts to provide foundations. And recent developments in analytical philosophy, as Rorty sees it, have tended to support their stance, and to vindicate the view that such inordinate ambitions for philosophy were fundamentally mistaken.[3]

It is very natural, as Rorty says, to conceive the ultimate sources of human knowledge as consisting of two components, a set of data which one immediately apprehends, and a self-evident method by which one proceeds on the basis of these to acquire knowledge of the sorts of things that we may in the ordinary sense be said to know – like that Australia is surrounded by water, and that Arctic Terns travel annually several thousand miles from their breeding grounds. But both the belief that there are data, and the conviction that there are self-evident methods by which we may proceed on the basis of these to state matters of fact, are subject to very damaging criticism, as has appeared from the work of recent philosophers. W. V. O. Quine has attacked the view, once very generally maintained among philosophers, that propositions may be strictly divided into 'synthetic' and 'analytic', or those which just happen to be true or false, and those which must be true by definition of their terms; thus destroying the most obvious means of articulating the two kinds of certainty required by this account. (It has been usual among philosophers to hold that some 'synthetic' propositions are certain by virtue of being direct records of experience; and that 'analytic' propositions, being certain by virtue to their meaning, express the rational principles by which we are to proceed on the basis of these.)

Wilfred Sellars has conducted an assault on what he calls 'the myth of the given', or the notion that we can apprehend data somehow uncontaminated with prior theories and assumptions.[4] It is clear that our talk of ordinary material objects is encrusted with such theories and assumptions; but talk of 'sense-data' or whatever, on which such talk has been supposed by philosophers to be based, is really even more so. There are compelling reasons for believing that we could never talk of 'sense-data' at all unless we could first talk of material objects. For instance, unless we could talk in the first place about objects in the public and material world which are red, how could we ever come to talk, in a way intelligible to one another, about private sensations as of red? The whole idea of a 'private language' supposed to be capable of describing such experiences has been shown to be incoherent, especially by the late work of Wittgenstein. The upshot is that neither sensations as such, nor observations of material objects – the most obvious candidates for the 'data' aspect of the foundations of knowledge – can properly be treated as foundational.

The objections to the allegedly self-evident procedures by which we are to build up our knowledge on the basis of such supposed 'data' are alleged to be no less fatal. As has been evident at least since the work of David Hume, there is no strictly logical way of proceeding from any set of observed facts to any generalization.[6] Even if we observe a million carrion crows to be black, there is nothing in reason to prevent the million-and-first turning out not to be so. And the kind of 'induction' which proceeds from observed events to scientific theories supposed to account for them appears to be still more hazardous and less subject to rule. Nearly all of our knowledge-claims depend upon the assumption of a regular connection between cause and effect, on what has been called 'the uniformity of nature'; but the question of how we can justify this assumption has proved a thorn in the side of philosophy.

A more sophisticated account, associated with the name of Sir Karl Popper, will have it that we freely create theories, and that logic becomes applicable once we make deductions from our theories; we may then reject those theories whose consequences are falsified by the data, and retain provisionally those which are corroborated in the sense that, while they might well have been thus falsified, they are not so.[7] (When Augustin Fresnel proposed his version of the wave theory of light, a very curious consequence, not at all to be expected on the basis either of common sense or of known rival theories, was deduced from it. That this consequence turned out to be true was regarded, surely rightly, as strongly in favour of the theory.[8]) But no theory is strictly speaking falsified by data; one always has to match deductions from a theory with data supposed to falsify or to corroborate it. (It is one thing to admit that there is a pattern of streaks on a photographic plate; another to say that one of them is due to the passage of some kind of fundamental particle.) And nearly all scientific theories are subject to anomalies or *prima facie* falsifications. If you wish to apply the criterion of falsification strictly, and abandon your theories in the face of any anomaly, science, which surely ought to be accepted as the paradigm case of genuine or well-founded knowledge, lies in ruins. But if you allow exceptions, where do you stop?[9]

It has been concluded on the basis of such considerations that the whole effort to determine the foundations of knowledge, and to justify them as such, is mistaken.[10] Should we infer from this the conclusion that 'anything goes', that no judgment is ever better founded than its contradictory? Some thinkers do indeed preach epistemological anarchism[11]; while others uphold the view that there are as many 'worlds' as there are views of the world, or that each human group or society constructs its own 'world'.[12] But as Rorty sees it, such sensational conclusions are quite unnecessary. We should disabuse ourselves of the 'correspondence theory' of truth – the view that statements are true by virtue of a kind of mirroring of reality such as no-one has ever been able clearly or convincingly to describe. If we want to know what the truth is on any matter, we simply go to the experts. The physicist knows what is true within the range of her specialty, the chemist and the zoologist what is true about things and events within *their* respective disciplines; no-one seriously expects such persons to be dictated to by philosophers. Really, when one reflects about the matter, there is no need for knowledge to have any 'foundations' at all of a philosophical kind; they are quite otiose.[13]

If we wish to find out about the nature of 'knowledge', we should go to the psychologists, who are the authorities on how people come to hold established opinions. For the fact is, that however much of a song and dance philosophers may have made in the past about the nature of 'truth', 'goodness' and the rest, 'true' beliefs are nothing other than beliefs held by the majority of the members of one's society, or at least the most prestigious group within it; while 'good' actions and persons are no more and no less than the actions and persons of which they approve. Of course this does not imply that pursuit of truth and goodness is any less noble or worthwhile an ideal than it is on a more metaphysical or foundationalist view.[14]

It might be wondered what task remains for philosophers, on this account of things. If philosophers are not concerned with the 'foundations' of knowledge, value or culture, what *are* they concerned with? Certainly, the surfacing of this question has given rise to a crisis of identity among philosophers, and very understandably so. However, even if the imperialistic pretentions of some earlier philosophers must now be abandoned, there remains the rather humbler but thoroughly worthy business of promoting conversation, and so mutual understanding, among persons of divergent interests and opinions. Such an activity will be a matter rather of persuasion and edification than of the proof and knock-down argument with which so many philosophers have been preoccupied, and will demand rhetorical rather than strictly logical skills.[15]

Thus far a sketch of the kind of 'post-analytic philosophy' which is represented so forcefully in Rorty's work. I think that it is indeed a tribute to Rorty's rhetorical skill, that he manages to conceal so effectively the radical cognitive and moral scepticism which is in fact the conclusion to be drawn from his premises. It seems at first sight an excessively facile objection to anti-foundationalism, that if it is true, no statement has any better foundation than its contradictory; and that this applies to the statements constitutive of anti-foundationalism itself. And yet it is hard to see how it can be effectively argued against.[16] One may indeed, in the manner recommended by Rorty, exert one's rhetorical skill to dissuade people from attending to such difficulties; but that is another matter. Nor is the paradox just mentioned the only one of which Rorty's position appears to fall foul. There is a principle which, I think, very few persons would deny, which has been emphasized by Alfred Tarski and Karl Popper.[17] This is, that a proposition 'p' is true if and only if the corresponding state of affairs p is the case. For instance, in accordance with the principle, 'Mercury is the only metal which is liquid at normal temperatures on the surface of the earth' is true if and only if mercury is the only metal which is liquid at normal temperatures on the surface of the earth; 'Jephtha Jones of Aberystwyth has a birthday in December' is true if and only if Jephtha Jones of Aberystwyth has a birthday in December. Now on Rorty's view, what makes any proposition true is the agreement of one's society, or of the most prestigious group within it. But it follows from this, if one adds Tarski's principle, that the agreement of one's society, or the most prestigious group within it, makes any state of affairs the case as well. In other words, it is by social *fiat* on our part that Alexander the Great conquered Persia, that life arose on earth over one hundred million years ago, and that the galaxy closest to the Milky Way contains over a million stars. Other societies than ours, whose view of the world differs from ours, make other such states of affairs to be the case. (Though the very existence of such other societies, and their holding of views different from our own, seems to depend on our social *fiat* too – the mind reels at the proliferation of nonsense and incoherence which appears inevitably to emerge from such a set of premisses.) I submit that such extreme subjective idealism, for all Rorty's protests, is a genuine consequence of his position; and also that it is a little hard to swallow.[18]

It will be remembered that it is a cardinal principle of Lonergan's thought that erroneous views on the nature of knowledge, when pressed to their conclusion, make knowledge impossible; that, as he expresses it, 'counter-positions invite reversal'.[19] So far as Rorty's position is representative of 'post-analytic' philosophy, the movement of ideas from analytic to post-analytic philosophy is as clear an example as one could wish of this process; the 'latent nonsense' of the early analytic account of the foundations of knowledge has been shown up as 'manifest nonsense', to use or abuse a phrase of Wittgenstein's.[20]

It looks as though the earlier analytic position on the foundations of knowledge has been rendered untenable by post-analytic criticism; but that the post-analytic position itself leads to some pretty remarkable paradoxes. Is there any solution to the difficulty? One may begin discussion of the question by pointing to another curiosity in Rorty's work. His book *Philosophy and the Mirror of Nature* is a sustained and very sophisticated argument to establish the truth of one philosophical position and the falsity of another. And yet it is a consequence of his position that the truth about things in general is *not* to be established by argument, but is a matter of social consensus. If what is so in general is *not* to be established by argument, then perhaps we may find in this fact a basis or foundation for knowledge of the kind that Rorty denies.

Let us suppose for a moment, in accordance with the assumptions both of common sense and of science as usually understood, that there is a real world which exists and is largely as it is prior to and independently of the existence of human societies and their systems of belief or knowledge. If this is the case, given the account of truth which I believe almost everyone would accept, and which is highlighted in Tarski's account, true judgments are judgments which assert how things actually are in this independently-existing world, false judgments those which fail to do so. Now either knowledge of how things are in this independently existing world is forever unavailable to us, or we are in principle at least capable of coming to know about them, or to make justified true judgments about them. The former view not only seems strange, but is incoherent on the last analysis. If we can know nothing about the independently-existing world, how can we know (*pace* Kant's teaching about 'things in themselves') that it is independent and existing?

Granted that there *is* such a world, then, it appears that we can get to know something about it. As to *how* we may do so, the point that we established a moment ago, that one can get to know what is so by argument, seems to provide the essential clue. After all, what could 'the real world' amount to in the last analysis, other than the totality of what is so? And short of some distinction between the process of argument taken only so far, and the same process pursued indefinitely, distinctions like those between 'reality' and 'appearance' or 'illusion', and between 'the world as it really is' and 'the world merely *for* or *of* our own particular group', could get no purchase on our thought or language.

'But', someone may object, 'to appeal to argument neglects rather than meets the point made by Rorty, that fundamental differences between views are not subject to resolution by rigorous proof, but only by persuasion of a rhetorical kind. Proof in the strict sense after all requires premises; and it is the very essence of radically opposed views that their fundamental premises are different.' However, rigorous proof on the geometrical pattern on the one hand, and the imposition of one's views on other people by sheer rhetoric on the other, do not exhaust the options. There is the possibility also that one might proceed in disputed questions on any subject on the basis of the kind of attention to experience, envisagement of possibilities grasped by understanding which might account for that experience, and reasonable judgment that that possibility is so which does apparently account best for the experience, which is the central characteristic of the epistemology of Lonergan.

That knowledge is based upon or founded in experience, whatever else besides experience it may consist in, is held by Lonergan in common with the empiricists. A difficulty about this has been raised by W. V. O. Quine, who points out that any judgement can be retained, in the face of the experience which appears to be incompatible with it, if one makes alterations elsewhere within the system of judgments within which the particular judgment in question finds its place.[21] Quine concludes that our judgments are not confirmed or disconfirmed by experience as it were piecemeal, but that our system of judgments as a whole is supported by our experience as a whole. But Rorty infers, I believe rightly, that at this rate the assumption that our judgments are founded on experience at all is emptied of content.[22] It appears to me that the difficulty about relating individual judgments to experience pointed out by Quine should be resolved in another manner than the one he himself has proposed. I believe that our justified judgments are typically related each to a range of experience, in such a way that while the non-occurrence of *no particular item* of that range would absolutely falsify the judgment, that of *the range of experience as a whole*, or any considerable proportion of it, would certainly do so. If the judgment is true, *you would expect* certain particular experiences to be enjoyed in certain circumstances, and *you would expect* certain others not to be so. However, *any particular experience*, whether corroborating or falsifying, can *at a pinch* be discounted, if there is compensation elsewhere.[23]

An analogy may serve to bring out the point which I am trying to make. There are books for small children in which dots are marked on some pages, and the owner of the book is invited to make up a picture by joining the dots. Let us think of an example where there are very many dots, and the picture to emerge is that of an elephant or a rabbit. In such a case, it is likely that the omission or displacement of *no single dot* will make it impossible for the owner of the book to apprehend the pattern. And yet it would obviously be absurd to say that apprehension of the pattern did not depend on the collocation of dots as a whole. Again, the alteration or omission of no single letter (type or token) constitutive of the sentence preceding the present one would have made the sentence unintelligible to the reader; perhaps even several such (token) anomalies would not unduly have taxed her ingenuity.[24] And yet it is obvious that her apprehension of the sentence and its meaning does depend on the collocation of letters as a whole.[25] The reader will easily see that the relation of the apprehended form or meaning to what is present to sensation in the examples just adduced, is exactly the same as the relation of the object of insight to the data of experience or imagination on Lonergan's account.

In a review of the first edition of this book, Professor William Frerking suggested the following questions as going 'to the heart of Lonergan's enterprise. Is there any mental *act* of understanding? And is the kind of appeal to introspection which Lonergan appears to make at crucial points of his argument valid?[26] Now it is true that Lonergan does rely for central theses of his philosophy on what may be called 'introspection.' But he also denies, as vehemently as any analytical philosopher, that it is appropriate in approaching basic questions in philosophy or elsewhere to take what he calls an 'inner look'. The point does seem correctly to have been made, in particular by Gilbert Ryle,[27] that in establishing the meaning of certain psychological terms, one has to attend rather to dispositions to behaviour than to supposed inner states. If I wish to ascertain whether someone knows how to load a Vickers machine gun, the way to set about it is to see how she behaves in circumstances where it is appropriate for her to load such a gun. Again, for it to be true that I believe some proposition at a particular time, nothing whatever has to be going on at that time in the inner theatre of my consciousness; it was true of me three minutes before I began to write the first draft of the last sentence that I believed that Genghis Khan was a conqueror and ruler of a great empire, though I was not then giving my mind to the matter at all. But it would be generally agreed, I think, that a Rylean analysis is more convincing as applied to some psychological states than to others; it is much more plausible, for example, to reduce a desire to a disposition to behaviour, than it is so to reduce a feeling of intense pain.

What is really pivotal to Lonergan's philosophy as a whole is not so much any kind of introspection as the difference between 'positions' and 'counterpositions'; that is, between judgments relating to philosophy, psychology and other topics, from which it may be inferred that persons can have experience, question intelligently and judge reasonably; and those from which it is to be inferred that they cannot. No 'introspection' is needed to articulate, justify or apply this distinction. Yet it is true that Lonergan does maintain that it is useful for philosophers and other persons to become aware of what it is for them to ask questions, come to understand, make judgments, reach decisions, and so on. But are these not conscious processes, to which one can give one's attention while one performs them or just after one has done so? And would it not be generally agreed, at least by those who are not concerned to defend some special philosophical doctrine, that it is at least sometimes useful for a person, in the interests of cognitive and moral integrity, to catch herself out on occasions when she has brushed aside relevant evidence, or failed to ask a significant question, or shirked an important decision?

One opponent of Lonergan has gone so far as to claim never to have experienced an act of understanding such as is described by Lonergan.[28] But really it does seem an implausible, not to say damaging, admission, that one has never had the experience of coming to understand, or even to misunderstand, the solution to a problem about which one has been previously puzzled. That is nothing more or less than what

Lonergan means by an act of understanding. (Perhaps he would have been better understood on this matter, if he had referred to the act of *coming* to understand.) And as Lonergan remarks, few writers of learned articles include in them a statement to the effect that they have never been conscious of weighing the evidence for a judgment, or of propounding a judgment for good reason; nor do books often begin with a declaration that their authors have never been aware of making a responsible decision, least of all in offering the present work to the public.[29] If they did, it would be obvious that it was ridiculous, assuming that one believed what they said on this particular matter, to take seriously anything else that they had to say. But the important point to be grasped is that many philosophers and psychologists (such as eliminative materialists and behaviourists), while they may seldom directly make such admissions, hold general theories about the nature of things or about human nature of which such admissions are a logically necessary consequence.

Followers of Wittgenstein quite rightly insist that, if we are to use our essentially 'public' speech to refer to 'private' states, there must be publicly observable criteria for the occurrence of these states.[30] But, of course, there are all sorts of behavioural signs by which persons other than ourselves betray to us by their speech and actions that they have just come to understand something, or that they have made a judgment or reached a decision. Granted that we need to have public criteria for the occurrence of such mental acts if we are to think and to talk about them, why should we not deepen our apprehension of them by the kind of attention to our mental acts which I have briefly described, and which Lonergan has treated at length?

Lonergan would profoundly agree with Wittgenstein and Ryle that there is something very wrong with the prevailing picture of mind as something *inside* our skins, from which we somehow, by a mysterious process which no-one has ever been able convincingly to articulate or to justify, break through the knowledge of what is *outside*. The self for Lonergan is not that at which each of us can take an intimate inner look, any more than the external world is, by way of contrast to this, what we have to take an outer look at through the medium of sense-contents or whatever. Indeed, he regards this conception of the matter as the most fundamental and pervasive of all philosophical errors.[31] As he sees it, in experience we do indeed have data on the self, but so we do on the 'external' world; we know both self and world by means of judgments founded on understanding of experience, neither more immediately than the other.

In fact, on Lonergan's view, the problem of conceiving how our minds can know the 'external' world 'is not a problem of moving from within outwards, of moving from a subject to an object outside the subject. It is a problem of moving from above downwards, of moving from an infinite potentiality commensurate with the universe towards a rational apprehension that seizes the difference of subject and object in essentially the same way that it seizes any other real distinction.' And within the immensity of the universe thus to be known 'we ourselves and all our acts of conceiving and judging are no more than particular and not too important items'.[32]

I have already argued at some length that, on the basis of Lonergan's general account of knowledge, one may find out what is actually good as well as what is true; and that there is no better reason to espouse a thoroughgoing subjectivism or relativism in ethics than there is in science.[33] It does not seem useful to add anything on the matter at this point.

Nietzsche notoriously declared that God is dead, and that as a consequence human beings must establish norms of cognition and evaluation for themselves.[34] His influence could be regarded as tending in two possible directions, towards nihilism on the one hand, and towards thorough human authenticity with respect to cognition and evaluation on the other. The nihilistic conclusion which might be derived from Nietzsche is that there are no norms for acquiring knowledge of what is true or of what is good either given or to be found. At this rate, no claim as to what is true or what is good is in the last analysis any better founded than its contradictory. Such a consistent and thoroughgoing scepticism is not socially or psychologically endurable, so the closely related positions of conventionalism and relativism are apt to be embraced instead. What any community assumes to be true and good, are what truth and goodness are; what any community says or assumes to be the norms by which what is true and what is good are to be established, are the norms by which they are to be established. To 'criticize' the assumptions and standards of one such community is nothing other than to apply to them the assumptions and standards of another; to try to discover the *real* standards is to pursue an illusion.[35]

The alternative inference is that there is a cognitive, and perhaps also a moral, authenticity, the norms of which it is the business of all human beings, and perhaps especially philosophers, to discover and apply. (What bearing this has on the question of God need not be considered in the immediate context.) At this rate, to expose false and inadequate norms is valuable above all as a means to showing up the real norms for what they are. As is well-known, Nietzsche emphasized the place in the acquisition and promulgation of knowledge of the will to power.[36] In accordance with an extreme version of this view, all knowledge-claims whatever are made more or less directly in the interests of the self-aggrandisement of those who make them. But one may also interpret the view – and many would say that this is more in accordance with the direction of Nietzsche's writings as a whole – as to the effect that the proper expression of the 'will to power' is the subordination of all one's energies to the true norms of cognitive and moral authenticity. The former strand of Nietzsche's influence seems well-expressed in the 'anti-foundationalism' and 'deconstructionism' which seem dominant at present in the 'Anglo-Saxon' and 'Continental' spheres of influence in philosophy. The latter strand may be said to have come to its full maturity of expression in the philosophy of Lonergan.

Which of these two strands is to be preferred, and why? The main point to be made here is that the former strand is self-destructive, in the manner that Lonergan has pointed out to be typical of 'counter-positions.' Any attempt to formulate it, even in the most qualified or elliptical possible way, invites the challenge: Is that a reasonable and responsible thing to say? Is the claim that it expresses better grounded than its contradictory? Does it or does it not consist of judgments propounded as a result of consideration of a sufficient range of hypotheses supposed to explain the whole extent of relevent evidence? (The issue is often obscured by the humorous style affected by such authors as Paul Feyerabend and Jacques Derrida; it seems bad taste to take what they say as though they really meant it, as though they were taking full responsibility for the statements that they make.) If it is not a reasonable and responsible thing to say, there is no reason whatever why anyone should accept it. If it is, then the utterer commits herself to the view that one tends to get at the truth by applying one's faculties of experience, understanding and judgement in the manner exhaustively described by Lonergan. To put the matter in Lonergan's terms, everyone who makes a claim implicitly commits herself to the 'positions' in doing so even if she explicitly expounds 'counter-positions', all of which imply, with varying degrees of directness or obviousness, that she cannot ever have good reason for what she says, or that even if she does, this has no bearing whatever on its truth or falsity.

The strong influence of Nietzsche is evident, and indeed acknowledged, in the writings of Michel Foucault and Jacques Derrida. On the most obvious reading of these authors, they both certainly represent the sceptical side of Nietzsche's influence. Foucault is noted for his detailed accounts of the manner in which the will to power has dominated the supposed acquisition and promulgation of knowledge in various fields; what has been put about as 'knowledge' about medicine, psychiatry or sexuality has in fact been, as he brings out, largely if not exclusively a means by which some persons can exercise control over others.[37] But the question should at some time strike the attentive reader of Foucault, of how far his basic principle, that what is called 'knowledge' is a matter of the exercise of power, is supposed to apply; and to what extent being affected by this motive invalidates knowledge-claims. If all knowledge-claims are entirely dominated by the will to exercise power, and this vitiates their status as knowledge of or justified true belief about that with which they deal, then Foucault's own knowledge-claims are vitiated. Certainly a corrective might be supplied, which would be such as to bring out the limited application either of the principle that knowledge-claims are in the last analysis simply a matter of the exercise of power, or of the assumption that they are vitiated for this reason; in that case, Foucault's work would indeed be an invaluable instrument for the critique of ideas and institutions. (This corrective would be a matter, to use Lonergan's terms, of 'developing the positions' as opposed to merely 'reversing the counter-positions' in Foucault's work.[38]) But the basis for such a corrective, so far as I can judge, is not to be found in the writings of Foucault himself.[39]

Similar considerations apply to the 'deconstruction' sponsored by Jacques Derrida. It seems to be of the essence of this enterprise to attend to and to subvert such 'hierarchical oppositions' as those between true and false, good and bad, right and wrong, sound and unsound, and so on.[40] But to say that all such hierarchical oppositions are mistaken is presumably to make a claim supposed to be true rather than false, and supportable by arguments which are sound rather than unsound. And to say that one ought to attempt to subvert them, and that one had better not accept them or take them for granted, is to recommend one course of action as good, as contrasted with another which is bad in comparison. Derrida admits that one cannot, at this stage of culture at least, entirely get away from such 'hierarchical oppositions';[41] but it would have been helpful if he had given some hints as to the limit, if any, in the scope of his criticism of them. To what extent and in what circumstances does 'deconstruction' destroy the norms of cognition and evaluation, and to what extent and in what circumstances does it found them on a firmer basis? If its scope and its destructiveness are unlimited, then all judgments of fact and value, including those asserted or assumed by Derrida himself, are equally baseless. The actual effect of this on ideas and institutions is, of course, profoundly conservative;[42] if any alternative to the *status quo* is no less subject to adverse criticism, the *status quo* might just as well be left intact, as it is obviously less trouble to put up with any situation than to alter it. A criticism so radical that it destroys equally all alternatives to what is criticised, and even all bases on which criticism can be mounted, is effectively no criticism at all.

In conclusion, there seem to be two possible ways out of the widely-acknowledged *impasse* in contemporary philosophy; the complete demise of the subject as traditionally understood, or moving to a position approximate to that of

Lonergan.[43] Not only is the first way in principle self-destructive, for reasons already given; but the consequences of following it would be culturally disastrous. What could be more important for culture than the articulation and implementation of general principles of truth and goodness in relation to which language, thought, and the human institutions based on them can be radically and comprehensively criticized? But it is just the existence of such principles that the most salient representatives of contemporary philosophy, whether 'Anglo-Saxon' or 'Continental', seem driven to deny. Short of the existence and availability of such principles, the many rival claims which besiege and torment us on the rather important questions of how the world is, and how we ought to live our lives, can be supported in their strife against one another by nothing but arbitrary methods of persuasion, or shouting one another down, or violence and bloodshed. Lonergan's fundamental putative achievement as a philosopher is that he has articulated and justified the principles in question; surely his claim, given that it is not clearly absurd, is worthy of serious investigation by the intellectual community. 'I set before you life and death; ... therefore choose life.'[44]

I no longer have the reservations expressed above[45] about Lonergan's argument for the existence of God. By its nature, the 'inverse insight' that intelligibility is not to be gained in one manner and at one level involves the corollary that it is to be gained in another manner and at another level. Thus there could not be a well-founded 'inverse insight' to the effect that the world is not after all due to the *fiat* of an unrestricted act of understanding.

Conclusion

It will be evident, from what I have written here, that, unless I am very much mistaken, Lonergan's philosophy is one of the outstanding achievements of our time, and applicable to a vast range of pressing intellectual, moral, social, political, educational and religious problems. Its neglect up to the present seems to me both astonishing and deplorable. Practitioners of the relevant fields of inquiry on the whole do not attempt either to use or to refute Lonergan's arguments, but take the simpler course of failing to advert to their existence. If this short introduction does anything at all to reverse this situation, it will have achieved its purpose.

NOTE. In a recent paper, *Insight Revisited*[1] , Lonergan has commented on some aspects of the book in the light of his more recent thinking. He remarks that his use of the terms 'mystery' and 'myth' to refer to 'symbolic expressions of positions and counterpositions' respectively, is somewhat out of line with current usage. He adds that in *Method in Theology* there is provided what amounts to an orderly set of instructions for achieving a universal viewpoint, in place of a systematic account of the problems of interpretation as propounded in *Insight*. In the same work, the good is envisaged not so much as the intelligent and reasonable, as what is intended in questions for deliberation; for example, Is this worthwhile? Is it really or only apparently so? (Evidently these differences are a matter rather of emphasis than of substance.)

In writings subsequent to *Insight*, Lonergan has been at pains to emphasise that arguments for the existence of God should on the whole take place within the context of systematic theology, or the understanding of a set of religious beliefs; otherwise one is apt to generate the well-known misapprehension that it is one God who is the focus of religious devotion, another who is the subject of philosophical arguments. The main function of such arguments is not in any case to demonstrate the existence of God to those who have not previously believed in it, though they may occasionally do so; it is rather to show the religiously converted that their beliefs are harmonious with an unrestricted exercise of intelligence and reasonableness.[2]

Notes

Introduction

1. *Insight*, xxviii. All other references in this book will be to *Insight* except those otherwise assigned. This introduction draws heavily on two articles, 'The Lonergan Phenomenon' (*The Month*, July 1970), and 'Bernard Lonergan as Theologian' (*Theology*, September 1970).

2. i.e. the science of interpretation.

3. A.S. Eddington, *The Nature of the Physical World*, xi—xiii.

4. David Hume, *A Treatise of Human Nature*, I, iv, 2.

5. Cf. Bertrand Russell, 'The Philosophy of Logical Atomism', in *Logic and Knowledge*, ed. R.C. Marsh, p. 279.

6. Cf. A.J. Ayer, *Language, Truth and Logic*, 19—20.

7. *A Treatise of Human Nature*, I, iv, 6.

8. The assumption that knowledge consists basically of taking a look is, as Lonergan sees it, at the basis of most erroneous theories of knowledge.

9. The best brief and simple accounts by Lonergan of his own cognitional theory are '*Cognitional Structures*' (*Spirit as Inquiry*, ed. F.E. Crowe, 230—42), and '*Metaphysics as Horizon*' (*Gregorianum* (1963), 307—18). These are reprinted in *Collection*, 202—20, 221—39. Cf. also Chapter 1 of *Method in Theology*. A preliminary note seems in place about this and subsequent references to the latter work. *Insight* is addressed to all intelligent and reasonable men; of these theologians, at best, constitute a sub-class. I have cited *Method in Theology*, therefore, only where it clarifies and amplifies what is said in *Insight*.

Chapter 1

1. In expounding Lonergan's philosophy in what follows, I shall distinguish sharply between summaries of his position and my own exegetical comments by putting the latter in brackets. It seems to me that the resulting loss of elegance in the text will be well offset by the gain in lucidity and objectivity.

2. *Insight*, 3—4.

3. 4—5.

4. 6. Cf. *Verbum*, 14, 25—6, 40, 77.

5. The reader may remember that it was this very point, that geometrical figures as such are not objects of sensation or imagination, which led Plato, e.g. in the *Meno* and the *Phaedo*, to argue that the human soul must once have had access to a world of ideas that

transcended the world of the senses. Lonergan, though he would not wish to follow Plato in arguing for the soul's pre-existence, is equally concerned to emphasise the independent power of the intelligence to reach mathematical and scientific abstractions on the basis of particular concrete observations and acts of imagination. One might say that classical empiricism, as exemplified, say, in Locke, does not properly advert to the difference between imagination and conception; and that the inevitable consequence of this is Humean scepticism, which draws the full consequences from the thesis that we cannot apprehend anything — for instance the causal nexus or the substantial self — which we cannot imagine. Kant, of course, was very vividly aware of the distinction, which he applied in his own way; he thought that only in sensation, and indirectly even there, did our minds apprehend whatever may exist independently of them; and that the conceptual scheme which our minds imposed upon sensation did not correspond to any reality existing outside our minds. For Lonergan, as for Aristotle and Aquinas, sensation, imagination and conception are all parts of the process by which our minds come to know the real world.

6. 7—9. Cf. *Verbum*, 28—9.

7. 11—12. It has been pointed out that Lonergan's theory of insight may be taken as a very general application of the postulational structure developed by David Hilbert in exploring the foundations of Euclidean geometry. Cf. R. Eric O'Connor in *Spirit as Inquiry*, 13—14.

8. It is instructive to compare these remarks with Wittgenstein's comments on following a rule (*Philosophical Investigations*, 1, § § 143—238).

9. 13—15.

10. Perhaps an advocate of 'the new mathematics' would wish to express this last point differently; but I see no reason why he should disagree with the fundamental matter at issue, which is the relation of lower to higher viewpoints in mathematics. 15—17; Cf. *Verbum* 51—2.

11. 17—19.

12. In *The Blue Book*, Wittgenstein compares the advance of human knowledge to the activity of picking up books scattered about on the floor of a library, and arranging them in their proper places on shelves (*The Blue and Brown Books*, 44—5). He remarks that some of the most important advances are parallel to taking down two books which had long been standing together on one of the shelves, and putting them arbitrarily onto different shelves. Surely the parallel in the advance of human knowledge is exactly what Lonergan calls an inverse insight.

13. 19—24. Cf. *Verbum*, 54.

14. 26—9.

15. 30—2. Since the writing of *Insight*, Lonergan has distinguished between the three realms of common sense, theory, and interiority; one enters the second by reflection on the first, and the third by reflection on the first and second. The realm of interiority is nothing else than what is constituted by the analysis of consciousness and its operations (*Method in Theology*, 81—5). Thus *Insight* as a whole could be called

an investigation of the realm of interiority, though the phrase does not occur in it.

Chapter 2

1. 33—4.
2. 36—8.
3. Cf. *Posterior Analytics* II,2
4. Cf. 'The Isomorphism of Thomist and Scientific Thought'. (*Collection*, 142—51).
5. 37.
6. 173, 175, 177—9.
7. 41.
8. The classical exposition of this paradox is due to Plato (*Meno* 79c et seq). The whole argument of Leslie Dewart's book *The Foundations of Belief* seems to me to be vitiated by lack of attention to its ramifications.
9. 44—5, 47.
10. 45—6, 48—52.
11. 53—7.
12. 58—9, 62—7.
13. 70—2, 578, Neglect of this last point, it might be suggested, is responsible for the paradoxes to which the original formulation of the Verification Principle by the Logical Positivists gave rise.
14. 74—6.
15. 76—8.
16. It is important to bear in mind that this distinction is *not* exactly equivalent to that made by Galileo and Locke between secondary and primary qualities, or by Kant between the qualities of phenomenal things and whatever qualities may be supposed to belong to things in themselves.
17. 78—80, 82—3.
18. Chapter V of *Insight* is a commentary on and justification of this point; it has not seemed suitable to treat it at length in this introduction to Lonergan's philosophy.
19. 84—5.
20. 89, 91, 94, 96—100.
21. 104—5, 116—7.
22. 117—9.
23. p. 21—5 above.
24. 119—21.
25. 122—3.
26. 124—8.
27. This sense of 'necessary' and 'contingent' is not of course, the same as that usual in modern philosophy.
28. 129—30.
29. 130—1.
30. 132—3.
31. 135—8.

32. Cf. G. Frege, *The Foundations of Arithmetic*, p. 42: 'The more the internal contrasts within a thing fade into insignificance by comparison with the contrast between it and its surroundings, and the more the internal connection among its elements overshadow its connections with its surroundings, the more natural it seems for us to regard it as a distinct object.'

33. 205, 441, 254—7, 259.

34. 248, 250—1, 253.

35. 459—61.

36. 462—3, 479.

37. 263, 266, 468, 466.

38. 533.

39. For detailed presentation of this theory, cf. Konrad Lorenz, *On Aggression*.

40. 479—82 Lonergan's conception of the nature of biological science is at once adumbrated and illustrated, it seems to me, in W.H. Thorpe's *Learning and Instinct in Animals*.

41. 485.

Chapter 3.

1. 324.

2. Cf. 'Metaphysics as Horizon' (*Collection*, 202—20).

3. Naturally, this will not apply so far as one regards psychology as reducible to the study of observable behaviour or neurology. But Lonergan would regard this as due ultimately to that mistaken theory of knowledge and reality which regards knowing as fundamentally taking a look.

4. 72—3, 81.

5. P. 10 above.

6. 378—81

7. 319—21.

8. 322—6.

9. Cf. Descartes' famous conclusion that at least I cannot really doubt that I am a doubter.

10. 331—2. For an interesting criticism of such an attitude, cf. J.W.N. Watkins, 'Comprehensively Critical Rationalism' (*Philosophy*, January 1969).

11. 334—6.

12. For a brief and clear survey of the problem, cf. S. Körner, *Kant*, 91—5.

13. On the relation of Lonergan's cognitional theory and metaphysics to the Critical Philosophy of Kant, cf. 'Metaphysics as Horizon' (*Collection*, 202—20), and the many references to Kant in *Verbum*.

14. 341.

15. Cf. F.H. Bradley's objections, in *Appearance and Reality*, Book I, to our ordinary claims to knowledge.

16. It is instructive to compare the doctrine at one time held by

Bertrand Russell, that 'this' and 'that' are 'logically proper names', i.e. that they refer directly to elements of experience (cf. *Logic and Knowledge*, ed. R.C. Marsh, 201).

17. 342—7.

18. Lonergan's use of the term 'being' may remind analytical philosophers rather painfully of neo-Scholasticism. I think it is very important not to be put off by this from taking seriously what he has to say; since as the succeeding paragraphs show, he is quite aware of what is wrong with that alleged 'intuition of being' affirmed by some neo-Scholastics.

19. Cf. the problem of what is sometimes called 'the Meinongian jungle'. Since I can easily think of centaurs or golden mountains, must not they have 'being' in some sense?

20. 348, 350, 353—6.

21. This sentence expresses succinctly the respect in which Lonergan's philosophy differs most centrally from that of Kant. For Kant, if one attends properly to the nature of human cognitional process one will come to understand that our theoretical knowledge can only be of a phenomenal world, not of things in themselves. For Lonergan, there are no other 'things in themselves' than what the mind comes to affirm as existing by means of intelligent grasp and reasonable affirmation on the basis of experience.

22. 360—2.

23. W.V.O. Quine, 'On What There Is' (*Review of Metaphysics*, September, 1948); also the Symposium between Quine, P.T. Geach, and A.J. Ayer, 'On What There Is' (*Proceedings of the Aristotelian Society*, Supplementary Volume XXV, 1951).

24. 364—6.

25. One is reminded of G.E. Moore's very similar reflections on the concept 'good' (*Principia Ethica*, 6—16, etc.)

26. Cf. A. Kenny's amusing application of the Scotist concept of being; that being is a quality shared by God, the battle of Thermopylae, and a potted shrimp. ('Aquinas and Wittgenstein', *The Downside Review*, Autumn, 1959).

27. 367—9.

28. i.e., 'What is it?', and 'Is it so?' or 'Does it exist?'.

29. Lonergan's questioning subject is equivalent to the 'agent intellect' of Aristotle and Aquinas; cf. *Verbum*, 47, 171—3, etc. For the whole historical discussion of the last three paragraphs, cf. *Verbum*, especially Chapters I, II and IV.

30. 369—70.

31. The change by a human subject from a false to a true view of the nature of knowledge, reality and objectivity has been termed 'intellectual conversion' by Lonergan, and compared with moral and religious conversion, which indeed tend to promote and be promoted by it. Cf. *Method in Theology*, 238—40.

32. The various aspects of human consciousness will be considered at greater length in Chapter 5.

33. 385—7

34. Cf. pp. 5—6.

35. 387, 514.

36. Hume's scepticism is, I take it, a classical instance of the reversal of a counter-position. Suppose that knowledge is to be had by taking a look at what is about us. We cannot apprehend causes by taking a look, since all we perceive is one event following another. Therefore we can have no knowledge of causes. Cf. also the remark in *Verbum*: 'Kant's critique was not of the pure reason but of the human mind as conceived by Scotus' (25).

37. 388—9.

38. Cf. Hegel '. . . the value of logic is only appreciated when it is preceded by experience of the sciences; it then displays itself to mind as the universal truth, not as a *particular* knowledge *alongside* other matters and realities, but as the essential being of all these latter', (*Science of Logic*, tr. A.V. Miller, p. 58. I owe this quotation to Professor A.R. Manser). It is worth saying that what Hegel understands by 'logic' is roughly what Lonergan understands by cognitional theory and metaphysics.

39. 390—1.

40. Examples of metaphysics at the problematic stage would be Marxist theories of knowledge and reality, and the Logical Positivist attempt to unify the sciences.

41. 391—4.

42. Socrates made the same point in comparing his office to that of a midwife.

43. 396—9.

44. 309—402.

45. Cf. Hume: 'The contrary of every matter of fact is still possible; because it can never imply a contradiction, and is conceived by the mind with the same facility and distinctness, as if ever so conformable to reality' (*An Enquiry Concerning Human Understanding*, iv, 1.).

46. Pp. 23, 25.

47. Cf. Wittgenstein: 'Concepts which occur in "necessary" propositions must also occur and have a meaning in non-necessary ones' (*Remarks on the Foundations of Mathematics*, IV, 41). I owe this citation to P.J. Sherry.

48. 402—4. Nicholas of Autrecourt's comment seems to be yet another example of a counter-position inviting its own reversal; no wonder he is sometimes called 'the medieval Hume'.

49. Cf. p. 22.

50. 404—5.

51. For a very brief account of Thomas Aquinas' theory of 'abstraction', and the way in which it differs from another notion to which philosophical objection may readily be taken, cf. P.T. Geach, *Mental Acts*, 130—1.

52. Cf. *Verbum*, Chapter IV.

53. 405—6.

54. 406—7.

55. *Verbum*, especially 65—75.

56. 407—8.

57. 408—11.

58. 411—3.

59. 413—6.

60. G.E. Moore would presumably be an exception in the twentieth century, and perhaps Thomas Reid in the eighteenth.

61. 416—8.

62. Cf. C.S. Peirce's attack on Hegel for misinterpreting what Peirce calls 'thirdness' (*Values in a Universe of Chance*, 201—2). The relation to Hegel is only one of many respects in which the philosophy of Lonergan approximates to that of Peirce, though apparently there is no direct influence.

63. 372—4; 422—3.

64. Cf. p. 64.

65. Cf. pp. 67—8, 32.

66. 423.

67. On 'patterns of experience', cf. p. 109—110.

68. Cf. p. 36—7 above.

69. 424.

70. 424—5, xx — xxi.

71. 425—7.

72. On this notion of 'belief', cf. *Method in Theology*, pp. 41—8. It is not identical with that usual in philosophical discussion.

73. 427—30.

74. Cf. p. 28 above.

75. 431—4. Cf. p. 29.

76. Cf. p. 37.

77. For Locke, 'substance' is characteristically not a concrete thing (e.g. a horse or a man), but a thing conceived as denuded of all its sensible properties (a horse or man apart from his visually, aurally, tactually perceived characteristics). The concept of substance has been in disrepute among subsequent empiricists partly owing to Berkeley's and Hume's criticisms of Locke (what could the horse possibly be over and above the amalgam of its sensible properties?) and partly owing to a confusion of Locke's doctrine with Aristotle's.

78. 431—4.

79. For a clear and concise account of physicalism, cf. R. Carnap, *The Unity of Science*.

80. 437—8.

81. P. 13 above.

82. 438—9.

83. 439—41.

84. 508—9.

Chapter 4

1. On the topics discussed in this chapter, cf. also *Method in*

Theology, Chapter 7. For application of these principles to generate a critical theory of history, cf. Chapters 8 and 9 of the same work.

2. Cf. Lonergan's comment on the limitations of E. Coreth's book on metaphysics, with which he is in general in substantial agreement (*Collection*, 219f).

3. 530–1.

4. 531, 535–6.

5. Cf. the conception of our knowledge of causality advanced by P. Alexander in 'Are Causal Laws Purely General?' (*Proceedings of the Aristotelian Society*, 1970, Supplementary Volume XLIV, 28–36).

6. 536, 538–40.

7. I think that R.G. Collingwood and Max Weber, in their very different ways, might be regarded as having made heroic efforts to establish it, or at least something approaching it. For the attitude to such efforts of the more positivistically minded sociologist, cf. R. Rudner, *The Philosophy of Social Science*, Chapter 4.

8. 540–1.

9. 542–3.

10. Cf. Chapter 6.

11. 546, 548–9. The success of J.R.R. Tolkien's *The Lord of the Rings*, and the general contemporary interest in mysticism and the occult, might be taken as confirmation of this point.

12. 563–4.

13. On the comparison of opposed viewpoints in the approach to the universal viewpoint, cf. *Method in Theology*, pp. 129, 153 and Chapter 10.

14. 565, 567–8.

15. It is one of the most disquieting aspects of the thoroughgoing and undiscriminating application of stimulus-response theory in psychology, that this distinction, between a critical and an automatic response, seems incapable of being made in terms of it.

16. 569–71.

17. For the notion of an operator, cf. pp. 43–4.

18. 571–5, 577. Cf. Aristotle's wise remark, that it is characteristic of the educated man not to look for greater precision in the discussion of a subject than the subject itself warrants (*Nicomachean Ethics*, 1,3).

19. 578–9.

20. 579–81.

21. Descartes was sure that, in order for one thing to exert force on another, there must be matter in between them. This gives rise to a puzzle if one holds that the space between the sun and the planets is largely empty, and yet that the sun does affect the motions of the planets. Descartes concluded that space was really a plenum, within which were vortices causing planetary motions.

22. In *Language, Truth and Logic*, Ayer argued that since experience of events in the past is unobtainable, it follows that the meaning of a statement about the past must be reducible to statements about what an investigator may observe here and now in documents and so on

(p. 147). This might be taken as a classic instance of a counter-position leading to its own reversal, since it surely is incredible that 'Queen Victoria came to the throne in 1837' *means* 'If a man open such-and-such a book, he will observe such-and-such marks'.

23. 581—2.

24. One may compare G. Frege's short way with the doctrine that numbers were nothing but marks on paper. Frege inferred from this that to say, for example, that the number three was greater than the number one meant simply that the mark '3' was larger than the mark '1'. When the mathematicians who upheld the doctrine complained crossly that this was a gross misinterpretation of it, Frege retorted that, on the contrary, it was simply a consequence of taking it literally. (I cannot find the reference for this; however, similar points are made in *Frege against the Formalists*, in *Translations from the Philosophical Writings of G. Frege*, ed. P.T. Geach and M. Black).

25. 582—3.

26. Cf. p. 109.

27. 583—5.

28. Cf. pp. 18—20.

29. 586—8.

30. 588—90.

31. Cf. pp. 54—6.

32. 590—1. Cf. pp. 15—16.

33. This process in the case of Christian doctrine, as it developed from the time of Jesus to that of the orthodox Trinitarian and Christological formulations, is exhaustively described and explained by Lonergan in *De Deo Trino* and *De Verbo Incarnato*.

34. 591—2.

35. 594.

Chapter 5

1. It is behaviourist doctrine that human behaviour, and therefore the history of persons and institutions, can usefully be studied without reference to the experience, understanding, judgement and decision of agents. This is pilloried by Lonergan as 'The Principle of the Empty Head' (*Method in Theology* 157—8, 204, 223). It is heroically defended in B.F. Skinner's *Beyond Freedom and Dignity*.

2. 173; x—xii. On the topics discussed in this chapter, cf. also Chapter 2 of *Method in Theology*, on 'The Human Good'.

3. Cf. p. 27.

4. Cf. Freud's tentative remarks on the function of art in *Wit and its Relation to the Unconscious*, tr. A.A. Brill, 136—7.

5. 181—5.

6. For a large number of examples, cf W.H. Thorpe, *Learning and Instinct in Animals*; K. Lorenz, *Studies in Animal and Human Behaviour*.

7. 185—9.

8. Many psychiatrists have complained of the misleading etymology

of the term 'neurosis'. (cf. O. Hobart Mowrer, *Abnormal Reactions or Actions?*, p. 19); but at least one suggested alternative, 'sociosis', invites one to identify mental disorder rather too closely with disharmony with one's fellows. 'Scotosis', with its aura of darkness and hence of the opposite of enlightenment, seems a useful coinage.

9. Cf. pp. 10—11.

10. 191—5; 206. The view of the dream as wish-fulfilment is of course due to Freud. Jung's conception of the dream as a compensation for some aspect of conscious life is perhaps more adequate (cf. e.g. *Two Essays in Analytical Psychology*, 177). Freud himself modified his theory late in his life (cf. his *Beyond the Pleasure Principle*).

11. 193—8, 206.

12. Marx would see religion in this light; but Lonergan, as will appear later on, regards social contingencies as rather affecting the manner and expression of religious belief than constitutive of its substance.

13. Lévi-Strauss, so far as I can see, regards myths more or less exclusively from this point of view.

14. 198—9.

15. Karen Horney's *Self-Analysis* is a book which may very readily be understood in these terms. Even more explicit is H. Fingarette's *Self-Deception*.

16. 200—3.

17. Pp. 36—9.

18. 203—5.

19. 207—8. Cf. Plato, *Republic*, II, 367C—375A; *Karl Marx; Selected Writings* (ed. T.B. Bottomore and M. Rubel), 86—7, 92—3, 99—100, 105—7 etc.

20. 208—9, 212, 215—17.

21. The notion of the good will be discussed at greater length on pp. 122—5.

22. The following remarks of E. Goffman (*Asylums*, 335) seem to have reference to individual and group bias: 'Whatever else these institutions (i.e. prisons, hospitals etc.) do, one of their central effects is to sustain the self-conception of the professional staff employed there . . . The farther one's claims diverge from the facts, the more effort one must exert and the more help one must have to bolster one's position'. Mao Tse-Tung says: 'Daring or not daring to deal with selfishness is to be or not to be revolutionary'.

23. 222—5.

24. 226—8.

25. Cf. the saying prevalent a few years ago in some circles, 'We must learn to live with the bomb'. Certainly, a scientific discovery once made can hardly be unmade; but there may be some question of whether it is intelligent and reasonable to acquiesce in a *status quo* where thermo-nuclear weapons were being extensively manufactured and stockpiled.

26. 229—31.

27. For a precise and vivid description of this process, cf.

A. MacIntyre, 'A Mistake about Causality in Social Science' (*Philosophy, Politics and Society*, Series II, ed. Laslett and Runciman: 48—70).

28. 231—3.

29. Cf. pp. 32—5 above.

30. 233—4.

31. 235—6.

32. Orwell and others have commented on the connection of totalitarian habits of thought with mystifying jargon, which prevents one from seeing the facts of coercion and repression as they are.

33. I suppose that so far as one *means* by classes sections of society whose ends are essentially in conflict, as I think Marx does (cf. *Selected Writings*, ed. T.B. Bottomore and M. Rubel, 79—80), a classless society would be conceded by Lonergan to be both possible and desirable.

34. 236—8.

35. 239—41.

36. 595—9.

37. This seems to be the essence of what Sartre would call 'bad faith'. Cf. *Being and Nothingness*, Part One, Chapter Two.

38. 599—600.

39. 600—1, 604.

40. Lonergan's conception of the good, in common with that of Aquinas and the scholastic tradition, is wider than the ordinary conception.

41. Pp. 30—2.

42. 605—7. The relation between the metaphysics and ethics in Whitehead's philosophy is very similar to that in Lonergan's. Cf. *Religion in the Making*, 95—8, 100—5; *Process and Reality*, 482 etc.

43. 608—9.

44. Corresponding to experience, understanding, judgement and decision are four 'transcendental precepts' later distinguished by Lonergan; 'be attentive, be intelligent, be reasonable, be responsible' (cf. *Method in Theology*, 20, 53).

45. 609—15.

46. 617—18. P.F. Strawson's distinction between the two sorts of basic particular, in *Individuals* (246—7, etc.), is comparable, though not identical.

47. Cf. Kant: 'Everything in nature works in accordance with laws. Only a rational being has the power to act in accordance with his ideas of laws — that is in accordance with principles — and only so has he a will' (*The Moral Law*, tr. H.J. Paton, p. 76).

48. 619, 622—7.

49. 627.

50. Cf. a comment by David Cooper: 'Recent psychiatric — or perhaps anti-psychiatric — research into the origins of the major form of madness in our age, schizophrenia, has moved round to the position that people do not in fact go mad, but are driven mad by others who are driven into the position of driving them mad by a peculiar convergence of social pressures' (Introduction to M. Foucault's *Madness and Civilization*).

51. 628—32
52. 632—3

Chapter 6

1. It seems fitting to borrow for the heading of this chapter the title of A.G.N. Flew's splendid book; though Flew's arguments and conclusions certainly differ from Lonergan's.

2. 731.

3. Cf. pp. 14—16.

4. Cf. pp. 10—11. It may be as well to remind the reader that what Lonergan means by 'abstraction' is not the doctrine of abstraction attacked, and as far as I can see conclusively refuted, by P.T. Geach in *Mental Acts.*

5. Thus it does at least make sense to suppose that the aspect of a man which is independent of the empirical residue might exist despite the destruction of that which is intrinsically conditioned by it; that one's 'soul' might survive the death of one's 'body'. Cf. the rather complex argument of 518—20.

6. 643, 517f., 645, 650f.

7. For modern discussions of this topic, cf. *The Ontological Argument,* ed. A. Plantinga. Quite popular among contemporary philosophers is what has been labelled 'the ontological disproof' of the existence of God, which is to the effect that, since the concept 'God' is incoherent, it makes no sense to suppose that God exists. More prevalent still is the view that neither rational proof nor rational disproof of God's existence is possible. In opposition to both views, Lonergan argues both that the concept 'God' makes sense, and that there are valid arguments for God's existence.

8. Cf. p. 69.

9. The more consistent logical positivists acknowledged that, by strict application of the verification principle, the laws of science could not be literally true, since their verification was not strictly a matter of sense-experience. Cf. the remark of M. Schlick (quoted J.O. Urmson, *Philosophical Analysis,* p. 112): 'Natural laws do not have the character of propositions which are true or false but rather set forth instructions for the formation of such propositions'.

10. 670—2. Cf. *Method in Theology,* 101—3, 342, for a summary of this argument for the existence of God. Lonergan admits that such a proof is very seldom a means to conversion, but rather comes to be acknowledged as valid as a result of it.

11. The internal causes of anything are its central and conjugate potency, form and act. Cf. pp. 83—5 above.

12. On the notion of proportionate being, cf. p. 65 above.

13. Lonergan is not involved in the well-known fallacy of the 'quantifier-shift' at this point — the kind of inference exemplified by that from 'Every wife has a husband' to 'There is some one individual who is the husband of all wives'. This fallacy is apt to vitiate arguments

for the existence of God which depend, as this one does, on causality. One cannot validly argue from 'Every event has a cause' to 'There is one and only one entity, which is the cause of all events'. In particular, Lonergan is aware that even if it were proved that there is *at least* one unrestricted act of understanding, it would still have to be proved that there is *only* one.

14. 651f., 655.

15. 656f., 661—3, 668f.

16. Cf. *Method in Theology*, 117, for a compact statement of the problem of evil and its solution, and the relevance of faith in God to social progress and decline.

17. Cf. pp. 32—5.

18. 665—7.

19. Cf. p. 125.

20. 665—8.

21. Cf. p. 21.

22. Cf. pp. 85—7.

23. 696—7.

24. 698—700, 721—5.

25. Cf. pp. 120—2 above.

26. 725—7.

27. For examples of the kind of humanism described, cf. the essays collected in *The Humanist Frame* (edited by Sir Julian Huxley) and in *Objections to Humanism* (edited by H.J. Blackham).

28. 728—9.

Chapter 7

1. Cf. R.G. Collingwood, *Autobiography*, 33, 39. This principle of Collingwood's is explicitly recognised and praised by Lonergan in *Method in Theology*, 164.

2. In this brief discussion of the philosophy of science, I owe a great deal to Alec Dolby.

3. Cf. Karl Popper, *The Logic of Scientific Discovery*, 16, 27ff., 32—3, 40, etc.

4. Cf. J.B. Conant, *On Understanding Science*, 99—101.

5. Thomas S. Kuhn, *The Structure of Scientific Revolutions*, especially 24—30, 77—91.

6. Cf. pp. 26—8.

7. Cf. p. 82.

8. Cf. Chapter 2.

9. Hume was the first to state clearly that, if knowledge is really confined to the limits of experience, the assumption of the existence either of an external world to cause the experience or a self to enjoy it is unjustified.

10. 'Sense-data' and 'sense-contents' are technical terms used to denote the elements of experience by some twentieth-century philosophers.

11. The paradox inherent in any view of reality which invalidates the

steps taken to arrive at it was adverted to by Wittgenstein, in the famous passage about throwing away one's ladder at the end of the *Tractatus Logico-Philosophicus* (6.54).

12. For a brief and clear exposition of physicalism, cf. R. Carnap, *The Unity of Science*. A more recent defence of the theory is J.J.C. Smart's *Philosophy and Scientific Realism*.

13. The remark of Richard Taylor is pertinent: 'Human beings, and perhaps other animals, are claimed by an increasing number of philosophers to be the causes of certain of the motions of their own bodies in a way that uniquely distinguishes them as 'agents'. This renders irreducible the difference between human behaviour and that of inanimate things . . .' ('Causation', in *The Encyclopaedia of Philosophy*, ed. Paul Edwards).

14. Gilbert Ryle (cf. *The Concept of Mind*, passim) objects to the treatment of the mental properties of human beings, their intelligence, their emotion, and so on, as though they were properties of some 'occult entity' somehow underlying human behaviour, as opposed to being a matter of that behaviour itself. So far as Ryle would mean by an 'occult entity' something *over and above what intelligence can grasp in the observable phenomena*, Lonergan would agree with his strictures; but so far as Ryle means that there is nothing to our mental characteristics but our observable behaviour (and perhaps our brain-states as well), he would certainly not do so. This also seems to be Lonergan's attitude to the tradition in psychological investigation and theory which follows Pavlov and J.B. Watson; cf. e.g. B.F. Skinner's *Verbal Behaviour* and H.J. Eysenck's *Dimensions of Personality*.

15. Cf. L. Wittgenstein, *Philosophical Investigations* I, § 38.

16. Karl Popper's opposition to the philosophers of ordinary language illustrates the philosophical aspect of the conflict between common sense and science.

17. A. Boyce Gibson, *Theism and Empiricism*, p. 11.

18. After writing *Insight*, Lonergan showed a far greater interest in phenomenology and existentialism.

19. This is abundantly illustrated in the writings of Freud and Jung; cf. also K. Horney, *Self-Analysis*; E. Berne, *Games People Play*; and H. Fingarette, *Self-Deception*. It is of interest that the writings of R.D. Laing (*The Families of Schizophrenics; The Divided Self*) seem to show that some schizophrenia at least is a reaction to self-deception by those in the immediate environment of the patient. (Cf. my article, 'Philosophy and Schizophrenia', in *The Journal of the British Society of Phenomenology*, May 1971.)

20. Among the finest of many descriptions of this process are A. Solzhenitsyn's novels, *The First Circle* and *Cancer Ward*.

21. Pp. 27–8.

22. For a brief discussion of these problems, cf. R. Marlé, *An Introduction to Hermeneutics*.

23. Cf. Chomsky's *Syntactic Structures*, especially p. 80–81.

24. Cf. the famous (or notorious) review of Skinner's *Verbal*

Behaviour; reprinted in *The Structure of Language*, ed. J.A. Fodor and J.J. Katz.

25. Cf. the two articles by Philippa Foot, 'Moral Arguments' (*Mind*, 1958) and 'Moral Beliefs' (*Proceedings of the Aristotelian Society*, 1958). Cf. also P. Corbett, 'Ethics and Experience' (*Aristotelian Society Supplementary Volume*, XLIII (1969)).

26. *Treatise of Human Nature*, III, 1, 1.

27. Cf. III, 2, 9: 'The general opinion of mankind has some authority in all cases; but in this of morals it is perfectly infallible'. If this is so, a moral judgement may be validly deduced from at least one kind of statement of fact, i.e. one about the universal moral opinion of mankind.

28. G.E. Moore, *Principia Ethica*, § 13 and *passim*.

29. Ibid., 10.

30. *Language, Truth and Logic*, Chapter 6. For a useful summary of the development very briefly described here, cf. Mary Warnock, *Ethics Since 1900*.

31. Cf. particularly R.M. Hare's *The Language of Morals* and *Freedom and Reason*.

32. I have defended this view at length in 'The Objectivity of Value Judgements' (*Philosophical Quarterly*, April 1971).

33. Barth's critique of natural theology is summarised and criticised in the first part of my *Grace Versus Nature*.

34. Considering the enormous differences between Barth and Lonergan in this and other matters, it is remarkable how similar are their methods in strictly dogmatic theology. (Cf. for example, *Church Dogmatics* IV, 2, 63–71; and Lonergan's 'The Dehellenization of Dogma', *A Second Collection*, 11–32.) Comparison of them could provide material for a long and useful book.

35. The same may be said for John Hick. Cf. his *Arguments for the Existence of God*.

36. *Honest to God*, p. 29.

37. *Theological Science*, ix.

38. Cf. John Hick, *Arguments for the Existence of God*, 102–7.

39. Cf. particularly the preface to the Second Edition of Kant's *Critique of Pure Reason*.

40. Ross, op. cit., 119f., 135f., 175f.

41. Ross does not claim that every real state of affairs is *actually* explicable, only that it is so *in principle*. He adds this qualification, which differentiates his Principle E from Leibniz's Principle of Sufficient Reason, because he thinks that if the existence of the contingent world as such is actually intelligible, it will follow that God was necessitated in bringing it into existence (op. cit., 294). But this depends on an assumption which Lonergan has shown good reason to reject (cf. 621, 656f., and p.   above) — that everything that is explicable is *ipso facto* necessitated.

42. Cf. also L. Wittgenstein, *Tractatus Logico-Philosophicus*, 2.027–2.0272.

43. W.C. Kneale, 'Time and Eternity in Theology', *Proceedings of the Aristotelian Society*, 1961, 104—6.

44. Cf. 656f.

45. Cf. the arguments for theism of C.S. Peirce and A.N. Whitehead (*Values in a Universe of Chance*, ed. P.P. Wiener, the final section; *Science and the Modern World*, 13). Both of these philosophers seem in effect to base their argument on (*a*) the fact that the world as we know it is characterised by intelligible order, and (*b*) the implausibility of the suggestion of Hume and Kant that this order is imposed by human understanding.

46. 'Evil and Omnipotence' (*Mind*, 1955, 200—12).

47. For a brilliant summary of the difficulties in the notion of human free-will, cf. R. Chisholm, 'Responsibility and Avoidability' (*Determinism and Freedom in the Age of Modern Science*, ed. S. Hook, p. 157ff.)

48. Pp. 30—2.

49. Mackie, p. 209. The rebuttal is due to A. Plantinga, 'The Free Will Defence' (*Philosophy in America*, ed. Max Black, 204—220.)

50. For the quest of the historical Jesus, cf. A. Schweitzer's classic work, with that title. To the copious literature on 'demythologizing', Volume I of the series *Kerygma and Myth* (by Bultmann and others) seems to be about the best introduction.

51. *Psychology and Religion*, 154—5.

52. Cf. W.F. Albright, *From the Stone Age to Christianity*, 380—90; B. Gerhardsson, *Memory and Manuscript*; and A.N. Sherwin-White, *Roman Society and Roman Law in the New Testament*.

53. *On Aggression*, 235ff.

54. Cf. p. 140.

55. Cf. p. 138.

56. *Method in Theology*, 108—9, 119.

57. Cf. his *Patterns in Comparative Religion*.

58. R.C. Zaehner, *Concordant Discord*, 443.

Conclusion

1. B. Lonergan, *A Second Collection*, 269—78; cf. especially 275—8.

2. Cf. *Method in Theology*, 338—40; 'Natural Knowledge of God' (*A Second Collection*, 117—33); *Philosophy of God, and Theology*,, especially 40—2, 55—6. Cf. also Bernard Tyrrell, *Bernard Lonergan's Philosophy of God*.

Afterword

1. Cf. the collection *Post-Analytic Philosophy*, edited by John Rajchman and Cornel West (New York: Columbia University Press, 1985).

2. See his *Philosophy and the Mirror of Nature* (Princeton, New Jersey: Princeton University Press, 1979), 8.

3. Ibid., 5, 6, 168—70.

4. W. C. Sellars, *Science, Perception and Reality* (London: Routledge

and Kegan Paul, 1963). Cf. Rorty, op. cit., 95, 104–8.

5. Rorty, op. cit., 173–4, 1983.

6. David Hume, *An Enquiry Concerning Human Understanding*, Section iV, Part II; Section V, Part I.

7. K. R. Popper, *Objective Knowledge* (Oxford: Clarendon Press, 1972), chapter 1.

8. Cf. A. E. E. McKenzie, *The Major Achievements of Science* (Cambridge: Cambridge University Press, 1960), 159.

9. See P. K. Feyerabend, 'Consolations for the Specialist' (*Criticism and the Growth of Knowledge*, ed. I. Lakatos and A. Musgrave (Cambridge: Cambridge University Press, 1970)), 215, 218; *Against Method* (London: New Left Books, 1975), 65–6, 143, 153–5, 159, 182ff.

10. Rorty, op. cit., 178.

11. E.g. Feyerabend, in the works cited above.

12. E.g. T. S. Kuhn. See *The Structure of Scientific Revolutions* (Chicago: Chicago University Press, 1962).

13. Rorty, op. cit., 178, 181.

14. Ibid., chapter 5.

15. Ibid., 6, 11–2.

16. The point is elegantly illustrated by the title of a recent anti-foundationalist work, M. E. Williams's *Groundless Belief* (Oxford: Blackwells, 1977). Except on the assumption that Williams provides grounds for believing in his basic contention that beliefs are groundless, it would be pointless to read his book – which is in fact excellent and so well worth reading.

17. See A. Tarski, *Logic, Semantics, Metamathematics* (Oxford: Clarendon Press, 1956), 152–278; Popper, op. cit., 44–51, 319–39.

18. For Rorty's position on idealism, cf. Rorty, op. cit., 273–84.

19. *Insight*, 389.

20. On the relation of Lonergan's thought to that of Wittgenstein, see H. Meynell, 'Lonergan, Wittgenstein, and Where Language Hooks Onto the World', in M. L. Lamb, ed., *Creativity and Method* (Milwaukee, Wisconsin: Marquette University Press, 1981).

21. Cf. Quine's seminal article, 'Two Dogmas of Empiricism', in *From a Logical Point of View* (Cambridge, Mass.: Harvard University Press, 1953).

22. Cf. Rorty, op. cit., 169–75, 177–82, 192–204.

23. See H. Meynell, 'The Objectivity of Value Judgments' (*Philosophical Quarterly*, April 1971), 129–30. In that article I labelled the relationship in question 'loose entailment.'

24. A note on the 'type-token ambiguity' may be useful for non-specialists. The three letters 'aaa' are the same as one another with respect to type, different with respect to token. 'Hubert and Reginald were wearing the same tie at a party', where 'the same tie' is understood with respect to type, records a fairly normal if slightly regrettable incident; understood with respect to token, it describes a curious arrangement indeed.

25. The crucial mistake here, I believe, is to see that relation of judgments to experience, which Lonergan exhaustively describes in *Insight*,

too narrowly in terms of the kind of calculus of truth-functions which is classically set out in Wittgenstein's *Tractatus Logico-Philosophicus* (London: Routledge and Kegan Paul, 1961). On this scheme, the truth or falsity of any proposition is precisely a matter of the truth or falsity of each of a precisely determined set of 'elementary propositions.'

26. *Philosophical Review*, April 1978, 283.

27. G. Ryle, *The Concept of Mind* (New York: Barnes and Noble, 1949).

28. Cf. Patrick McGrath in P. Corcoran, ed., *Looking at Lonergan's Method* (Dublin: Talbot Press, 1975), 16–17.

30. Cf. Wittgenstein, *Philosophical Investigations* (Oxford: Blackwells, 1958), I para. 269.

31. Cf. *Insight*, chapter Xi.

32. Lonergan, *Verbum, Word and Idea in Aquinas* (London: Darton, Longman and Todd, 1968), 88.

33. Cf. p. 155–8 above. Once again (cf. note 23 above), it is neglect of 'loose entailment' which seems to be at the heart of the trouble.

34. Cf. F. Nietzsche, *Thus Spoke Zarathustra* (Harmondsworth: Penguin Books, 1969); W. Kaufmann, *Nietzsche* (Cleveland and New York: World Publishing Company, 1956).

35. For expositions of this view, see S. B. Barnes, *Scientific Knowledge and Social Theory* (London: Routledge and Kegan Paul, 1976); David Bloor, *Knowledge and Social Imagery* (London: Routledge and Kegan Paul, 1976).

36. Kaufmann, op. cit., Part III.

37. Cf. especially M. Foucault, *Power/Knowledge* (Brighton: Harvester Press, 1980).

38. Pp. 62–4 above.

39. For a longer discussion of Foucault, see H. Meynell, 'On Knowledge, Power, and Michel Foucault' (*The Heythrop Journal*, October 1989).

40. See J. Derrida, *Of Grammatology* (Baltimore: Johns Hopkins University Press, 1976). For a longer discussion of Derrida, see H. Meynell, 'On Deconstruction and the Proof of Platonism' (*New Blackfriars*, January 1989).

41. Cf. J. Culler, *On Deconstruction, Theory and Criticism After Structuralism* (Ithaca, N.Y.: Cornell University Press, 1982), 7, 88.

42. Cf. Culler, op. cit., 156; where he quotes from Derrida's 'The Conflict of the Faculties.'

43. This seems to be the main thrust of *The Crisis of Philosophy*, by Michael H. McCarthy (Albany: State University of New York Press, 1990).

44. Deuteronomy 30:19.

45. P. 163.

Glossary

Absolutely unconditioned	that which has no conditions whatever
Abstraction	the act of grasping the essential and avoiding the inessential; of apprehending the intelligible in the sensible, the general in the particular, in arriving at an insight.
Act	*see* potency, form, act.
Analytic principles	analytic propositions whose constituent terms refer to what really exists.
Analytic propositions	propositions true by virtue of the meanings of their constituent terms.
Basic counterposition	the false assumption that the real is whatever confronts the pre-critical extroverted consciousness common to men and animals.
Basic position	that the real is what is to be known by the three-fold cognitional process of attentive experience, intelligent inquiry, and reasonable reflection.
Bias, general and group	*see* general bias *and* group bias
Canons of empirical method	basic rules of procedure to be followed in scientific inquiry.
Canons of interpretation	basic rules of procedure to be followed in getting to know what any man at any time meant by what he said or wrote.
Central potency, form, act	A thing or concrete individual as to be experienced or imagined; as to be grasped by understanding as a unit; and as to be affirmed to exist.
Classical heuristic structure	A heuristic structure which anticipates the kind of intelligibility that may be grasped by direct insight,
Conditioned series	*see* scheme of recurrence
Conjugate, experiential	*see* experiential conjugate
Conjugate, explanatory	*see* pure conjugate

Conjugate potency, form, act	A quality or type of event as to be experienced or imagined; as to be grasped by understanding as what it is; and as to be affirmed to occur.
Conjugate, pure	*see* pure conjugate
Cosmopolis	an institution demanding man's first loyalty, devoted to the discovery and implementation of intelligent and reasonable policies, and to the exposure of the myths and falsifications generated in the interests of group and general bias.
Counter-position	a philosophical pronouncement on any epistemological, metaphysical, ethical, or theological issue which is derived from the basic counter-position and inconsistent with the basic position.
Cycle, long and shorter	*see* shorter cycle *and* longer cycle
Dialectical method	the method of inquiry appropriate to that type of development in which the relationship between successive stages cannot be grasped by direct insight.
Effective freedom	the ability to implement decisions arrived at by the exercise of essential freedom
Emergent probability	the immanent order or design of that which conforms both to classical and to statistical laws and which consists of a conditioned series of schemes of recurrence; in fact, the immanent order or design of our universe.
Empirical residue	the class of matters of fact which have no immanent intelligibility; e.g. actual differences between individuals of the same class, or between different places and different times.
Essential freedom	the ability to inquire, to judge, and to decide, without constraint.
Experiential conjugate	a quality or type of event defined by reference to experience.
Explicit metaphysics	the integral heuristic structure of proportionate being; i.e. the ordered set of notions by means of which the overall content of the universe may correctly though provisionally be determined. It expels from the deliverances of science and common-sense whatever is not due to experience, intelligent inquiry, and reasonable reflection.
False values	objects of choice founded on the flight from understanding, or rationalisation, or moral renunciation.
Form	*see* potency, form, act.

Freedom, effective and essential	*see* effective freedom *and* essential freedom
Genera and species	Each explanatory genus is characterised by conjugates on its own level and all lower levels; e.g. plants constitute an explanatory genus, since they not only grow and assimilate foreign matter in a way that chemical elements do not, but in addition have chemical and physical properties. Each genus subsists by virtue of its own scheme of recurrence, and all those other schemes of recurrence on which that depends; it consists of a number of types of thing or species.
General bias	The tendency of common sense in practical affairs to avoid the exercise and implementation of sustained intelligence and reasonableness.
Generalised empirical method	that method of inquiry which is appropriately applied to the data of consciousness in general, as scientific method is to the data of sense. (It is this method which is followed by *Insight*.)
Genetic method	the method of inquiry appropriate to that type of development in which the relationship between successive stages can be grasped by direct insight.
Heuristic structure	that structure of concepts by means of which the inquirer gives a preliminary description of what is to be known, such as will serve to direct his inquiry.
Higher viewpoint	a set of later insights which show the shortcomings and limitations of an earlier set.
Insight	the act of apprehending the answer to a question, of coming to understand a set of data.
Inverse insight	the act of understanding by which one grasps that a set of data is not directly intelligible; that questions of a certain type cannot be answered.
Known unknown	what one knows that one does not know.
Latent metaphysics	the stage of metaphysics typical of the lowest level of human consciousness and thought, at which attempts to unify knowledge are haphazard and spasmodic.
Longer cycle	the cycle of deterioration and self-destruction in a society which results from general bias.
Material being	what is intrinsically constituted by the empirical residue, and so cannot conceivably exist without it.
Metaphysics	*see* explicit, latent, problematic metaphysics

Mystery and myth	emotion-laden images connected with the known unknown, which in the case of myth involve the distortion of reality, in the case of mystery do not do so
Mythic consciousness	that kind of consciousness which functions entirely without the benefit of critical reflection, for which the real is either what is emotionally satisfying or what has immediate practical implications
Oversight	lack of an appropriate insight
Patterns of experience	characteristic sequences of sensations, images, memories etc. which realise particular types of end; e.g. the *biological* pattern realising the ends of intussusception, reproduction, etc.; the *aesthetic* pattern, in which experience occurs for the sake of experience; the *intellectual* pattern, where it is harnessed to serve the ends of intelligent inquiry and reasonable reflection; and the *dramatic* pattern, where it promotes the roles which each man plays out in relation to his fellows.
Polymorphic consciousness of man	the consciousness of man varying according to the patterns of experience, in which the other patterns, each appropriate in its place, are apt to interfere in the operation of the intellectual.
Position	a philosophical pronouncement on any epistemological, metaphysical, ethical or theological matter which is derived from the basic position.
Potency, form, act	the real as to be experienced or imagined; as to be grasped by understanding; as to be affirmed to exist or occur.
Practical insight	insight into what is to be done.
Probability, emergent	*see* emergent probability.
Problematic metaphysics	the stage of metaphysics where need for unification of human knowledge is felt, but where this end cannot be achieved owing to entanglement in the counter-positions.
Proportionate being	whatever is to be known by the human cognitional process of experience, understanding and judgement.
Protean notion of being	the notion of whatever can possibly be judged to exist or be the case in the light of any possible understanding or misunderstanding of any possible experience.
Pure conjugate	quality or type of event defined by reference to empirically established laws and theories.
Pure formulation	formulation of anyone's meaning that proceeds

from the universal viewpoint and is addressed to it.

Scheme of recurrence
a state of affairs characterised by a set of classical laws, which begins, continues and ceases to function in accordance with statistical probabilities; if P, Q and R are such schemes, they form a *conditioned series* so far as R cannot exist if Q does not exist, and Q cannot exist unless P does so.

Scotosis
a psychic condition resulting from the flight from insight, by which images which might give rise to the avoided insight or insights are prevented from occurring

Shorter cycle
the cycle of deterioration and destruction within a society which results from group bias.

Social surd
the unintelligible element in a social situation generated by general bias.

Spiritual being
what is subject of acts of understanding, judgement, decision, etc. Since it may abstract from the empirical residue, it is not intrinsically constituted by it.

Statistical heuristic structure
a heuristic structure which anticipates the kind of intelligibility which cannot be grasped by direct insight.

Transcendent being
whatever may exist apart from proportionate being

True values
the objects of fully intelligent and reasonable choice

Unconditioned, absolutely and virtually
see virtually unconditioned *and* absolutely unconditioned.

Universal viewpoint
that in virtue of which one may in principle apprehend the meaning of any other subject's words and actions as the result of a certain genetically and dialectically ordered course of experience and lack of experience, of understanding and failure to understand, of judgements and absences of judgement, of decisions and failures to decide.

Unsystematic process
that kind of process which cannot be mastered by a single insight or coherent set of insights.

Viewpoint, higher
see higher viewpoint

Viewpoint, universal
see universal viewpoint.

Virtually unconditioned
what is grasped by true judgement, as apprehending both *under what conditions* a state of affairs will be the case, and *that* these conditions are fulfilled.

Bibliography

Alexander, P. 'Are Causal Laws Purely General?', *Proceedings of the Aristotelian Society* Supplementary Volume XLIV (1970).

Albright, W.F. *From the Stone Age to Christianity* (New York: Doubleday, 1957).

Aristotle, *The Ethics of Aristotle*, translated by J.A.K. Thomson (Harmondsworth: Penguin Books, 1955).

Ayer, A.J. *Language, Truth and Logic* (London: Gollancz, 1946). Contribution to Symposium, 'On What There Is'. *See* Quine, W.V.O.

Barden, G. 'Insight and Mirrors', *Method*, October 1886. *See* McShane, P.

Barnes, S.B. *Scientific Knowledge and Sociological Theory* (London: Routledge and Kegan Paul, 1974).

Barth, K. *Church Dogmatics* (Edinburgh: T. and T. Clark, 1936–64).

Beards, A. 'Kenny and Lonergan on Aquinas', *Method*, (October 1986).

Berne, E. *Games People Play* (Harmondsworth: Penguin Books, 1968).

Blackham, H.J. (ed.), *Objections to Humanism* (London: Constable, 1963).

Bloor, D. *Knowledge and Social Imagery* (London: Routledge and Kegan Paul, 1976).

Bradley, F.H. *Appearance and Reality* (London: Oxford University Press, 1930).

Braxton, E.K. 'Bernard Lonergan's Hermeneutic of the Symbol', *Irish Theological Quarterly*, 1976.

Bultmann, R. (*et al.*) *Kerygma and Myth* (London: SPCK. Vol. 1, 1953; Vol. 2, 1962).

Burns, R.M. 'Bernard Lonergan's Proof of the Existence and Nature of God', *Modern Theology*, January 1987.

Burrell, D.B. 'Lonergan and Philosophy of Religion', *Method*, March 1986.

Byrne, P.H. 'The Fabric of Lonergan's Thought', *Lonergan Workshop* VI (ed. F. Lawrence; Atlanta, Ga.: Scholars Press, 1986).

'The Thomist Sources of Lonergan's World-View', *The Thomist*, January 1982.

Carnap, R. *The Unity of Science* (London: Kegan Paul, 1934).

Chisholm, R. 'Responsibility and Avoidability', in *Determinism and Freedom in the Age of Modern Science*, ed. S. Hook (New York: Collier Books, 1961).

Chomsky, N. *Syntactic Structures* (The Hague and Paris: Mouton, 1957).

Language and Mind (New York: Harcourt, 1968).

'A Review of Skinner's *Verbal Behaviour*', in *The Structure of Language*, ed. J.A. Fodor and J.J. Katz (New Jersey: Prentice Hall, 1964).

Collingwood, R.G. *An Autobiography* (London: Oxford University Press, 1939).

Conant, J.B. *On Understanding Science* (New York: Mentor Books, 1956).

Conn, W.E. *Conscience: Development and Self-Transcendence* (Birmingham, Alabama: Religious Education Press, 1981).

'Bernard Lonergan on Value' *The Thomist*, April 1976).

Corcoran, P. (ed.) *Looking at Lonergan's Method* (Dublin: Talbot Press, 1975). (Note: Readers should be warned that this symposium is very varied in quality, and that some of the contributions are misleading.)

Crowe, F.E. (ed.) *Spirit as Inquiry. Studies in Honor of Bernard Lonergan* (Minnesota: North Central Publishing Company, 1964).

The Lonergan Enterprise (Cambridge, Mass.: Cowley, 1980).

Appropriating the Lonergan Idea (Washington, D.C.: Catholic University of America Press, 1989).

'Transcendental Deduction: A Lonerganian Meaning and Use', *Method*, April 1984.

'An Exploration of Lonergan's New Notion of Value', *Lonergan Workshop III* (ed. F. Lawrence; Chico., Ca.: Scholars Press, 1982).

'An Expansion of Lonergan's Notion of Value', *Lonergan Workshop VII* (ed. F. Lawrence; Atlanta, Ga.: Scholars Press, 1988).

Cullen, J. *On Deconstruction and Criticism after Structuralism* (Ithaca, N.Y.: Cornell University Press, 1982).

Dalferth, I. *Theology and Philosophy* (Oxford: Blackwell, 1988).

Darwin, C. *The Origin of Species* (London: Oxford University Press, 1919).

Davis, C. 'Lonergan's Appropriation of the Concept of Praxis', *New Blackfriars*, March 1987.

Dewart, L. *The Future of Belief* (London: Burns and Oates, 1967).

Doran, R.M. *Subject and Psyche: Ricoeur, Jung, and the Search for Foundations* (Washington, D.C.: University of America Press, 1979).

'Psychic Conversion', *The Thomist*, January 1977.

'Subject, Psyche, and Theology's Foundations', *The Journal of Religion*, July 1977.

'The Theologian's Psyche: Notes Towards a Reconstruction of Depth Psychology', *Lonergan Workshop I* (ed. F. Lawrence; Missoula, Montana: Scholars Press, 1978).

'Suffering Servanthood and the Scale of Values', *Lonergan Workshop IV* (ed. F. Lawrence; Chico, Ca.: Scholars Press, 1983).

'Primary Process and the Spiritual Unconscious', *Lonergan Workshop V* (ed. F. Lawrence; Chico, Ca.: Scholars Press, 1985).

'From Psychic Conversion to the Dialectic of Community', *Lonergan Workshop VI*.

'Duality and Dialectic', *Lonergan Workshop VIII* (Atlanta, GA.; Scholars Press, 1988).

Theology and the Dialectics of History (Toronto: University of Toronto Press, 1990).

Eliade, M. *Patterns of Comparative Religion* (London: Sheed and Ward, 1958).

Eysenck, H.J. *Dimensions of Personality* (London: Routledge and Kegan Paul, 1950).

Feyerabend, P.K. *Against Method* (London: New Left Books, 1975).

'Consolations for the Specialist', in *Criticism and the Growth of Knowledge* (ed. I. Lakatos and A. Musgrave; Cambridge: Cambridge University Press, 1970).

Fingarette, H. *Self-Deception* (London: Routledge and Kegan Paul, 1969).

Fitzpatrick, J. 'Strawson and Lonergan on Person', *Method*, October 1984.

'Lonergan's Notion of Belief', *Method*, October 1983.

'Lonergan and Poetry.I', *New Blackfriars*, October 1978.

'Lonergan and Poetry.II', *New Blackfriars*, November 1978.

'Lonergan and Hume I. Epistemology (1)', *New Blackfriars*, March 1982.

'Lonergan and Hume II. Epistemology (2)', *New Blackfriars*, May 1982.

'Lonergan and Hume III. Critique of Religion (1)', *New Blackfriars*, June 1982.

'Lonergan and Hume IV. Critique of Religion (2)', *New Blackfriars*, September 1982.

Flanagan, J. 'Culture and Morality', *Lonergan Workshop II* (Chico, Ca.: Scholars Press, 1981).

'Transcendental Dialectic of Desire and Fear', *Lonergan Workshop I*.

'Culture and Morality', *Lonergan Workshop II*.

'The Self-Causing Subject: Intrinsic and Extrinsic Knowing', *Lonergan Workshop III*.

Flew, A.G.N. *God and Philosophy* (London: Hutchinson, 1966).

Foot, P.R. 'Moral Arguments', *Mind*, October 1958.

'Moral Beliefs', *Proceedings of the Aristotelian Society* (1958–9).

Foshay, T. 'Bernard Lonergan and James Joyce. Literature as Deconversion', *Lonergan Workshop VI*.

Foucault, M. *Power/Knowledge* (Brighton: Harvester Press, 1980).

Madness and Civilization (London: Tavistock, 1967).

Frege, G. *The Foundations of Arithmetic* (Oxford: Blackwell, 1953).

Translations from the Philosophical Writings of Gottlob Frege, ed. and tr. P.T. Geach and M. Black (Oxford: Blackwell, 1960).

Freud, S. *Beyond the Pleasure Principle* (London: Hogarth Press, 1948).

The Interpretation of Dreams (London and New York: Allen & Unwin, and Macmillan, 1945).

Wit and its Relation to the Unconscious, translated by A.A. Brill (London, Kegan Paul, 1922).

Geach, P.T. *Mental Acts* (London: Routledge and Kegan Paul, 1957).

Contribution to symposium, 'On What There Is'. See Quine, W.V.O.

Gerhardsson, B. *Memory and Manuscript* (Uppsala, 1961).

Gibson, A. Boyce. *Theism and Empiricism* (London, SCM Press, 1970).

Goffman, E. *Asylums* (Harmondsworth: Penguin Books, 1971).

Going, C. ' "Persons as Originating Values": A Primer (Reader) from Lonergan's Thought on the topic of Values', *Lonergan Workshop III*.

Gregson, V. *Lonergan, Spirituality, and the Meeting of Religions* (Lanham, MD: College Theology Society, 1985).

Hanink, J.G. 'A Reply from the Clapham Omnibus', *Method*, October 1983.

'A Worthy Fellow Wonders', *Method*, October 1983.

Hare, R.M. *The Language of Morals* (Oxford: Clarendon Press, 1952).

Freedom and Reason (Oxford: Clarendon Press, 1963).

Hefling, C. 'Turning Liberalism Inside Out', *Method*, October 1985.

Hegel, G.W.F. *The Science of Logic*, translated by A.V. Miller (London: Allen and Unwin, 1969).

Hick, J. *Arguments for the Existence of God* (London: Macmillan, 1970).

Horney, K. *Self-Analysis* (London: Routledge and Kegan Paul, 1950).

Hughes, Glenn. 'A Critique of "Lonergan's Notion of Dialectic" by Ronald McKinney S.J.', *Method*, March 1983.

'The Discussion of Mystery in *Insight*', *Method*, March 1986.

Huxley, J. (ed.) *The Humanist Frame* (London: Allen and Unwin, 1961).

Jossua, J.-P. 'Some Questions on the Role of Believing Experience in the Work of Bernard Lonergan', *Irish Theological Quarterly*, October 1973.

Jung, C.G. *Psychology and Religion, West and East* (London: Routledge and Kegan Paul, 1956).

Kant, I. *Critique of Pure Reason*, translated by N. Kemp-Smith (London: Macmillan, 1929).

The Moral Law, translated by H.J. Paton (London: Hutchinson, 1962).

Kaufmann, W. *Nietzsche* (Cleveland and New York: World Publishing Company, 1956).

Kelly, A.J. 'Is Lonergan's *Method* Adequate to Christian Mystery?', *The Thomist*, July 1975).

Kerr, Fergus *Theology After Wittgenstein* (Oxford: Blackwell, 1986).

'Objections to Lonergan's Method', *New Blackfriars*, July 1975.

'Beyond Lonergan's Method: A Response to William Mathews', *New Blackfriars*, February 1976.

Kidder, P. 'Lonergan and the Husserlian Problem of Transcendental Subjectivity', *Method*, March 1986.

Körner, S. *Kant* (Harmondsworth: Penguin Books, 1955).

Kuhn, T.S. *The Structure of Scientific Revolutions* (Chicago: Chicago University Press, 1962).

Lukatos, I. and Musgrave, A. (eds) *Criticism and the Growth of Knowledge* (Cambridge: Cambridge University Press, 1970).

Lamb, M.L. *History, Method and Theology: A Dialectical Comparison of Wilhelm Dilthey's Critique of Historical Reason and Bernard Lonergan's Meta-Methodology* (Missoula, Montana: Scholars Press, 1978).

(ed.) *Creativity and Method. Essays in Honor of Bernard Lonergan, S.J.* (Milwaukee, Wisconsin: Marquette University Press, 1981).

'The Production Process and Exponential Growth: A Study in Socio-Economics and Theology', *Lonergan Workshop I*.

'Methodology, Metascience, and Political Theology', *Lonergan Workshop II*.

'The Dialectics of Theory and Praxis Within Paradigm Analysis', *Lonergan Workshop V*.

Lash, N. 'In Defence of Lonergan's Critics', *New Blackfriars* March 1976.

Lawrence, F. 'Political Theology and "The Longer Cycle of Decline"', *Lonergan Workshop I.*

'"The Modern Philosophic Differentiation of Consciousness" or What is the Enlightenment?', *Lonergan Workshop II.*

'Elements of Basic Communication', *Lonergan Workshop VI.*

Lonergan, B.J.F. *Insight. A Study of Human Understanding* (London: Longman's 1957).

Collection (Collected Works of Bernard Lonergan, Vol. 4. Toronto: University of Toronto Press, 1988).

Verbum. Word and Idea in Aquinas (London: Darton, Longman and Todd, 1968).

Understanding and Being (Collected Works of Bernard Lonergan, Vol. 5. Toronto: University of Toronto Press, 1990).

Method in Theology (London: Darton, Longman and Todd, 1972).

Philosophy of God, and Theology (London: Darton, Longman and Todd, 1973).

A Second Collection (London: Darton, Longman and Todd, 1974).

A Third Collection (ed. F.E. Crowe. New York/Mahwah: Paulist Press, 1985).

Introducing the Thought of Bernard Lonergan. Three papers from *Collection*, with an introduction by P. McShane (London: Darton, Longman and Todd, 1973).

De Deo Trino I Pars Dogmatica II Pars Systematica (Rome: Gregorian University Press, 1964). *De Verbo Incarnato* (Rome: Gregorian University Press, 1964).

De Constitutione Christi (Rome: Gregorian University Press, 1956).

'Questionnaire on Philosophy: Response', *Method*, October 1984.

'The Original Preface to *Insight*', *Method*, March 1985.

'Religious Knowledge', *Lonergan Workshop I.*

'A Post-Hegelian Philosophy of Religion', *Lonergan Workshop III.*

Lorenz, K. *On Aggression* (London: Methuen, 1967).

Studies in Animal and Human Behaviour Vol. II (London: Methuen, 1971).

MacIntyre, A. *After Virtue* (London: Duckworth, 1981).

'A Mistake about Causality in Social Science', in *Philosophy, Politics and Society, Series Two* ed. P. Laslett and W.G. Runciman (Oxford: Blackwell, 1962).

MacKenzie, A.E.E. *The Major Achievements of Science* (Cambridge: Cambridge University Press, 1960).

Mackie, J.L. 'Evil and Omnipotence', *Mind*, April 1955.

Marlé, R. *Introduction to Hermeneutics* (London: Burns and Oates, 1967).

Marx, K. *Selected Writings in Sociology and Social Philosophy*, ed. T.B. Bottomore and M. Rubel (Harmondsworth: Penguin Books, 1963).

Mathews, W. 'Lonergan's Awake: A Reply to Fergus Kerr', *New Blackfriars*, January 1976.

'Lonergan: A Final Word', *New Blackfriars*, August 1977.

'Intellectual Conversion and Science Education', *Lonergan Workshop V*.

Matustik, M.J. *Mediation of Deconstruction. Bernard Lonergan's Method in Philosophy* (Lanham, Maryland: University Press of America, 1987).

McCarthy, M.H. *The Crisis of Philosophy* (Ithaca, New York: State University of New York Press, 1989).

McKinney, R.M. 'Lonergan's Notion of Dialectic', *The Thomist*, April 1982.

'A Reply to Glenn Hughes', *Method*, March 1983.

McShane, P. *Randomness, Statistics and Emergence* (Notre Dame, Indiana: University of Notre Dame Press, 1970).

'Lonergan's Challenge to the University and Economy' (Lanham, Maryland: University Press of America, 1979).

(ed.) *Foundations of Theology*, Papers from the International Lonergan Congress, 1970 (Dublin: Gill and Macmillan, 1971).

(ed.) *Language, Truth and Meaning*, Papers from the International Lonergan Congress, 1970 (Dublin: Gill and Macmillan, 1972).

with Barden, G. *Towards Self-Meaning* (Dublin: Gill and Macmillan, 1969).

Melchin, K.R. *History, Ethics and Emergent Probability* (Lanham, Maryland: University Press of America, 1987).

Meynell, H.A. *The Theology of Bernard Lonergan* (Atlanta, Ga.: Scholars Press, 1986).

'Foundation and Empiricism', *Method*, October, 1983.

'Reversing Rorty', *Method*, March 1986.

'Lonergan's Theory of Knowledge and the Social Sciences', *New Blackfriars*, September 1975.

Moore, G.E. *Principia Ethica* (Cambridge: Cambridge University Press, 1956).

Moore, S. 'Christian Self-Discovery'. *Lonergan Workshop I*.

'The Language of Love', *Lonergan Workshop III*.

'The New Life', *Lonergan Workshop V*.

Morelli, M.D. *Philosophy's Place in Culture* (Lanham, Maryland: University Press of America, 1984).

'Reversing the Counter-Position: The *Argumentum ad Hominem* in Philosophic Dialogue', *Lonergan Workshop VI*.

Nietzsche, F. *Thus Spoke Zarathustra* (Harmondsworth: Penguin Books, 1969).

Nilson, J. *Hegel's Phenomenology and Lonergan's Insight* (Meisenhein am Glan: Hain, 1979).

'Transcendent Knowledge in *Insight*. A Closer Look', *The Thomist*, April 1973.

O'Callaghan, M. *Unity in Theology* (Lanham, Maryland: University Press of America, 1980).

O'Leary, J. 'The Hermeneutics of Dogmatism' (*Irish Theological Quarterly*, 1980).

Oyler, D. 'Emergence in Complex Systems', *Method*, March, 1983.

Peirce, C.S. *Values in a Universe of Chance*, ed. P.P. Wiener (Stanford: Stanford University Press, 1958).

Piscitelli, E. 'The Fundamental Attitudes of the Liberally Education Person: Foundational Dialectics', *Lonergan Workshop V*.

Plantinga, A. 'The Free Will Defense', in *Philosophy in America*, ed. M. Black (London: Allen and Unwin, 1965).

(ed.) *The Ontological Argument* (London: Macmillan, 1968).

Plato *Great Dialogues of Plato*, translated by W.D. Rouse (New York: Mentor Books, 1956).

The Last Days of Socrates, translated by H. Tredennick (Harmondsworth: Penguin Books, 1954).

Popper, K.R. *The Logic of Scientific Discovery* (London: Hutchinson, 1959).

Objective Knowledge. An Evolutionary Approach (Oxford: Clarendon Press, 1972).

Quesnell, Q. 'Pinning Down the Meaning', *Lonergan Workshop VII*.

'The Foundations of Heresy', *Lonergan Workshop II*.

Quine, W.V.O. *From a Logical Point of View* (Cambridge, Mass.: Harvard University Press, 1953).

'On What There Is' (*Review of Metaphysics*, 1948).

Contribute to symposium, 'On What There Is' (*Proceedings of the Aristotelian Society*, Supplementary Volume XXV, 1951).

Rajchman, J. and West, C. (eds) *Post-Analytic Philosophy* (New York: Columbia University Press, 1985).

Reiser, W.E. 'Lonergan's Notion of the Religious A Priori', *The Thomist*, April 1971.

'Foundational Reality and Three Approaches: MacKinnon, Harvey, and Lonergan', *The Thomist*, July 1972.

Ring, N. 'Language, Prayer, and the Dynamics of Transformation', *Lonergan Workshop IV*.

Rorty, R. *Philosophy and the Mirror of Nature* (Princeton: Princeton University Press, 1979).

Ross, J.F. *Philosophical Theology* (Indianapolis and New York: Bobbs-Merrill Company, 1969).

Rudner, R.S. *The Philosophy of Social Science* (Englewood Cliffs, New Jersey: Prentice Hall, 1966).

Russell, B. *Logic and Knowledge*, ed. R.C. Marsh (London: Allen and Unwin, 1956).

Ryle, G. *The Concept of Mind* (London: Hutchinson, 1949).

Sala, G. *Das A priori in der menschlichen Erkenntnis: Eine Studie über Kants Kritik der reinen Vernunft und Lonergans Insight* (Meisenheim am Glan: Hain, 1971).

Sartre, J.-P. *Being and Nothingness* (London: Methuen, 1957).

Schweitzer, A. *The Quest of the Historical Jesus* (London: Black, 1922).

Sellars, W.C. *Science, Perception and Reality* (London: Routledge and Kegan Paul, 1963).

220   *Introduction to the Philosophy of Bernard Lonergan*

Sherwin-White, A.N. *Roman Society and Roman Law in the New Testament* (Oxford: Clarendon Press, 1963).
Skinner, B.F. *Verbal Behaviour* (New York: Appleton, 1957).
Beyond Freedom and Dignity (London: Jonathan Cape, 1972).
Smart, J.J.C. *Philosophy and Scientific Realism* (London: Routledge and Kegan Paul, 1963).
Solzhenitsyn, A. *Cancer Ward* (Harmondsworth: Penguin Books, 1971).
The First Circle (London: Collins, 1968).
Strawson, P.F. *Individuals* (London: Methuen, 1964).
Tarski, A. *Logic, Semantics, Metamathematics* (Oxford: Clarendon Press, 1956).
Taylor, R. 'Causation', in *The Encyclopedia of Philosophy*, ed. Paul Edwards (London: Collier-Macmillan, 1967).
Tekippe, T.J. 'The Crisis of the Human Good', *Lonergan Workshop VII*.
Thorpe, W.H. *Learning and Instinct in Animals* (London: Methuen, 1963).
Torrance, T.F. *Theological Science* (London: Oxford University Press, 1969).
Tracy, D. *The Achievement of Bernard Lonergan* (New York: Herder and Herder, 1970).
'Theological Models: An Exercise in Dialectics', *Lonergan Workshop II*.
Tyrrell, B. *Bernard Lonergan's Philosophy of God* (Dublin: Gill and Macmillan, 1974).
'On the Possibility and Desirability of a Christian Psychotherapy', *Lonergan Workshop I*.
'"Dynamics of Christotherapy" and the Issue of a De Jure Psychotherapeutic Pluralism', *Lonergan Workshop II*.
'Psychological Conversion, Methods of Healing, and Communication', *Lonergan Workshop VI*.
'Feelings as Apprehensive-Intentional Responses to Values', *Lonergan Workshop VII*.
Vertin, M. 'Philosophy of God, Theology, and the Problems of Evil', *Lonergan Workshop III*.
'Dialectically-Opposed Phenomenologies of Knowing: A Pedagogical Elaboration of Basic Ideal-Types', *Lonergan Workshop IV*.

Warnock, M. *Ethics Since 1900* (London: Oxford University Press, 1966).

Watkins, J.W.N. 'Comprehensively Critical Rationalism', *Philosophy*, January 1969.

West, C. See Rajchman, J.

Whitehead, A.N. *Science and the Modern World* (New York: Mentor Books, 1948).

Religion in the Making (Cambridge: Cambridge University Press, 1926).

Process and Reality (Cambridge: Cambridge University Press, 1929).

Williams, M.E. *Groundless Belief* (Oxford: Blackwell, 1977).

Wilson, P. 'Human Knowledge of God's Existence in the Theology of Bernard Lonergan', *The Thomist*, April 1971.

Wittgenstein, L. *Tractatus Logico-Philosophicus* (London: Routledge and Kegan Paul, 1961).

Philosophical Investigations (Oxford: Blackwell, 1958).

Philosophische Bemerkungen (Oxford: Blackwell, 1964).

The Blue and Brown Books. Preliminary Studies for the Philosophical Investigations (Oxford: Blackwell, 1978).

Zaehner, R.C. *Concordant Discord. The Interdependence of Faiths* (Oxford: Clarendon Press, 1970).

Index

222